International Political Economy Series

General Editor: **Timothy M. Shaw**, Professor of Commonwealth Governance and Development, and Director of the Institute of Commonwealth Studies, School of Advanced Study, University of London

Titles include:

Hans Abrahamsson
UNDERSTANDING WORLD ORDER AND STRUCTURAL CHANGE
Poverty, Conflict and the Global Arena

Sandra Braman (*editor*)
THE EMERGENT GLOBAL INFORMATION POLICY REGIME

James Busumtwi-Sam and Laurent Dobuzinskis
TURBULENCE AND NEW DIRECTIONS IN GLOBAL POLITICAL ECONOMY

Elizabeth De Boer-Ashworth
THE GLOBAL POLITICAL ECONOMY AND POST-1989 CHANGE
The Place of the Central European Transition

Bill Dunn
GLOBAL RESTRUCTURING AND THE POWER OF LABOUR

Myron J. Frankman
WORLD DEMOCRATIC FEDERALISM
Peace and Justice Indivisible

Helen A. Garten
US FINANCIAL REGULATION AND THE LEVEL PLAYING FIELD

Randall D. Germain (*editor*)
GLOBALIZATION AND ITS CRITICS
Perspectives from Political Economy

Barry K. Gills (*editor*)
GLOBALIZATION AND THE POLITICS OF RESISTANCE

Richard Grant and John Rennie Short (*editors*)
GLOBALIZATION AND THE MARGINS

Graham Harrison (*editor*)
GLOBAL ENCOUNTERS
International Political Economy, Development and Globalization

Patrick Hayden and Chamsy el-Ojeili (*editors*)
CONFRONTING GLOBALIZATION
Humanity, Justice and the Renewal of Politics

Axel Hülsemeyer (*editor*)
GLOBALIZATION IN THE TWENTY-FIRST CENTURY
Convergence or Divergence?

Helge Hveem and Kristen Nordhaug (*editors*)
PUBLIC POLICY IN THE AGE OF GLOBALIZATION
Responses to Environmental and Economic Crises

AF698873

Takashi Inoguchi
GLOBAL CHANGE
A Japanese Perspective

Jomo K.S. and Shyamala Nagaraj (*editors*)
GLOBALIZATION VERSUS DEVELOPMENT

Dominic Kelly and Wyn Grant (*editors*)
THE POLITICS OF INTERNATIONAL TRADE IN THE 21st CENTURY
Actors, Issues and Regional Dynamics

Craig N. Murphy (*editor*)
EGALITARIAN POLITICS IN THE AGE OF GLOBALIZATION

Michael Niemann
A SPATIAL APPROACH TO REGIONALISM IN THE GLOBAL ECONOMY

Morten Ougaard
THE GLOBALIZATION OF POLITICS
Power, Social Forces and Governance

Markus Perkmann and Ngai-Ling Sum
GLOBALIZATION, REGIONALIZATION AND CROSS-BORDER REGIONS

Leonard Seabrooke
US POWER IN INTERNATIONAL FINANCE
The Victory of Dividends

Timothy J. Sinclair and Kenneth P. Thomas (*editors*)
STRUCTURE AND AGENCY IN INTERNATIONAL CAPITAL MOBILITY

Fredrik Söderbaum and Timothy M. Shaw (*editors*)
THEORIES OF NEW REGIONALISM
A Palgrave Reader

Amy Verdun
EUROPEAN RESPONSES TO GLOBALIZATION AND FINANCIAL MARKET INTEGRATION
Perceptions of Economic and Monetary Union in Britain, France and Germany

---

International Political Economy Series
Series Standing Order ISBN 978-0-333-71708-0 hardback
Series Standing Order ISBN 978-0-333-71110-1 paperback
(*outside North America only*)

You can receive future titles in this series as they are published by placing a standing order. Please contact your bookseller or, in case of difficulty, write to us at the address below with your name and address, the title of the series and one of the ISBNs quoted above.

Customer Services Department, Macmillan Distribution Ltd, Houndmills, Basingstoke, Hampshire RG21 6XS, England

---

Confronting Globalization

Humanity, Justice and the Renewal of Politics

Edited by

Patrick Hayden
Senior Lecturer in Political Theory
Victoria University of Wellington
New Zealand

and

Chamsy el-Ojeili
Lecturer in Sociology
Victoria University of Wellington
New Zealand

palgrave
macmillan

Editorial matter, selection and Chapter 1 © Patrick Hayden and Chamsy el-Ojeili 2005

Individual chapters (in order) © Peter Beilharz, Roger Deacon, James Brassett and Federico Merke, Barry Smart, François Debrix, Michael A. Peters, Mark Evans, Luis Cabrera, Timothy W. Luke, Douglas Kellner, Martin Weber, Andrew Robinson and Simon Tormey, Manfred B. Steger, Darrel Moellendorf, Daniele Archibugi 2005

All rights reserved. No reproduction, copy or transmission of this publication may be made without written permission.

No paragraph of this publication may be reproduced, copied or transmitted save with written permission or in accordance with the provisions of the Copyright, Designs and Patents Act 1988, or under the terms of any licence permitting limited copying issued by the Copyright Licensing Agency, 90 Tottenham Court Road, London W1T 4LP.

Any person who does any unauthorized act in relation to this publication may be liable to criminal prosecution and civil claims for damages.

The authors have asserted their rights to be identified as the authors of this work in accordance with the Copyright, Designs and Patents Act 1988.

First published 2005 by
PALGRAVE MACMILLAN
Houndmills, Basingstoke, Hampshire RG21 6XS and
175 Fifth Avenue, New York, N.Y. 10010
Companies and representatives throughout the world

PALGRAVE MACMILLAN is the global academic imprint of the Palgrave Macmillan division of St. Martin's Press, LLC and of Palgrave Macmillan Ltd. Macmillan® is a registered trademark in the United States, United Kingdom and other countries. Palgrave is a registered trademark in the European Union and other countries.

ISBN 978-1-349-52305-4 ISBN 978-0-230-59882-9 (eBook)
DOI 10.1057/9780230598829

A catalogue record for this book is available from the British Library.

Library of Congress Cataloging-in-Publication Data
Confronting globalization : humanity, justice, and the renewal of politics / edited by
Patrick Hayden, Chamsy el-Ojeili.
p. cm. — (International political economy series)
Includes bibliographical references and index.

1. Globalization. 2. Globalization—Social aspects. I. Hayden, Patrick. II. El-Ojeili, Chamsy. III. Series.
JZ1318C6573 2005
303.48′2—dc22 2004065450

10 9 8 7 6 5 4 3 2 1
14 13 12 11 10 09 08 07 06 05

Transferred to Digital Printing 2011.

Contents

Notes on the Contributors

Daniele Archibugi is a Director of the Italian National Research Council. He has worked at the Universities of Sussex, Naples, Cambridge and Rome. In 2003–4 he was Leverhulme Visiting Professor at the London School of Economics and Political Science and in 2004–5 he was Lauro De Bosis Professor at Harvard University. He works on globalization, technological change and the political theory of international relations. He is an adviser to the European Commission, the OECD and several UN specialized agencies, and has worked on the reform of international organizations. Among his publications in the field of political theory, he has co-edited *Cosmopolitan Democracy: An Agenda for a New World Order* (1995) and *Re-Imagining Political Community: Studies in Cosmopolitan Democracy* (1998), and edited *Debating Cosmopolitics* (2003).

Peter Beilharz is Professor of Sociology and Director of the Thesis Eleven Centre for Critical Theory at La Trobe University in Australia. He was Professor of Australian Studies at Harvard University in 1999–2000, and William Dean Howells Fellow at Harvard in 2002. He is Faculty Associate in Sociology at Yale University. He has published twenty books, including *Imagining the Antipodes* (1997), *Zygmunt Bauman* (1999), and most recently *Postwar American Critical Thought* (2005). He is now working on a major project tracking the antipodes across the twentieth century.

James Brassett is a research student at the University of Warwick based in the ESRC Centre for the Study of Globalisation and Regionalisation. His work covers theories of globalization, international political economy and ethics with a special focus on the normative possibilities presented by global civil society. He has co-authored an article with Richard Higgott, 'Building the Normative Dimension(s) of a Global Polity', in *Review of International Studies* (2003).

Luis Cabrera is Assistant Professor of Political Science at Arizona State University West. He has published articles on cosmopolitan distributive justice and global political integration, and he is the author of *Political Theory of Global Justice: A Cosmopolitan Case for the World State* (2004).

Roger Deacon is Honorary Research Fellow in Human and Social Studies and Honorary Lecturer in Education at the University of KwaZulu-Natal, and managing editor of *Theoria: A Journal of Social and Political Theory*. He publishes in the fields of political philosophy, the history of ideas and educational theory, and his most recent publication is *Fabricating Foucault* (2003). His current research interests are in the origins of early modern education, and the art and politics of war.

François Debrix is Associate Professor of International Relations at Florida International University. His publications include *Re-Envisioning Peace-keeping: The United Nations and the Mobilization of Ideology* (1999), *Language, Agency and Politics in a Constructed World* (2003, editor), and *Rituals of Mediation: International Politics and Social Meaning* (2003, co-editor). His work in the domains of international relations theory, postmodern theory and culture, and critical world order studies has been published in journals such as *Alternatives, Geopolitics, New Political Science, Philosophy and Social Criticism, Postmodern Culture, Strategies* and *Third World Quarterly*. He is currently working on a new book-length manuscript that explores the politics of fear-making in the transnational polity through a critical analysis of the 'mad cow' crisis.

Chamsy el-Ojeili is Lecturer in Sociology at Victoria University of Wellington, New Zealand. He is the author of *From Left Communism to Postmodernism: Reconsidering Emancipatory Discourse* (2003), and co-editor of *New Zealand Sociology*.

Mark Evans is Senior Lecturer in Political Theory at the University of Wales, Swansea. His publications include *The Edinburgh Companion to Contemporary Liberalism* (2001), *Ethics in International Relations: New Directions* (2004), *Just War Theory: A Reappraisal* (2005) and *Liberal Justifications* (2005). He is associate editor of *Politics and Ethics Review*. His research interests include human rights, international ethics, the ethics of individual character in liberalism, and the distinction between ideal and non-ideal theory in the analysis of moral and political problems.

Patrick Hayden is Senior Lecturer in Political Theory at Victoria University of Wellington, and editor of *Politics and Ethics Review*. His publications include *Cosmopolitan Global Politics* (2005), *America's War on Terror* (2003, co-editor), *John Rawls: Towards a Just World Order* (2002), and *The Philosophy of Human Rights* (2001). His research interests include international ethics and human rights, theories of war and peace, democratic theory, and the application of social and political theory to the study of international relations and global politics.

Douglas Kellner is George Kneller Chair in the Philosophy of Education at UCLA and is author of many books on social theory, politics, history, and culture, including *Camera Politica: The Politics and Ideology of Contemporary Hollywood Film* (with Michael Ryan); *Critical Theory, Marxism, and Modernity; Jean Baudrillard: From Marxism to Postmodernism and Beyond; Postmodern Theory: Critical Interrogations* (with Steven Best); *Television and the Crisis of Democracy; The Persian Gulf TV War; Media Culture;* and *The Postmodern Turn* (with Steven Best). Recent books include *Grand Theft 2000: Media Spectacle and the Theft of an Election, The Postmodern Adventure: Science, Technology, and Cultural Studies at the Third Millennium* (with Steve Best), and *September 11, Terror War, and the Dangers of the Bush Legacy.*

Timothy W. Luke is Programme Chair, Government and International Affairs, School of Public and International Affairs, and University Distinguished Professor in the Department of Political Science at Virginia Institute Polytechnic and State University. He is the author of numerous books, including *Museum Pieces: Power Plays at the Exhibition* (2002), *Capitalism, Democracy, and Ecology: Departing from Marx* (1999), *Ecocritique: Contesting the Politics of Nature, Economy and Culture* (1997), and *Social Theory and Modernity: Critique, Dissent and Revolution* (1990).

Federico Merke is a PhD candidate at the Latin American Faculty of Social Sciences (FLACSO) in Buenos Aires. He received his first degree from the Universidad del Salvador before studying at the University of Warwick where he attained an MA in International Studies. He is Deputy Director of Academic Affairs at the Argentine Council for International Relations and teaches International Relations Theory at the Universidad del Salvador. He recently published the article, 'Entre el 9/11 y el 11/9: Debates y Perspectivas sobre el Cambio en las Relaciones Internacionales', in *Foro Internacional* (2004).

Darrel Moellendorf is Associate Professor of Philosophy and Director of the Institute for Ethics and Public Affairs at San Diego State University. He is the author of several articles and chapters in books, as well as *Cosmopolitan Justice* (2002). Additionally, he has guest co-edited special issues of *Developing World Bioethics* (with Michael Selgelid) on resource distribution and *Journal of Ethics* (with Gillian Brock) on global justice. A reprint of the latter will be published in 2005 in book form.

Michael A. Peters is Professor of Education at the University of Glasgow and the University of Auckland. He has research interests in educational theory and policy, and in contemporary philosophy, and has published many articles and books on these topics.

Andrew Robinson is an activist based in Derby, UK, and a part-time tutor in the School of Politics, University of Nottingham. He recently submitted his doctoral thesis on the work of John Rawls having graduated with a First and Distinction in his BA and MA studies. His research focuses on social exclusion and oppressive discourse in contemporary political thought. He has published numerous scholarly articles and has extensive research and writing interests, including populism, postcolonial theory, Marxism and social constructions of 'delinquency' and 'madness'.

Barry Smart is Professor of Sociology at the University of Portsmouth. His books include *Foucault, Marxism, and Critique* (1983), *Michel Foucault* (1988), *Modern Conditions: Postmodern Controversies* (1991), *Postmodernity* (1992), *Facing Modernity* (1999), and *Economy, Culture, and Society* (2003).

Manfred B. Steger is Professor of Politics and Government at Illinois State University and Research Fellow at the Globalization Research Center at the University of Hawai'i-Manoa. He has written widely on ideologies of globalization, theories of non-violence and international politics. His book, *Globalism: The New Market Ideology* (2003) won the 2003 Michael Harrington Award of the New Political Science Section of the American Political Science Association and a new edition was published in 2005.

Simon Tormey is Senior Lecturer in Politics and Critical Theory at the University of Nottingham. He is the author of numerous books and articles including *Making Sense of Tyranny: Interpretations of Totalitarianism* (1995), *Agnes Heller: Socialism, Autonomy and the Postmodern* (2001), *Anti-Capitalism* (2004), and *Exploring Post-Marxisms* (2005). He is series editor for 'Reappraising the Political' with Manchester University Press (with Jon Simons) and on the editorial board of *Contemporary Political Theory*. His recent work concerns globalization and resistance, postmodern and neo-Marxian theory, and the work of Wittgenstein, Deleuze and Guattari.

Martin Weber is Lecturer in Politics and International Relations at the University of Aberdeen, Scotland. His research interests are in international political theory/critical theory, green political thought, social movements in world politics, and international political economy. Among his publications are 'Competing Political Visions: WTO Governance and Green Politics' (*Global Environmental Politics*, 2001); 'Engaging Globalization: Critical Theory and Global Political Change' (*Alternatives*, 2002); 'The Politics of Global Health Governance: Whatever Happened to "Health for All by the Year 2000"?' (with C. Thomas, *Global Governance*, 2004); and 'The Critical Social Theory of the Frankfurt School, and the Social Turn in IR' (*Review of International Studies*, 2005).

List of Abbreviations

BE	Biocomplexity in the Environment
FBI	Federal Bureau of Investigation
FDI	Foreign Direct Investment
FTAA	Free Trade Area of the Americas
GATS	General Agreement on Trade in Services
GATT	General Agreement on Tariffs and Trade
GDP	Gross Domestic Product
GIF	Group-in-Fusion
IMF	International Monetary Fund
IPCC	Intergovernmental Panel in Climate Change
IPSs	International Public Spheres
IR	International Relations
IT	Information Technology
MFN	Most Favoured Nation
MGJ	Movement for Global Justice
NAFTA	North American Free Trade Agreement
NATO	North Atlantic Treaty Organization
NGO	Non-Governmental Organization
NSF	National Science Foundation
NSMs	New Social Movements
OECD	Organisation for Economic Co-operation and Development
PPP	Purchasing Power Parity
TRIPS	Agreement on Trade-Related Intellectual Property Rights
TU	Thin Universalism
UN	United Nations
UNCTAD	United Nations Conference on Trade and Development
UNDP	United Nations Development Programme
USIA	United States Information Agency
WHO	World Health Organization
WSF	World Social Forum
WTO	World Trade Organization

1

Confronting Globalization in the Twenty-first Century: An Introduction

Patrick Hayden and Chamsy el-Ojeili

The literature on globalization is truly prodigious and wide-ranging. The process, after all, encompasses a plurality of phenomena. Consider, for instance, the following: the US$1.5 trillion turned over per day in foreign exchange; the size and power of many large multinational corporations; the new technologies such as the Internet which spell the 'death of distance',[1] recomposing communities and identity and providing the possibility of a new public sphere; the emergence of a new system of global governance, with local bodies, non-governmental organizations, multinational corporations, transnational global bodies and treaties reconfiguring the nature of rule, and perhaps making the state more of a 'strategic actor'[2] rather than a prime political mover; a new polarization of wealth, with the three richest people in the world controlling more assets than the 600 million people in the 48 less developed countries; the development of a new international division of labour, and the transformation of work, with its personal and social consequences;[3] the spread of Western cultural products so that 'America is everybody's second culture'; the emergence of a global environmental commons in the face of a host of threatening ecological catastrophes;[4] and the much talked of global scission between McWorld, on the one hand, and Jihad, on the other. The aim in this Introduction will not be to extensively analyse these complex issues, or to exhaustively trace the diverse attempts to confront globalization, but rather to provide some key landmarks – theoretical and political – as ways to set the scene for the chapters that are to follow.

A preliminary consideration must be the very meaning of 'globalization'. Globalization has been conceptualized in a variety of ways, including as time/space compression;[5] as the extension of social relations over the globe;[6] as the stretching of social relations, the intensification of flows, increasing interpenetration, and global infrastructures;[7] as 'the worldwide diffusion of practices, expansion of relations across continents, organization of social life on a global scale, and the growth of a shared global consciousness';[8] as 'cross-national flows of goods, investment, production and technology';[9] and as 'A social process in which the constraints of geography on economic, political, social and cultural arrangements recede, in which people become increasingly aware that they are receding and in which people act accordingly.'[10] We believe, though, that as a working conceptualization, Held and McGrew's expansive definition is most useful:

> globalization denotes the expanding scale, growing magnitude, speeding up and deepening impact of interregional flows and patterns of social interaction. It refers to a shift or transformation in the scale of human social organization that links distant communities and expands the reach of power relations across the world's major regions and continents.[11]

In short, globalization is most fundamentally about *growing world interconnectedness and its social and political implications*.

Such a definition avoids focusing on one dimension alone – as Marxists, for example, do when they insist on economics, capitalism or class as primary. It also emphasizes world interconnectedness as an uneven and complex thing; it is not all of a piece, and Held and McGrew elsewhere provide an important historical dimension in delineating different periods of globalization, from premodern, to early modern, modern, and contemporary globalization.[12] This periodization avoids ahistorical approaches to globalization and suggests that contemporary globalization has had important precursors over time, although arguably the distinctive scale and scope of contemporary globalization has led to virtually unprecedented global shifts in the conditions of people's lives.

Some implications of globalization for social and political theory

A host of recent books have sought to theorize the particularity of contemporary globalization by accenting certain features of growing world interconnectedness. For Bauman, we have a multifaceted set of processes, but the new stratification born of differentials around mobility – from tourists to vagabonds – stands out.[13] According to Giddens, detraditionalization, risk and reflexivity loom large as aspects of late modernity.[14]

In his monumental trilogy, *The Information Age,* Castells characterizes the emerging new world as contoured by three strands: the information and technology revolution, the crises of capitalism and statism and their subsequent restructurings, and the impact of cultural social movements.[15] Thinkers of a postcolonialist cast of mind have accented the hybridity and mutual contamination of all identity today; inescapably overlapping and intertwined histories, in Said's words, mean an end to aspirations of purity – 'No one today is purely *one* thing' – and a cosmopolitan utopian urge emerges where there might be 'a place for all at the rendezvous of victory'.[16] For John Urry, a turn to complexity theory provides the most promising avenue for addressing the disorderliness of global systems – unpredictability, non-linearity, a dialectic of moorings and mobility, and emergent systems that are far from reaching equilibrium.[17] And, for Hardt and Negri, a new decentred structure of rule – Empire – has emerged, extending sovereignty progressively over the whole of social life.[18]

The above is simply a taste of the sorts of ways theorists have approached globalization as a novel and pivotal moment requiring both theoretical and political-social confrontation. We will turn, in the following section, to the utopian dimension, to the realm of critique and of what might be called 'alternative globalization'. But here we will set out some of the essential ways that social, political, economic and environmental issues raised by the intense processes of globalization have major implications for the trajectory of social and political theory and practice. On the one hand, of course, are the various attempts to theorize the disputed nature, meaning and phenomenon of globalization itself, some of the approaches to which have been outlined above. On the other hand are efforts to engage with the multiple constitutive and consequential agents, movements, institutions, challenges and opportunities which both define and redefine the kinds of transformations occurring as a result of, or in response to, processes of globalization. Significantly, these latter efforts have lent themselves to normative reflection on the various issues associated with globalization, staking out a place for moral and political theorizing that seeks to reconsider some of the fundamental concepts, premises and principles of modern political life in order to elucidate the specific challenges that confront these under conditions of globalization, and articulate alternative visions for them.

What are some of the core features of globalization that have transformed many of the innermost structures of the contemporary world, and what types of theoretical concerns have these provoked which compel us to interrogate established social and political concepts, norms and practices? First, globalization points to both an intensification of cross-border interactions and a growing interdependence between national and transnational actors through a 'deterritorialization' whereby social spaces, distances and borders lose some of their previously overriding influence as political, cultural, social and economic relations become more global over time.[19] Accompanying these changes, of course, have been other notable aspects of globalization such as the integration of markets through trade, surging investment and information flows, the rapid spread of technologies such as the Internet, mobile telephone systems and satellite communications which allow people on different sides of the globe to communicate instantaneously, and the escalation of environmental issues which respect no borders, such as depletion of the ozone layer, transboundary pollution and global warming.[20]

As a result of these developments, over the last decade or so the entrenchment of globalization has generated an extraordinarily complex debate around the concept of sovereignty. A variety of theorists across the analytical spectrum have sought to redefine, reconceptualize, re-examine and revision the nature and meaning of sovereignty in the global age.[21] Despite this diversity, efforts at retheorizing sovereignty have illuminated three interrelated problems: first, the concept of sovereignty was introduced and adopted under conditions that are no longer pertinent or existent in the world today; second, the constraints on state behaviour that sovereignty imposed through the principle of non-intervention either have ceased to be effective or now serve as unjustifiable barriers to seemingly necessary forms of transnational action; and, third, the close historical alliance between sovereignty, national identity and state interests now serves to obscure not only proper understanding of the fundamental concepts of social and political morality, including rights, justice, self-determination and toleration, but also the values, norms and institutional requirements of the democratic project.

As a second core feature, then, a significant effect of globalization is transformation of the domain of sovereignty, from the partial dispersal of powers and authority to the construction of new modes of governance between states, intergovernmental institutions, and non-state actors. Changes in the domain of state sovereignty both restrain and enable or foster state action – such as through the mutual constraints and sanctions occasioned by formal regimes, as well as by providing expanded options and opportunities for globally public, shared schemes for addressing common areas of concern such as transboundary pollution, trade and finance, telecommunications, international crime, infectious diseases, terrorism and global warming.[22] The extent and impact of these changes may be accommodated to some degree by the international system of autonomous states but, for the most part, globalization raises important questions that cannot be suitably answered in conventional state-centric terms.

Third, globalization thus entails not only the intensification of interactions and interconnections that have led to the 'shrinking' of our world, but also the emergence of a system of global governance that seeks to regulate and manage various areas of transnational activity. The movement towards global governance initiated at the close of the Second World War has intensified as the capacity of states to effectively govern the range of issues that extend beyond (yet intersect) their territorial boundaries has declined.[23] In addition a host of non-state actors – including non-governmental organizations (NGOs), activist groups, the mass media, and economic institutions – have become increasingly influential in traditional political forums, and have also helped to shape global decision-making and policies through transnationally-networked forms of organization that operate beyond and supplement formal state and interstate functions and settings. This is not to suggest that the state is disappearing or becoming irrelevant, but that it is now enmeshed within horizontal and vertical networks of multiple suprastate, substate and non-state actors whose roles and contributions to global governance can no longer be confined to the boundaries and dictates of the nation-state.[24]

Fourth, the diminishing efficacy and pertinence of sovereign territoriality raises the question of the justice of the order (or disorder) bolstered by globalization. Traditionally questions of social justice have been restricted to the domestic sphere. Under conditions of globalization, however, the parties affected by the causes and consequences of injustice have been seen increasingly in transnational terms. With the influence of normative discourses and practices such as those of human rights and human development the fact that, for instance, there is an ever-growing global inequality of resources and goods, of extreme poverty and world hunger seems to many theorists to provide ample evidence of the manifest yet avoidable injustice of the existing economic order. Consequently, it is argued that the terms and scope of justice must be conceived as applying not only within but also across state borders.[25] The shared fates and interests of persons – what Held refers to as 'communities of fate' – extend beyond political boundaries, as economic, social, cultural and political life becomes increasingly global.[26] Nevertheless, it has also been noted that the 'backlash' against globalization has tapped into strong sentiments of cultural diversity and identity that often run counter to the sense of global solidarity which may be needed to underpin moves towards more inclusive conceptions and practices of global justice.[27]

Fifth, the challenges of distributive justice under globalization raise other pressing issues concerning the justness of the world order. Among these issues are the democratic credentials and legitimacy of international institutions. While it is by no means clear that only one set of institutional arrangements will satisfy appropriate standards of legitimacy, it has become obvious to many that the global order suffers from a palpable 'democratic deficit'.[28] This position is reflected in, for example, the worldwide call for democratic reform of international organizations and greater inclusiveness in global governance that has been most visible since the 1999 World Trade Organization (WTO) meeting in Seattle. In much of the literature on globalization there is a general consensus that the present system of global governance is distorted in so far as it reflects a hierarchy of power at the international level which too frequently promotes the interests of the most powerful states and global social forces at the expense of the majority of the world's inhabitants. In particular, the new supranational layers of governance created by nation-states seeking to promote or regulate the effects of globalization generally have few mechanisms of accountability accessible to the general population. They tend to operate according to non-democratic principles and, as such, fail to represent a large segment of international society.[29]

Finally, in response to the demand for greater participation and accountability in the processes of globalization, a global public domain commonly referred to as 'global civil society' is emerging and is widely regarded as playing a central role in fostering global governance.[30] Civil society is defined as a realm of cooperative public engagement and social relations that involves individuals who act collectively yet who are separate or autonomous from the state. In the context of globalization civil society has assumed a significant global dimension on the basis of transnational networks of non-state actors, especially NGOs such as Amnesty International, Greenpeace, Oxfam International and Doctors Without Borders whose memberships, common purpose and organizational activities have spread across national borders. Global civil society has served not only as a source of governance per se, but more importantly as a force for *good* global governance through dissemination of information, formation of open forums for dialogue and debate, and advocacy of greater democracy, transparency and accountability in governmental and multilateral institutions.[31] Thus the globalization of political life associated with the emerging global civil society moves beyond the sense of greater connectedness between state-based actors identified with neoliberal institutionalism, and embraces the growing engagement with and influence of a host of non-state actors. In addition, global civil society has played a crucial role in expanding debates on citizenship in light of the deterritorialization of political life. With the de-linkage of social relations, forms of identity, modes of communication, and pathways for individual and collective action from the nation-state, the concept of what it means to be a citizen – including the rights, responsibilities and 'virtues' of citizenship – may be increasingly determined by forces, interests and forms of community that constitute, in Habermas's words, a 'postnational constellation'.[32]

A critical theory approach to confronting globalization

It seems clear, then, that globalization stands as the insurmountable political and intellectual horizon of our age. Because globalization has perhaps become 'the central thematic for social theory',[33] it is incumbent on critical theory to be querulous in the face of both the 'chronocentrism' that might be signalled in globalization's rising fortunes and the fast polarized political reactions to it. Hence globalization is a complex notion that requires unpacking; and we must – for this is critical theory's vocation – avoid taking it at face value, either imagining that we are locked into some triumphal end of history, or believing that a reversal is hidden in history in line with what Gramsci called the 'stupefying drug' of orthodox Marxism. To do so would be to succumb to a sterile and totalizing opposition between 'pro' and 'anti' globalization camps, in which the contours of globalization and what opportunities it either opens or forecloses become polarized around either the dominant discourse of neoliberalism and its sweeping valorization of the transnational flow of capital, commodities and labour, or the marginalized but indefatigable discourse of the Old Left and its indiscriminate condemnation of the same phenomenon. However, given the suspect legacy of the Old Left and the increasingly apparent failures of neoliberalism, an attempt to examine what globalization represents today and what potential it might hold for the future, from the fresh perspective of critical social and political theory, is called for.

Broadly speaking, there are two primary ways of identifying and defining critical theory and its concerns. The first, and perhaps most widely recognized version of critical theory is that associated with the body of work developed by members of the Frankfurt Institute of Social Research, or 'the Frankfurt School'. Drawing upon a wide-ranging cast of thinkers, including Kant, Hegel, Marx, Nietzsche, Weber and Freud, the Frankfurt School theorists – most notably Max Horkheimer, Theodor Adorno, Herbert Marcuse and, more recently, Albrecht Wellmer, Axel Honneth and Jürgen Habermas – sought to recover the liberatory potential of modern social and political life from the forms of domination and exploitation concomitant with the emergence of modernity.[34] The Frankfurt School theorists challenged orthodox Marxism's adherence to historical materialism and its reductive and positivistic views of economics and science, advocating instead a self-reflective version of immanent critique by which theory and its prescriptions for social transformation are regarded as inseparable from the historical, social and material contexts of its own genesis.

Second, critical theory is understood more broadly to refer to any social and political theory that is reflexive, in the sense that it is aware of the values, beliefs and interests which inform it; attuned to immanent critique, in so far as acknowledges its social and historical embeddedness and the fact that knowledge and specific political and material conditions are indivisible; and oriented towards facilitating and supporting emancipatory social transformation, both by diagnosing various dimensions of domination and proposing alternative or counterhegemonic social and political arrangements in order to improve human existence.[35] Consequently, critical theory by its very nature constitutes a pluralistic field populated by an eclectic mix of progressive theoretical and political perspectives. Despite this diversity, however, it can be said that what unites the different strands of critical theory is a shared commitment to human emancipation and a common concern to analyse the causes of, and prescribe solutions to, domination, exploitation and injustice. As Marcuse suggested, 'any critical theory of society' is committed to two basic normative claims, namely, 'the judgment that human life is worth living, or rather can be and ought to be made worth living' and 'the judgment that, in a given society, specific possibilities exist for the amelioration of human life and the specific ways and means of realizing these possibilities'.[36]

In the context of this book, critical theory is deployed pluralistically but also for the shared purpose of challenging existing practices and values, in order to reconsider the prospects for justice and social change within the context of a globalizing world. The critical theory we have in mind therefore draws pragmatically and non-dogmatically on the broad spectrum of Kantian, Marxist and Nietzschean traditions, as well as on other contemporary critical theoretical paradigms – such as poststructuralism, radical democracy, postcolonial theory and cosmopolitanism – as resources in the critique of ideology and the transformation of existing conditions of domination and oppression. It takes theory to be an important force in emancipatory projects, but rejects the positivism and rigidity of much of the Marxist tradition. It also rejects the paralysis often associated with postmodernism's seemingly interminable self-critique and relentless negativity. This critical theory reads the world as construction and change – as transformative potential – thus underscoring the primacy of the political. It seeks what is perhaps best described as a practice and 'principle of hope' in the extension and deepening of the emancipatory struggle for justice, freedom and equality under the conditions of globalization.[37]

Another way of casting the critical theoretical approach embraced by the essays in this volume is to think of them as reclaiming the constructive and committed terrain of what McLennan and Osborne refer to as 'oracular' ideas.[38] McLennan and Osborne suggest that, today, social and political ideas operate more and more in the modality of the vehicular rather than the oracular. Oracular ideas are predictive, long-term vocabularies of where we stand and where we are or should be going, 'something to stake your life upon'.[39] Vehicular ideas, on the contrary, are more instrumentally diagnostic, concerned narrowly with where we are, functioning as modest problem-solving devices that 'take us from A to B'. A critique of such vehicular ideas would contest the cheap, marketing, gimmicky orientation involved, the thinness and waning of utopian imagination, and the demise of the normative or evaluative dimension in the theory and practice of neoliberalism and the reactionary Right, as well as the old-fashioned Left. In these cases, the problems lie at both the level of analysis and of vision. These are the two, inextricably intertwined dimensions that this volume seeks to address, planting flags in order to map both the uneven and complex territory of globalization and the possibilities ahead, insisting on the inescapability of the visionary, utopian dimension.

There are, of course, both Left-progressive and Right-wing attempts to confront globalization, and the results of these efforts provide useful resources or markers for critical theoretical engagements with the dynamics associated with the intensification of global interconnectedness. The Right has been concerned about the erosion of ways of life ('cultural pollution', foreign control of resources) and about diminishing self-determination.[40] For Žižek, the revival of the ultra-Right is partly a signal of the movement of the Left, particularly social democracy, away from the terrain of class politics: it is only the Right, today, which appeals to working-class concerns.[41] For Castells, the dislocations of the past two or three decades have generated a new network society and have called forth a host of what he calls 'defensive identities'.[42] Thus, Islamic fundamentalism emerges as a response to the demise of nationalist and socialistic hopes for development and autonomy in the Middle East; thus, the revival of reactive national- and ethnic-based political projects; thus, a communitarian turn, which searches for meaning against growing atomization. For Castells, these confrontations with the new order are destined to produce merely havens, not the heavens of the now lost utopian movements.

In interrogating the emergence of a new, globalized economy – one of the central dislocating features of the network society – Castells underscores the advent of new information communication technology and the worldwide spread of neoliberal commonsense. This commonsense is for many thinkers an inescapable ideological horizon of the globalized present. Perry Anderson, for instance, designates it the *most successful ideology in history.*[43] Unsurprisingly, confronting globalization has frequently meant confronting neoliberalism. In this vein, Bourdieu devoted his last years to fighting against the 'banker's fatalism' that was concerned only with profit, that reduced the social world to economic language, that fetishized the productive forces, and that combated 'all forms of civilization associated with the social state'.[44]

One of the most noted features of the contemporary political and ideological landscape is the near-total submission of all parties to an agenda of 'tight fiscal policy' characteristic of neoliberalism, meaning, it is often said, a closing of the political universe, so that it is now easier to imagine the world destroyed in an environmental or supernatural disaster than it is to imagine a less spectacular alteration in the social formation.[45] In particular, social democracy's declining fortunes have been singled out as signalling a closure of political alternatives. One of the central characteristics of those works that seek to confront globalization has been a reassertion of the social or the public in the face of the apparently growing domination of the economic. This retrieves, in a sense, the mission of classical social democracy, which sought to install a specifically socially and economically democratic dimension alongside a political democracy that otherwise might remain merely formal, subordinated to capitalism's 'dull compulsion of the economic'.

In his *The Third Way*, Giddens reached for a way to respond to the apparent death and lingering ghost of socialism. The only way forward, beyond both classical social democracy and neoliberalism was, for Giddens, to seek to 'adapt social democracy to a world which has changed fundamentally over the past two or three decades'.[46] Here the aim was to reassert socialism's values where socialism's economic programme had fallen into disrepute – the failures of 'really existing socialism', social democracy's inadequate appreciation of capitalism's capacities, globalization and technological changes from the 1970s, transformations in class structure, and the arrival of postmaterialist values. Neoliberalism, though, insisted Giddens, could not be taken as victorious; witness the debilitating tension, for example, between market fundamentalism and conservatism. Of globalization, Giddens contended that nations retained and would continue to retain considerable power but this would necessarily be wielded in collaboration with other sources of authority, such as in the shift from government to governance as noted in the preceding section. Globalization, Giddens maintained, should be approached by Third Wayers in a positive and multifaceted manner. Protectionism could not serve as an answer, and neither could the uncritical defence of free trade: social justice and equality must not drop away as goals. A host of programmatic and values axioms, then, became vital – positive welfare, equality as inclusion, a new mixed economy, an active civil society, a social investment state and cosmopolitan democracy, for example. The nation remained an important stabilizing force against fragmentation, as well as new modes of global governance, and contestation of market fundamentalism.

Giddens's work subsequently attracted a number of combative and lucid critics who regarded the Third Way as a mere softening out of neoliberalism, as the best ideological shell for neoliberalism, and as completely evacuating the class elements from social democracy.[47] In response, Giddens has recently attempted to redraw the lines of a rejuvenated social democracy with his notion of 'neoprogressivism'. Neoprogressivism, in brief, stands for 'a strong public sphere, coupled to a thriving market economy; a pluralistic, but inclusive society; and a cosmopolitan wider world, founded upon principles of international law'.[48] Giddens contends that we need a period of publicization, or a defence of the 'core importance of the public sphere', to follow the period of privatization.[49] The public interest is the test for the functioning of both the state and the market, in line with greater public scepticism about the approach of corporates, and towards what Giddens calls a 'civil economy'. The 'ensuring state' replaces the enabling state of the Third Way: that is, the state has responsibilities – regulation – beyond enabling. Citizenship, now, involves *co*-production of public goods. In the realm of globalization, Giddens mentions managed diversity as a move beyond naïve multiculturalism, and he also endorses David Held's insistence on the need to create a global social democracy.

Held, in line with his recognition of the complexity and multidimensionality of globalization, rejects arguments that equate globalization with a 'race to the bottom' in welfare, labour and environmental terms, insisting on the continuing significance of political institutions. In fact, 'states remain the primary actors' in world politics.[50] However, with the information technology (IT) revolution, the end of the Cold War and the universalization of liberal democracy, the emergence of global markets, the reconfiguration of political power, the advent of a new type of global civil society, and the growing movement of people, something more than classical, nation-based, social democracy is called for. Social democracy's traditional concerns – 'the rule of law, political equality, democratic politics, social justice, social solidarity and community, economic efficiency and effectiveness' – must be extended to the regional and global levels.[51] Finding both neoliberal and anti-globalization approaches to globalization deeply flawed (the problem of market failure versus the naïveté of locally-based solutions), Held proposes a set of concrete interventions towards such global social democracy, or cosmopolitan democracy:

> promoting the rule of law at the international level; greater transparency, accountability and democracy in global governance; a deeper commitment to social justice in the pursuit of more equitable distribution of life chance; the protection and reinvention of community at diverse levels (from local to global); and the regulation of the global economy through the public management of global financial and trade flows, the provision of global public goods and the engagement of leading stakeholders in corporate governance.[52]

Perhaps the most savage criticisms of Third Way proposals have come from the Marxists.[53] In this reading, the Third Way offers nothing for those excluded from the benefits of globalization, and Third Wayers are considered either naïve or ill-intentioned in maintaining the possibility of a reform of voracious late capitalism. For orthodox Marxists such as Petras and Veltmeyer, globalization denotes merely a new (American) imperialism in the twenty-first century, an ideological tool ('globaloney') that seeks to make alternatives unimaginable.[54] While accepting that contemporary capitalism has been transformed, Petras and Veltmeyer read the new configuration as largely about the deepening and extension to all areas of the globe of exploitative capitalist relations, generated by the combined forces of multinational corporations (MNCs), banks, and imperial states. Far from signalling a demise of the nation-state, the new imperialism has meant a 'New Statism', and a 'new authoritarianism', masked by the spread of formal parliamentary democracy. This is made clear in the rise of extra-parliamentary action worldwide against the interests of the globalist ruling class. In familiar Marxian fashion, Petras and Veltmeyer imagine the objective conditions ripe and the subjective factors as maturing; price controls on essentials; freezing bank accounts of the wealthy; mobilizing unused resources to deepen and extend the domestic economy; undertaking agrarian reform; reducing profits and putting a moratorium on debt repayments; moving from hyper-specialization to a more balanced economy; implementing financial controls to eliminate speculative activity; and replacing privatization with socialization.

Hardt and Negri's recent work, *Empire,* derives from a completely different, libertarian tradition of socialist thought – Italian workerism – encompassing a challenging mixture of Manifesto Marxism, theories of post-Fordism and postindustrialism, and poststructuralism.[55] Empire is a deterritorializing form of sovereignty, ruling in new ways such as 'virtuous war' and the society of control (biopolitical power), yet without a centre (no Rome, no Winter Palace to storm). Postmodernism and informationalism stand as the coordinates of this new order, with immaterial labour – knowledge- and service-based – as the new modality of social and economic structuring. At the same time as Empire is forming, however, the multitudes are busy constructing counter-Empire. These multitudes – visible, variously, in Tiananmen Square in 1989, the LA riots of 1992, the uprisings in Chiapas in 1994, the French industrial strikes of 1995, and the Palestinian Intifada – are able to challenge Empire at any point and are the real force behind Empire's construction and dynamism. Fighting by means of desertion, migration and defection, these multitudes struggle to generate a new mode of life and a new community. Hardt and Negri mention as particularly important tendencies that move towards global citizenship, a social wage for all, and the right to re-appropriation.

Hardt and Negri's vision of Empire in the global age is mirrored in the events of, and those following, 11 September 2001. The terrorist attacks of '9/11' have been presented both as ushering in a 'new kind of war'[56] and as representing the mere continuation of a centuries-old 'clash of civilizations'.[57] To Huntington, the actions of al-Qaeda crystallized the challenges of Muslim societies to the dominance of Western-led globalization, and forged the latest in a series of struggles between rival civilizations.[58] Rather than signalling a genuine weakening of American hegemony, though, the pervasive sense of insecurity following the attacks then served as the basis of the ensuing 'war on terrorism'. For this reason, the prevalence of fear and insecurity throughout the USA can be regarded as the justificatory moment of resurgent American imperial power. As Hardt and Negri suggest, 'imperial rule functions by breaking down'.[59] For Bush and the neoconservative ideologues that form the foundation of his administration, globalization functions as a civilizing process through which the West – and especially the USA – is able to secure order, stability and economic freedom for the rest of the world, by force if necessary. The 'war on terrorism', then, serves as an almost inevitable extension of the alleged civilizational conflict between US capitalism (in conjunction with militarism and conservative Christian values) and anti-modernist Islamic fundamentalism. Indeed, following his victory in the 2004 presidential elections, Bush portrayed his re-election as a 'mandate' to pursue America's 'special responsibility' for asserting world order in spite of the nation's vulnerability as the 'heart' of civilization. This conception of America's 'special responsibility' fosters what Michael Ignatieff refers to as 'empire lite', a global sphere of influence or 'hegemony without colonies' producing an empire 'without consciousness of itself as such'.[60] However, while the spirit of American exceptionalism animates the drive towards empire,[61] resistance to US hegemony – both in the guise of militant and particularist fundamentalism, and in the form of transnational social movements for peace and justice – runs deep throughout an interdependent world.

While imaginatively and enthusiastically analysing this new world and providing a buoyant sense of the possibilities ahead, *Empire* suffers from a lack of specificity in terms of 'what is to be done'. Nevertheless it chimes well with much of what is new and exciting in the alternative or 'alter-globalization' movement. This movement has frequently been viewed as a reinvigoration of, or a replacement for, the lost socialist movement. For instance, Immanuel Wallerstein considers the decline of social and national anti-systemic movements which emerged in the nineteenth century. After 1968, there was greater scepticism about parties of both these types and they and the state in general lost much legitimacy as agents of fundamental social transformation. Since that time, there has been a search for a better kind of anti-systemic movement that would lead to a more democratic, egalitarian world, and here the alternative globalization movement looks promising. The alternative globalization movement is also notable as an instance of global civil society in action. In particular it can be viewed as the actualization of what Richard Falk has termed 'globalization from below', in which people-centred transnational social movements introduce new forms of radical, counterhegemonic political activism that challenge statist and corporatist 'globalization from above'.[62]

The alternative globalization movement is, of course, a heterogeneous grouping, focusing on a range of issues such as fair trade, the unaccountable power of multinational corporations, genetic engineering, Third World debt, environmental degradation, and labour rights. Thus this movement does not represent a direct programmatic replacement for socialism. This is clear in the case of the World Social Forum (WSF), focusing on capitalist-led globalization from above (acting as a counterweight to the World Economic Forum), built around the slogan 'another world is possible', and representing a plurality of organizations from around the world.[63] The accent on the WSF as an 'open forum', the 'free exchange of experiences and interlinking for effective action', the inclusion of different trends and lack of a common political manifesto all move significantly from the theory and practice of socialist orthodoxy, and seem in line with the nomadic, deterritorializing ambitions of Hardt and Negri's multitudes. And in the means of interlinking and in the new forms of political action (for instance, the more culturalist and ludic tendencies of counterglobalizing groups such as Indymedia, adbusters and the Yes Men; and the less vanguardist and more inclusive movements such as the Zapatistas, and the anti-WTO and anti-G-8 protests), we again have something quite different from the means and goals of the old socialist movement.

Strategically – and usefully in thinking about the utopian dimension of confronting globalization – Wallerstein views the alternative globalization movement as needing to address four issues in the period of transition we are currently in.[64] First, we need an *open debate* about the transition we are hoping for. Second, the movement cannot ignore short-term, defensive action, including electoral action, against an older revolutionary socialist tradition which, at times, was content with an orientation to the present contained in the startlingly inadequate judgement, 'the worse the better'. Third, middle-range goals must be established as well. Here, Wallerstein suggests progressive de-commodification against neoliberal attempts to commodify everything. In this way, he moves from the orthodox Marxist hopes for nationalization to the need to create structures that will perform and survive rather than necessarily generate profit. Last, it is necessary to develop the substantive meaning of long-term emphases, most crucially a world that is democratic and egalitarian.

Finally, it is important to briefly explore a progressive postmodern mode of confronting globalization, namely Derridean cosmopolitanism. Deconstruction's 'political turn', with its interrogations of friendship, community, hospitality, justice and democracy, are all profoundly relevant to globalization, even if Derrida sees the concept as often confused and linked to 'political tricks and political strategies' (arguments that promote the free market).[65] In the light of a host of plagues that press upon the world and transformations that fall under the category of 'globalization', Derrida seeks to trouble the canonical conceptions of friendship and democracy and to move them beyond territory, the nation-state, citizenship, and so forth. Derrida's idea of a 'New International' means the necessary transformation of the sovereignty of the state, new international laws and new practices, but it relies on the category of the 'to come' in these transformed concepts. That is, democracy (which embodies 'equality for everyone and respect for singularity') is not a regime, but is about a promise, an injunction, an impossibility, which keeps things open to endless debate and improvement; such destabilization of all identity and such a move from the category of necessity lends us real responsibility and turns us perpetually towards the future.

Cosmopolitanism has occupied a central role in other critical theoretical approaches that, while sharing many of Derrida's concerns, deviate from his particular epistemology and methodology. The theory of cosmopolitan democracy developed by Held, Anthony McGrew and Daniele Archibugi, for instance, outlines a project for multiple layers of democratized governance (from the local to the global) that, among other goals, attempts to resolve the shortcomings of global governance, in particular the perceived deficit of democratic legitimacy. For advocates of cosmopolitan democracy, any role that global governance can have in achieving human development through poverty reduction and the provision of both welfare and human security often is marginalized by the self-interested considerations of the realist power system. In essence, the current system of global governance privileges its market enhancing functions over its market correcting ones, an imbalance that has perhaps only grown in the wake of the recent expansion of neoliberal ideas and 'the existence of organized transnational interests far removed from any popular mandate'.[66] In addition, Held notes that although the end of the Cold War offered the possibility of a 'new international order' based on the extension of democracy across the globe and increasingly peaceful international relations, this potential remains largely unfulfilled, as demonstrated by the crises in Bosnia, Rwanda, Afghanistan, Iraq and elsewhere. Under these circumstances Held asserts the need for the creation of a global democratic polity and culture, the only framework in which the ideals of autonomy and democracy can be fully realized. The cosmopolitan model of democracy seeks to expand the levels of participatory politics and means of accountability through an adaptive 'system of diverse and overlapping power centres, shaped and delimited by democratic law'.[67] Despite the deficiencies of the existing system of global governance, Held is cautiously optimistic about the prospects for cultivating cosmopolitan democracy, especially considering that some cosmopolitan ideas, especially that of human rights, are already at the centre of post-Second World War legal and political developments.

As we have seen, many of the developments in critical social and political theory surveyed above challenge the presumptions of certainty which underpin the respective positions of neoliberalism and orthodox Marxism in regard to globalization. Contemporary critical theorists also seek to transcend the political apathy at times found in the works of postmodernists trapped in a cycle of perpetual incredulity. For this reason, the studies collected in this work have three main objectives: first, to critically assess simplistic attempts either to valorize or to condemn globalization and thereby to advance our understanding of current conditions and forms of globalization; second, to evaluate the possibilities for constructing forms of critical social and political theorizing which are not pregiven by the polarized positions of neoliberalism and orthodox Marxism; and third, to assess the immediate and future prospects of emancipatory political practice and to derive both theoretical and policy lessons that will foster critical interrogations of globalization now and in the immediate future.

Hence, it is towards an embracing approach that exemplifies what Bourdieu has termed a 'reasoned utopianism',[68] or Hudson has called a 'decentred utopianism'[69] – with social ideals as ethically and culturally oriented, attentive to difference, and theoretically open and multi-dimensional while remaining committed to democratic inclusiveness, the community of humanity and the expansion of justice across the globe – that we want to gesture in this book. The progressive confrontations with globalization all have their gains (here-and-now policy alternatives, bold theoretical innovation for greater illumination, revived utopianism, and renewed optimism against a Left that has been maudlin and withdrawn for so long, a greater caution *vis-à-vis* orthodox Marxian alternatives of the past) and drawbacks (a weak reformism that threatens to jettison social democratic values, a return to outworn class and economic determinism as well as outmoded Leninist and statist solutions, and a politically vague messianism). But a better way ahead is provided by a more theoretically and normatively ambitious cast of mind, holding to a more open approach characteristic of both the rich analytical resources of critical social and political theory and the alternative globalization emphasis that announces, first and most importantly, that 'another world is possible'.

Notes

1 Cairncross quoted in J. Urry, *Global Complexity* (Cambridge: Polity, 2003), p. 2.
2 M. Castells, *The Information Age: Economy, Society and Culture: The Rise of the Network Society* (Oxford: Basil Blackwell, 2000).
3 R. Sennet, *The Corrosion of Character: The Personal Consequences of Work in the New Capitalism* (New York: W. W. Norton, 1998); R. Sennett, 'Street and Office: Two Sources of Identity', in W. Hutton and A. Giddens (eds), *Global Capitalism* (New York: New Press, 2000).
4 V. Shiva, 'The World on the Edge', in Hutton and Giddens, *Global Capitalism*, p. 118.
5 Z. Bauman, *Globalization: The Human Consequences* (New York: Columbia University Press, 1998).
6 M. Mann, 'Globalization and September 11', *New Left Review*, 12 (2001), 51–72.
7 Cochrane and Pain quoted in R. Robertson, 'Globalization Theory 2000+: Major Problematics', in G. Ritzer and B. Smart (eds), *Handbook of Social Theory* (London: Sage, 2000), pp. 458–71.
8 Lechner quoted in G. Ritzer, *The Globalization of Nothing* (Thousand Oaks, CA: Pine Forge, 2004), p. 72.
9 J. Petras and H. Veltmeyer, *Globalization Unmasked: Imperialism in the 21st Century* (London: Zed Books, 2001), p. 26.
10 M. Waters, *Globalization*, 2nd edn (London: Routledge, 1995), p. 5.
11 D. Held and A. McGrew, *Globalization/Anti-Globalization* (Cambridge: Polity, 2002), p. 1.
12 D. Held and A. McGrew, *Global Transformations: Politics, Economics and Culture* (Cambridge: Polity, 1999).
13 Bauman, *Globalization.*
14 A. Giddens, *Runaway World: How Globalization is Shaping Our Lives* (Reith Lectures, 1999), online at http://news.bbc.co.uk/hi/english/static/events/reith_99/default.htm. On risk, see U. Beck, *World Risk Society* (Cambridge: Polity, 1998); U. Beck, *What is Globalization?* (Cambridge: Polity, 2000).
15 M. Castells, *The Information Age: Economy, Society and Culture: The Power of Identity* (Oxford: Basil Blackwell, 1997).
16 E. W. Said, *Culture and Imperialism* (London: Vintage, 1994), pp. 207, 339.
17 Urry, *Global Complexity.*
18 M. Hardt and A. Negri, *Empire* (Cambridge, MA: Harvard University Press, 2000).
19 J. A. Scholte, 'The Globalization of World Politics', in J. Baylis and S. Smith (eds), *The Globalization of World Politics: An Introduction to International Relations* (Oxford: Oxford University Press, 2001), pp. 14–15.
20 D. Held and A. McGrew (eds), *The Global Transformations Reader* (Cambridge: Polity, 2002), p. 1.
21 See, for instance, S. Sassen, *Losing Control: Sovereignty in an Age of Globalization* (New York: Columbia University Press, 1998).
22 See R. O. Keohane, *Power and Governance in a Partially Globalized World* (London: Routledge, 2002), and Andreas Hasenclever *et al.* (eds), *Theories of International Regimes* (Cambridge: Cambridge University Press, 1997).
23 See the Commission on Global Governance, *Our Global Neighbourhood: The Report of the Commission on Global Governance* (Oxford: Oxford University Press, 1995).

24 A. M. Slaughter, 'Disaggregated Sovereignty: Towards the Public Accountability of Global Government Networks', *Government and Opposition*, 39 (2004), 159–90.
25 See D. Moellendorf, *Cosmopolitan Justice* (Boulder, CO: Westview, 2002); T. Pogge, *World Poverty and Hunger* (Cambridge: Polity, 2002); and P. Singer, *One World: The Ethics of Globalization* (New Haven, CT: Yale University Press, 2002).
26 D. Held, *Democracy and the Global Order: From the Modern State to Cosmopolitan Governance* (Cambridge: Polity, 1995).
27 S. Benhabib, *The Claims of Culture: Equality and Diversity in the Global Era* (Princeton, NJ: Princeton University Press, 2002).
28 Held and McGrew, *The Global Transformations Reader*, p. 13.
29 D. Archibugi, 'Principles of Cosmopolitan Democracy', in D. Archibugi, D. Held and M. Kohler (eds), *Re-imagining Political Community: Studies in Cosmopolitan Democracy* (Cambridge: Polity, 1998), p. 204.
30 J. G. Ruggie, 'Taking Embedded Liberalism Global: The Corporate Connection', in D. Held and M. Koenig-Archibugi (eds), *Taming Globalization: Frontiers of Governance* (Cambridge: Polity, 2003), p. 95.
31 See M. Kaldor, *Global Civil Society: An Answer to War* (Cambridge: Polity, 2003), and J. Keane, *Global Civil Society?* (Cambridge: Cambridge University Press, 2003).
32 J. Habermas, *The Postnational Constellation: Political Essays* (Cambridge, MA: The MIT Press, 2001).
33 Featherstone and Lash quoted in J. Rosenberg, *The Follies of Globalisation Theory* (London: Verso, 2000), p. 2.
34 R. Wiggershaus, *The Frankfurt School: Its Histories, Theories and Political Significance* (Cambridge, MA: The MIT Press, 1995).
35 See D. Rasmussen, *The Handbook of Critical Theory* (Oxford: Basil Blackwell, 1996).
36 H. Marcuse, *One-Dimensional Man* (Boston, MA: Beacon Press, 1964), pp. x–xi.
37 See E. Bloch, *The Principle of Hope* (Cambridge, MA: The MIT Press, 1995).
38 G. McLennan and T. Osborne, 'Contemporary "Vehicularity" and "Romanticism": Debating the Status of Ideas and Intellectuals', *Critical Review of International Social and Political Philosophy*, 6 (2003), 51–66.
39 Ibid., p. 53.
40 M. B. Steger, *Globalism: The New Market Ideology* (Lanham, MB: Rowman & Littlefield, 2002).
41 S. Žižek, 'Why We All Love to Hate Haider', *New Left Review*, 2 (2000), 37–45.
42 Castells, *The Information Age: Economy, Society and Culture: The Power of Identity*.
43 P. Anderson, 'Renewals', *New Left Review*, 1 (2000), 5–24.
44 P. Bourdieu, *Acts of Resistance: Against the Tyranny of the Market* (New York: New Press, 1998b). See also Barry Smart's recent *Economy, Culture and Society* (London: Sage, 2003), which seeks to return sociology to the relationship between economy and society, bringing together critiques of neoliberalism.
45 S. Žižek, 'Multiculturalism, or, the Cultural Logic of Multinational Capitalism', *New Left Review*, 225 (1997), 29–51.
46 A. Giddens, *The Third Way: The Renewal of Social Democracy* (Cambridge: Polity, 1998), p. 26.
47 Anderson, 'Renewals'; Žižek, 'Why We All Love to Hate Haider'.

48 A. Giddens, *The Progressive Manifesto* (Cambridge: Polity, 2003), pp. 6–7.
49 Ibid., p. 11.
50 D. Held, 'Global Social Democracy', in Giddens, *The Progressive Manifesto*, p. 140.
51 Ibid., p. 145.
52 Ibid., p. 145. Much of this appears close to Habermas's on-going philosophical-political concerns – recently expressed in his dialogue with Derrida on Enlightenment, US unilateralism, terrorism and global cosmopolitanism (based on human rights and extending the international rule of law). G. Borradori (ed.), *Philosophy in a Time of Terror: Dialogues With Jürgen Habermas and Jacques Derrida* (Chicago, IL: University of Chicago Press, 2003)
53 See, for instance, A. Callinicos, *Against the Third Way* (Cambridge: Polity, 2001); Žižek, 'Why We All Love to Hate Haider'.
54 Petras and Veltmayer, *Globalization Unmasked: Imperialism in the 21st Century*.
55 Hardt and Negri, *Empire*.
56 G. W. Bush, 'President Pledges Assistance for New York Call with Pataki, Giuliani'. Remarks by the President in Telephone Conversation with New York Mayor Giuliani and New York Governor Pataki, 13 September 2001, Washington, DC: The White House, Office of the Press Secretary.
57 S. Huntington, *The Clash of Civilizations and the Remaking of World Order* (London: Touchstone Books, 1998). See also S. Huntington, 'The Age of Muslim Wars', *Newsweek*, Special Davos Edition, December 2001–February 2002.
58 For a powerful critique of the clash of civilizations thesis, and the pervasive simple-mindedness of commentary on Islamism in general, see A. Al-Azmeh, 'Postmodern Obscurantism and "The Muslim Question"', *Journal for the Study of Religions and Ideologies*, 5 (2003), 20–46, online at http://hiphi.ubbcluj.ro/JSRI/html%20version/index/no_5/aziaalazmeh-articol.htm.
59 Hardt and Negri, *Empire*, p. 202.
60 M. Ignatieff, *Empire Lite: Nation-building in Bosnia, Kosovo and Afghanistan* (London: Vintage, 2003), p. 2.
61 For a neoconservative statement to this effect see M. Boot, 'The Case for American Empire', *The Weekly Standard*, 7 (15 October 2001).
62 R. Falk, 'Resisting "Globalization from Above" through "Globalization from Below"', in B. Gills (ed.), *Globalization and the Politics of Resistance* (London: Macmillan, 2000); see also R. Falk, *Predatory Globalization: A Critique* (Cambridge: Polity, 1999).
63 Consult the WSF web site online at http://www.forumsocialmundial.org.br/home.asp.
64 I. Wallerstein, 'New Revolts Against the System', *New Left Review*, 18 (2002), 29–39.
65 J. Derrida, 'Politics and Friendship: A Discussion With Jacques Derrida', (1997), online at http://www.sussex.ac.uk/Units/frenchthought/derrida.htm.
66 D. Archibugi, 'Cosmopolitical Democracy', in D. Archibugi (ed.), *Debating Cosmopolitics* (London: Verso, 2003), p. 9.
67 Held, *Democracy and the Global Order*, p. 234.
68 P. Bourdieu, 'A Reasoned Utopia and Economic Fatalism', *New Left Review*, 227 (1998), 125–30.
69 W. Hudson, *The Reform of Utopia* (Aldershot: Ashgate, 2003).

Part I

Understanding Globalization's Challenges: Post-Marxism and Beyond

2
Postmodern Socialism Revisited

Peter Beilharz

Globalization rules, or at least globalization talk rules. All talk of socialism, meanwhile, melts into air. How has this come to be? A decade ago, at least in critical circles, the dominant keyword rather was the idea of the postmodern and it, also, had its influence, spreading into the dailies and talk shows. Whatever else it was, the idea of the postmodern was temporal, and it mixed anxiety and hope in the characteristic figure of the sublime. The postmodern was, notoriously, a negative or at best chronological marker, claiming a sense of 'being after', being after the modern, being after the postwar dream, the Keynesian Welfare State, after Fordism, after aesthetic modernism. It replayed an earlier period sense of boredom or *ennui*, a sense of loss, boredom, of only potential movement, later. Globalization, in contrast, is predominantly a spatial, and active term. It indicates boosterism, dynamism, or else rapaciousness and ruin.

These words matter, though it is always possible that they matter more for us, the critics, than for others. Sociologically, they work as symptoms, or semiological markers. We use terms like this to name our anxiety, that the world continues moving and therefore keeps eluding us both intellectually and politically. The object of our critical analysis is always necessarily ahead of us. Globalization talk rules, today, because it is a larger and more open-ended category than the postmodern ever was or could be. It has a historic referent – for Marxists, back to *The Communist Manifesto* or else to the Bolshevik theory of imperialism – but it is primarily future-oriented. And unlike the postmodern, however slippery that category was, the idea of globalization is open to fundamental contestation. Everybody experiences it, and many of us both love and hate it with a vehemence. Globalization represents the defining ambivalence of postmodern times.

Postmodern socialism

Some years ago I published a book called *Postmodern Socialism: Romanticism, City and State*, and I want to revisit it here as a way to open these questions again.[1] *Postmodern Socialism* was a second-order, global reflection on another book, the study of Australian Labour which was also published in 1994, *Transforming Labour: Labour Tradition and the Labour Decade*.[2] This second book was an obituary for the Australian Labour Party as an instrument of progressive social change, an argument that its pyrrhic victory was indeed as an active agent of globalization rather than of any kind of socialism, no matter how diluted its definition. But globalization was only just announced, in either of these books, where the postmodern and modern were more like the constituent terms of reference.

Globalization talk began to proliferate into this period, but its markers were uneven. Globalization was often made to stand for something else, as in imperialism, or the development of world systems. Plainly this was the logic of the most powerful period critique, in Paul Hirst and Grahame Thompson's *Globalization in Question*.[3] In terms of critical sociology the two most significant books were probably Roland Robertson's *Globalization*[4] and Manuel Castells' *The Information Age*.[5] Robertson's approach was as essayistic as Castells' was monumental. The main results of these innovations included the idea of 'glocalization', from Robertson, and the sense from Castells that there was a multiplicity of levels of globalization. The undercurrent in the Castells' project, however, is one of global swarming or *schwärmerei*, as though nothing will ever be the same again. Against the anthropological sensibility, implicit in the hybridity of Robertson's glocalization, Castells' new world has a distinctly vitalistic feel to it, and this is of some significance, for in the meantime vitalism has made a massive comeback, whether in the more scholarly work of Deleuze or the Manichean Marxism of Hardt and Negri.

The best explanation of globalization known to me in summary form is that of Michael Mann's brilliant essay in *New Left Review*, 'Globalization and September 11'.[6] For Mann, it follows that if modernities are multiple, so are globalizations, and this in more ways than one. Globalization refers not only to culture, economy and politics but also has a military dimension. The really revolutionary dimension remains that of the new Industrial Revolution powered by IT; finance is globalized more thoroughly than production, and the realm of culture is that most open to contestation.

The frame of *Transforming Labour*, in dull contrast to all this buzz, was Gramscian in intent. The image of transformation, *trasformismo* or incorporation into the mainstream, was a Gramscian motif which eluded all reviewers of the book. Here the approach was to think of the transformation of Labour from a social movement to a party of state as a dual process, where Labour was both transformed and acted as transformer, becoming the practical precedent for Blair's New Labour in the process. To view Labour in this way meant to look back, rather than forward, to local and imperial history, and to manoeuvre categories such as modernity and tradition in order to seek to begin to explain the peculiar configuration of settler capitalism in Australia and its attendant cultural peculiarities; modern, in many ways, yet without the industrial base of modernism in the American sense. To begin to understand the deregulative, neoliberal impulses of Labour in the 1980s it was necessary to construct senses of its hopes and fears against images of the 1970s (the Whitlam experiment), the 1940s (the culmination of classical labourism), and their earlier precedents. Whether postmodern or not – whether postmodern in culture, while modern or premodern in economy – globalization at this point burst through the door. For the standard view on the experiences of the antipodes was that Australia and New Zealand had traded on world primary commodity markets while protecting their citizens, keeping them out of the way of the world's more hazardous risks by cultivating social and economic protection, none of which was any longer sustainable.

In Australia, the key advocate of this narrative, where globalization was the proper remedy for a century of closure was Paul Kelly, in *The End of Certainty*.[7] On this account, the so-called social laboratory pioneered by Australia and New Zealand into the twentieth century now impeded growth and closed out all future prospects. A new epoch of openness would fix all this. Globalization, on this reading, was simply necessary; to argue against it was to fall victim to the nostalgia of traditionalism. Now nostalgia, famously, has been defined as memory with the pain cut out; and it does not take much condescension towards the history of ordinary citizens in their everyday lives to obliterate their own suffering, even in the good times of antipodean capitalism. Meantime, at a conceptual level, what is more pertinent here than charges against nostalgia is the persistent presence of romanticism in the critique of modernity.

The standard radical critique of modernity is that it is a victim of Enlightenment, the cult of reason, science, word and number. One argument in *Postmodern Socialism*, which follows a current in *Transforming Labour*, is that Enlightenment always travels with its inseparable partner, romanticism, and that this is as true of the experience of the antipodes as it is of the metropolis. *Postmodern Socialism* considers the view that romanticism, or anti-modernism, is as essential to modernity as it is to modernism. There can be no progress without loss, no movement of enlightenment without its attendant romanticism. Modernity generates futurism and hypermodernism, but it also evokes romanticism and nostalgia for lost worlds, real or imagined. The idea of the postmodern, in this way, was sometimes used as a romantic foil to modernity's enlightenment. Historically and culturally, however, it is in fact difficult to separate the two, as is well demonstrated for example in Cassirer's *Rousseau, Kant and Goethe*, or as we can see later in the work of the two greatest sociologists of modernity, Marx and Weber.[8] On any interpretation, in any case, modernity routinely generates its own sense of loss or alienation from the world it proclaims and powers forth. Modernity routinely generates its own anti-modernism: there can be no modernity without critique.

The residual issue in period arguments about the postmodern, then, was how to address the question of the novelty of the postmodern. Surely the postmodern could not be reduced to the historical precedent of the romantic, no matter how powerful the romantic critique of modernity then appeared? Earlier enthusiasms for the postmodern, such as those of Zygmunt Bauman, were precisely for the sense of novelty or release from modernist formulae, whether those of social engineering or international architectural style.[9] Modernism, notoriously for Baudelaire, proclaimed the *new*; surely this was something that the postmodern could offer again, if only as pastiche? Could the postmodern then be what came after socialism?

In an earlier text, *Socialism: The Active Utopia*, Bauman defined socialism as the counterculture of modernity.[10] Only socialisms reflect historically this ambivalent bonding of modernism and anti-modernism, enlightenment and romanticism. Romantic socialism, for its part, is often caught up with the image of the pastoral or identified with nature, where capitalism is associated with artifice. Yet, again, as Bauman insists, all culture becomes a matter of second nature, which means that nature is artificial at the same time as capitalism is naturalized for us.[11] The central figure in the formative tradition of critical theory here is neither Marx nor Rousseau, but Schiller. Schiller's anticipatory critique of alienation, fragmentation and the anti-human effects of the division of labour is crucial to understanding Marx's work.[12] And like Marx's work, it is indicative of a kind of naturalism which too easily ascribes all ills to civilization, as though we moderns could live without differentiation, specialization or the sweet smell of gasoline on asphalt.

The suburbs which many of us inhabit in the antipodes and elsewhere are both utopian and practical in intent. Their purpose is to avoid the intensity and stink of this city life, but also to connect to the pastoral. Suburbia is the last urban connection to the image of the green and pleasant land, which in the Australian case is an imperial rather than empirical fantasy, as it might be more closely in the arcadia of New Zealand. The argument in *Postmodern Socialism* is that socialists as modernists sought not only to divert factory civilization into garden cities, but also to close up the underground, the image of Hades which resurfaced as the factory in Birmingham or the rookery in London. By this time American cities such as Chicago and New York had their own 'little hells' or 'hell's kitchens'. The utopia of modern city-building included as part of its moral purpose the closing up of these undergrounds or nether worlds, by lifting up the submerged and making a society (or nation-state) of all citizens. My argument, in 1994, was that the dissociation of socialism and the social question and the global eclipse of socialism by capitalism, or of social democracy by globalization, however, saw the end of this dream.

The dualization of the world via the principle of uneven development shows this; no metropolis is without its underground. The cultures of the peripheries are insinuated in the centres as firmly as the centres penetrate the peripheries. Inequality more and more presents itself to us as spatial and geographical as well as political and economic. And no amount of genuflection to the value of inclusion can shift this, for the life chances of the excluded will necessarily refer to the informal, or underground economy and its own forms of slavery, those which predate and outstretch the dialectics of wage slavery in the public face of modernity. Dualization works at both global and national levels, and this is nothing new. Marx's image of hell was on the factory floor; ours may be in the brothel of sex slaves, in the stomachs of mules, in the fight club, on the street, or just in the endless stacking of the shelves of commodities that dominate all our lives, whether as consumers or producers.

In either case, here or there, as consumers or producers, we are awash in excess, waste, in the potlatch culture where there is enough surplus stuff for us to drown in while others still starve. In the suburbs of cities such as Melbourne or Auckland the underground, today, is spatially contiguous with society rather than literally underneath it. The underclass is metaphorically beneath us, because the hopes and dreams of its people are constrained by us and our consumption habits and expectations. This much has not changed, in its basic configuration, since

Marx or Dickens. At the imaginary or ideological level, all the same, we are united. Utopia is a hamburger.[13]

Marx revisited

These reflections on a text over ten years old necessarily raise other curiosities, in turn, about a tradition whose formative phase was over a century ago – that of Marxism itself. As we were told, not so long ago, that we were now postmodern, so are we also told now that we are, or should be, post-Marxist. What might this mean? I turn now to offer some reflections on the post-Marxist, beginning with the *via media* offered by Hardt and Negri in *Empire*.[14] *Empire* is an expression of our moment. It connects the postmodern, and the post-Marxist, to the dynamic of globalization and the immanent logic of empire. Its rapturous reception is equalled only by the extraordinary desire which is its impulse. It is a sign of the times, where the fantasy of communist victory is seized from the jaws of socialist defeat and the automatic logic of classical Marxism is blindly reinstated in the breast of capitalism, against all odds. The logic of *Empire* represents a kind of magical Marxism, whose impulse comes from the uncontainable revolutionary dynamic of *The Communist Manifesto* matched to the idea of automatic revolution from within in the arguments concerning technology in the *Grundrisse*. This fantasy was earlier connected by radical American Trotskyists to Engels' notion of the 'invading socialist society'.[15]

Marx had left at least two alternative ways open to socialism across the path of his work: either socialism was the result of the various efforts of the workers' movement, or else it was the immanent and necessary logical result of the path of capitalist development itself. Negri's work manages miraculously to hold these two together, so that the autonomous workers remain the agent of socialism but the inner dynamic also revolutionizes capitalism from within. While others had earlier viewed capitalism as doing socialism's work, globalization here becomes a kind of socialization from within. Capital and Empire are the autopoetic machines of power. Capital vanquishes the planet, but prepares the way for socialism in so doing. Proletarian struggles nevertheless persist in constituting the motor of capitalist development, for Labour remains the heart of Capital. The primary task, for Negri and Hardt, however, is not getting into but getting out of modernity. Globalization opens the real possibility of the postmodern, of being after Capital, after Capitalism and therefore after modernity. Information technology, in this way of thinking, involves immaterial labour, which offers the potential for a new kind of spontaneous and elementary communism. Immaterial labour, that is to say, represents the possibility of labour after labour, or labour after Capital. In Marx's thought, for Negri and Hardt, the relationship between the inside and the outside of capitalist development is completely determined in the dual standpoint of the proletariat, which is both inside and outside capital. Under the reign of the new Empire, abstract labour is an activity without place. The new productive forces have no place.[16] Empire is no place, which must also mean that it is everywhere. Globalization is good, in this view, because it provides greater possibilities for creation and liberation. 'The Multitude, in its will to be – against its desire for liberation, must push through Empire to come out the other side.'[17] The extent of this fantasy in Negri and Hardt is enough to make Marx's desire look radically modest. Here there is too much infinity, too much multiplicity, and no sense of limits or finitude.

The extraordinary reception of *Empire* can only be viewed as a symptom of its reaction. By the 1990s, for Marxists, all hopes were gone. The renewed driving force of capitalism via globalization had plainly become the main game. Then Negri and Hardt arrive with a new version of the old automatic Marxism argument, now in postmodern, informational guise. All that we have hitherto seen as symptomatic of the growth of capitalism, via globalization, is now revealed to be the subject of mistaken identity. It is socialism which drives all this along. But the argument is, to any detached reading, lost in space. Its language is mystical:

> The posse [of socialism] produces the chromosomes of its future organization. Bodies are in the front lines in this battle, bodies that consolidate in an irreversible way the results of past struggles and incorporate a power that has been gained ontologically... This is the point when the modern republic ceases to exist and the postmodern posse arises.[18]

Or: 'Here the militant is the one who best expresses the life of the multitude... This is the irrepressible lightness and joy of being communist.'[19]

Empire revives the worst of Bolshevism and the worst of automatic Marxism together. This Empire has its Emperors, but their readers are apparently oblivious to their nakedness. That such a book should become a bestseller tells only of the remaining fantasies of these well-heeled academic militants. The lost souls of New Bolshevism now enthusiastically embrace these bearers of good tidings. The broader appeal of the argument, as a consolation book prize for disappointed mock revolutionaries, reflects the revival of *The Communist Manifesto* and its installation as the *Urtext* of the radical critique of globalization. Here, alongside metaphors of liquidity, the central symbol is Marx's, 'all that is solid melts into air'. Marx's phrase has become all the more notorious since the publication of Marshall Berman's book fixing upon it, *All That is Solid Melts into Air,* in 1984.[20] Since then the radical sense of vitalism or *schwärmerei* has accelerated to the point that the image of acceleration itself is moot. Post-Marxists are addicted to speed.

Gilles Deleuze cannot be blamed for this, and neither should his inspiration, in the figure of Bergson.[21] Yet the generalized sense of vitalism, of movement as frenzy, melting or infinite contingency is discernable across the range of European social theory, not least in the standard equation of the images of movement and liquidity. Liquidity is an idea looking for trouble. But before there were textual liquids, it seems, there were meltings, and this then began with Marx's image in *The Communist Manifesto.* What is remarkable about this presupposition is that it rests on a mistranslation, or at best a symbolic expansion of Marx's humbler prose in that text. In the original German, Marx's prose is as follows: 'Alles Stehende and Ständische Verdampft'. This was translated into English for the first edition of the *Manifesto* by Samuel Moore forty years after its original enunciation as 'All that is solid melts into air.' Marshall Berman observes this fact in the papers collected as *Adventures in Marxism,* where he suggests that Moore's translation, not seen by Marx (d.1883) but overseen by Engels, was 'free' but not 'outrageous'. 'The cosmic scope and visionary grandeur of this image, its highly compressed and dramatic power, its vaguely apocalyptic undertones, the ambiguity of its point of view – the heat that destroys is also superabundant energy, an overflow of life – all these qualities are supposed to be hallmarks of the modernist imagination.'[22] Supposed by whom? By us, its modernist readers, looking for echoes of Rimbaud or Nietzsche, Rilke or Yeats, all of which seems to talk to a later moment, after the 1888 translation of the *Manifesto* into English.

A closer rendition of the famous phrase, however, would be something like 'all that is standing and estatelike turns into steam'. My own hunch is that steam or vapour was a carefully chosen image, for it informs the context of the *Manifesto,* where it is the spectre of steam power that makes the new capitalist dynamism possible. Steam-power explodes the estate-relations of feudalism; the famous passage may indeed amount to no more than that, with a trill of alliteration on 'Ständische' and 'Stehende'.

A different translation, offered by Martin Lawrence in 1922, instead gives the passage as follows: 'All that has been regarded as solid, crumbles into fragments.' A much later translation, by Terrell Carver, seeks to maintain the integrity of the passage while bridging the critical distance between us and it, and keeping up the alliteration: 'Everything feudal and fixed goes up in smoke.'[23] Against this, and against my suggestion here, it could be objected that while the Samuel Moore translation adds, it also adds value. This is a winning mistranslation. The new image, 'all that is solid melts into air', represents a symbolic expansion of Marx's phrase, which gives the image wings. It travels, and it travels wide and far, together with its comrade, the mistranslated image of the 'iron cage' in Weber. This objection is powerful, but it shifts the terms of reference here more fully from hermeneutics to reception history. The point that I want to make here is that by our own times a certain mischief also ensues. There are exceptions to this charge. Zygmunt Bauman, for example, uses the image in a more specific manner when he argues that the initially corrosive effects of modernity lead to the installation of a newly ossified or traditionalistic hard modernism, the image of which then serves to obscure more interesting movement on the ground. This process he characterizes not as the postmodern but as liquid modernity.[24] More concretely, this is an image of Fordism. The image of liquidity may be a useful antidote to that of the fixity of the solids of modernist tradition, but my own sense is that this does not quite capture the novelty of the moment. If we need a category such as liquid modernity, a strong qualifier added to a firmer noun, I would rather suggest as an alternative the idea of pneumatic modernity. The idea of pneumatic modernity has associations of its own. Initially, it is automotive rather than locomotive. More substantively, it is pumped up, inflated, inflationary, breathless, restless. Pneumatic modernity, in contrast to the idea of hydraulic modernity, evokes images of air, breath, gas, wind. Its sense of compression is also semantically connected to the sense of spirit, to the Holy Ghost, or to that other defining spirit, the spirit of capitalism.

Back to the present

This is merely a tease, a hint, a touch of breath on the nape of the neck, however; it is not a theory. The great achievement of Bauman's sociology, in contrast, is to frame the postmodern as the reinvention of modernism. The later introduction in Bauman's work of the image of liquidity seeks to avoid both the merely negative definition of being after the modern, and the sense of empty celebration for the postmodern as a consumer item, after its critical impulse itself was exhausted. The resulting image of liquid modernity, for Bauman, is presented as a metaphor, as a contrast to high or fixed modernism, not a description of an actually existing state of affairs. The point here is not that every aspect of our lives is permeated by absolute contingency, but rather that we are encouraged by the culture of the new individualism to think and act as though it were.[25] As individuals, say, in relationships, we can choose contingency, but we can also choose commitment. We have still not escaped from the scenario sketched out by Weber as the necessity to choose between the warring gods in our lives.

The idea of uncertainty or conditionality has always been a part of the Marxist tradition, understood as a radical rather than teleological historicism. To use this as an orienting point within the Marxian tradition would be to align not with *The Communist Manifesto* but with the *German Ideology*. From a different perspective, it might mean taking as the point of orientation from the *Manifesto* not the melting, but the power of the image of the sorcerers of the world out of control. Yet if the world is a trap, it may still be possible to think about ways of springing it. The claim about the globalized world which we now inhabit, meantime, is only that it accentuates the extent to which uncertainty and contingency mark our lives. Yet global culture also becomes second nature, and is ossified in the process. The political trick of globalization talk is exactly in this, in its capacity to present contingency as necessity. Marxists should have no business substituting their own miraculous schemes of necessitarianism in the stead of globalization. The case for a postmodern socialism remains that it is necessary only to commit to the in principle possibility in which we know that there is a better way to live. Utopia still counts, in this way of thinking, not as an immanent state of affairs or dynamic in the process of realizing itself, but rather as an ethic. This postmodern ethic, after all, is also a reinvention of the modern socialist ethic which preceded it. To think in this way is exactly the opposite of the logic of *Empire*. The idea of socialism is desirable precisely not because it is inevitable but because it is unachievable as a fact. Socialism ought be understood neither as a systemic imperative nor as a vital impulse: its ethical value – choice – is an indicator rather of autonomy. The idea of socialism always lies before us. It moves, and it moves with us.

Notes

1 P. Beilharz, *Postmodern Socialism: Romanticism, City and State* (Melbourne: Melbourne University Press, 1994).

2 P. Beilharz, *Transforming Labour: Labour Tradition and the Labour Decade in Australia* (Melbourne: Cambridge University Press, 1994).

3 P. Hirst and G. Thompson, *Globalization in Question: The International Economy and the Possibilities of Governance* (Cambridge: Polity, 1996).
4 R. Robertson, *Globalization: Social Theory and Global Culture* (London: Sage, 1992).
5 M. Castells, *The Information Age* (three volumes) (Oxford: Basil Blackwell, 1997, 1998, 2000).
6 M. Mann, 'Globalization and September 11', *New Left Review* 12 (2001), pp. 51–72.
7 P. Kelly, *The End of Certainty: The Story of the 1980s* (London: Allen & Unwin, 1992).
8 E. Cassirer, *Rousseau, Kant, Goethe: Two Essays* (Hamden: Archon Books, 1961).
9 Z. Bauman, *Legislators and Interpreters: On Modernity, Post-Modernity and Intellectuals* (Cambridge: Polity, 1987).
10 Z. Bauman, *Socialism: The Active Utopia* (London: George Allen & Unwin, 1976).
11 Z. Bauman, *Towards a Critical Sociology: An Essay on Commonsense and Emancipation* (London: Routledge & Kegan Paul, 1976).
12 F. W. S. Schiller, *Letters on the Aesthetic Education of Man* (Oxford: Oxford University Press, 1967).
13 P. Beilharz, *Labour's Utopias: Bolshevism, Fabianism, Social Democracy* (London: Routledge, 1992).
14 M. Hardt and A. Negri, *Empire* (Cambridge, MA: Harvard University Press, 2000).
15 P. Beilharz, *Trotsky, Trotskyism and the Transition to Socialism* (London: Croom Helm, 1987).
16 Hardt and Negri, *Empire*, pp. 208–10.
17 Ibid., p. 218.
18 Ibid., pp. 410–11.
19 Ibid., pp. 411, 413.
20 M. Berman, *All That is Solid Melts into Air: The Experience of Modernity* (London: Verso, 1983).
21 The presence of Deleuze in the text of *Empire* is marginal, but the spirit of vitalism is everywhere. Compare G. Deleuze, *Bergsonism* (New York: Zone, 1988).
22 M. Berman, *Adventures in Marxism* (London: Verso, 1999).
23 D. Ryazanoff (ed.), *The Communist Manifesto of Karl Marx and Friedrich Engels* (New York: Russell & Russell, 1963), p. 29; T. Carver, in M. Cowling (ed.), *The Communist Manifesto: New Interpretations* (New York: New York University Press, 1998), p. 16; cf. K. Marx and F. Engels, *Werke*, Vol. 4 (Berlin: Dietz, 1956–), p. 465.
24 Z. Bauman, *Liquid Modernity* (Cambridge: Polity, 2000); cf. J. Urry, *Sociology Beyond Societies: Mobilities for the 21st Century* (London: Routledge, 2000).
25 Z. Bauman, *Liquid Love: On the Frailty of Human Bonds* (Cambridge: Polity, 2003); Z. Bauman, *Society Under Siege* (Cambridge: Polity, 2002).

3
Despotic Enlightenment: Rethinking Globalization after Foucault

Roger Deacon

Introduction

Globalization is no less than a development of the Enlightenment project of modern social theory and practice, the urge to control the world so as to explain it, to explain the world so as to promote change, and to change the world so as to control it. During the Enlightenment, that 'moment when the West for the first time affirmed the autonomy and sovereignty of its own rationality',[1] a series of ancient disciplinary technologies (aimed at rationalizing the management of individuals) was first consolidated on a national scale. According to Michel Foucault, the Enlightenment has also become central to contemporary preoccupations due to widespread disillusionment with its promise of revolutionary social and political transformation, and a questioning of its cultural and scientific universals, associated with Western economic and political hegemony. This chapter focuses upon three central effects of globalization – the transformation of politics and the state, the reconceptualization of sovereignty, and the incipient militarization of human rights – and argues that they can be best understood in terms of their Enlightenment rationality, 'the autonomy of whose structures carries with it a history of dogmatism and despotism'.[2]

Totalization and individualization

Though he produced most of his work before globalization fully impinged upon the minds of intellectuals in the closing decades of the twentieth century, the concepts and analyses that Foucault developed are extremely helpful in making sense of our globalizing present. Ranging as far back as the ancient empires of the Near East, Foucault traced the rise of pastoral techniques for producing truth and governing oneself and others. These techniques, which drew upon Stoic practices of mastery of the self as much as Christian monastic and penitential practices, relied initially on hierarchy, surveillance and examination to normalize subjects; later, as polities became larger and more centralized and their populations increased, the spread of these disciplinary technologies throughout the social body, coupled with systems of enclosure and habits inculcated through interdependence, helped to fabricate self-determining modern human subjects.

Foucault was particularly interested in the manner in which large-scale mechanisms of social regulation have intersected in different ways throughout history with local or small-scale technologies of self-discipline. He insisted that 'discipline' is neither something which is done to people nor something that people simply do. Rather, it exists and develops precisely at the points where the actions of people and the effects of structures are almost indistinguishable, the points of 'governance' where relations of power intersect with 'technologies of the self', especially 'the points where the technologies of domination of individuals over one another have recourse to processes by which the individual acts upon himself. And conversely ... the points where the techniques of the self are integrated into structures of coercion and domination.'[3] Discipline, as much about governing oneself as about governing others, has over the course of two millennia mutated from pastoral relations of power first into absolutist reason of state and then into modern disciplinary power, and '[i]ts inevitable effects are both individualisation and totalisation';[4] the former referring to 'the development of power techniques oriented towards individuals and intended to rule them in a continuous and permanent way', and the latter to the centralization of political power in the state.[5]

The centralization of political power in the modern state and its accompanying levelling and standardizing bent was a product of its absolutist predecessors' success in monopolizing the means of legitimate violence and taxation. Such monopolies permitted 'the birth of meticulous military and political tactics by which the control of bodies and individual forces was exercised within states', and at the same time brought emerging nation-states into confrontation with each other.[6] As Foucault put it, while democratic representation made it possible for the 'will of all to form the fundamental authority of sovereignty', disciplinary technologies guaranteed 'the submission of forces and bodies. The real, corporal disciplines constituted the foundation of the formal, juridical liberties ... The

"Enlightenment", which discovered the liberties, also invented the disciplines', which often function as 'a sort of counter-law'.[7] Totalization assembles and disarms us and renders us amenable to ourselves.

The disciplines which accompanied this centralization and progressive democratization of political power consisted of once-ancient techniques intended to fabricate individuals. Foucault traced these techniques back to the likening of rulers to shepherds whose power over their flocks required not only presence and vigilance but also responsibility and, if necessary, sacrifice in order to ensure both the general welfare and individual salvation.[8] This pastoral practice, involving 'a power which individualizes by attributing, in an essential paradox, as much value to a single lamb as to the entire flock',[9] also demanded detailed knowledge, which in turn led to practices of self-examination and confession. The modern regime of 'power/knowledge' combines a totalizing 'economic and ideological state violence which ignore[s] who we are individually' with an individualizing 'scientific or administrative inquisition which determines who one is'.[10] Individualization thus oversees and examines us and subjects us to freedom.

That the oversight and management of people in their multitudes as in their individuality depends as much upon themselves as upon their division and enclosure by a flexible planetary grid of simultaneously sovereign and interdependent states, remains relevant in our globalizing world. Globalization transfers the disciplinary technologies first refined in the West, and generalized on a national scale since the Enlightenment, to the international level. The totalizing trend towards political centralization has not yet exhausted all of its effects; neither has the accompanying tendency for centralized units to become internally differentiated and to develop their own relatively autonomous subregions and identities. On the one hand, we witness the political unification of Europe, the expansion of the North Atlantic Treaty Organization (NATO), the rapid economic integration of Latin America and the formation of the African Union. On the other hand, potentially disintegrative political tendencies remain evident in central Africa, south-eastern Europe and ex-Soviet Asia; amongst the ethno-federal regions of the Russian Republic itself; and even, to a lesser degree, in the long centralized states of the West, from Spanish Basques and Catalans to Irish Unionists, Quebecois separatists and American militiamen.

As a consequence of the new information and communications technologies which typify our rapidly evolving 'epoch of simultaneity',[11] the time which the disciplines apportioned is speeding up, and the space they divided is shrinking. Heightened world trade, instantaneous financial flows, adaptable production techniques, proliferating service activities and growing consumerism form the basis for increasing and irreversible interdependence among ever-greater numbers of people and places. As distance is attenuated and interactions increase, cultures steadily if asymmetrically interpenetrate and diffuse worldwide: 'it is precisely because the whole world is Westernizing that the West is becoming relatively more permeable to Indian philosophy, to African art, to Japanese painting, to Arabic mysticism'.[12] In so far as globalization is the Westernization of the world, it is at the same time the transformation of the West (albeit disfigured by huge power differentials), prompting the emergence of new, multicultural identities amongst individuals and groups, but also threatening and giving a harder edge to certain existing traditions. As traditional political and economic boundaries blur and become more porous and flexible, totalizing and individualizing processes (once confined to national structures such as schools, prisons and factories) now also manifest themselves in the parliaments of superstates, the bureaucracies of international agencies and the global operations of transnational corporations.

These effects of globalization suggest that the bifurcated focus of disciplinary mechanisms aimed at policing entire populations, and of pedagogical and ethical technologies of self-formation intended to fabricate individual subjects, has become more important – and more integrated – than ever before. The phenomenon of 'descending individualization', which Foucault analysed in the context of a shift in penitentiary practices at the start of the nineteenth century, and an associated 'ascending totalization',[13] are equally applicable in the present context of a globalizing and despotic enlightenment. Foucault suggested that '[t]he disciplines mark the moment when the reversal of the political axis of individualization – as one might call it – takes place', the moment of enlightenment when 'individualization is "descending"'.[14] Then, 'ordinary' individuals – especially children, patients and delinquents of all sorts – began to have their lives more closely examined, while great and powerful individuals such as kings began to merge into the collective background of governments, elites and ruling classes. Now, too, on an international level, the individual dictator, the extremist sect and the ethnic minority – contrasted against a once ill-defined, amorphous and now defunct 'Third World' – have become more individualized, as much the focus of the media as of foreign powers, while an accompanying 'ascending totalization' has seen a firmer delineation (or limning) of such entities such as the 'international community', 'Islam', the 'coalition forces' and the 'axis of evil'. Still underpinning these now global processes of totalization and individualization are the same principles of hierarchy, surveillance, examination, enclosure, interdependence and normalization, fashioning new forms of political practice, transforming the state, reconceptualizing sovereignty and imposing rights.

Politics and the state

To begin with, we observe the decline of older forms, the emergence of new forms, and the interpenetration of once discrete domains, of political practice and public life. Media-induced virtual reality turns public events into soap operas, actors become politicians and disparate pressure groups make common cause across sectors and countries. While we are certainly not 'experiencing the end of politics', as Foucault once provocatively suggested,[15] there is no doubt that globalization is inducing the *transformation of politics*. Politics as it has been known over the past few centuries, organized almost exclusively around self-reflective sovereign identities engaged in or resisting large-scale, usually progressive and often revolutionary social change, is increasingly being assimilated or displaced (though not replaced), and these effects of globalization have been amplified by a pervasive disenchantment with revolution. The hopes that the 'Revolution' originally inspired in disaffected individuals and oppressed masses alike were dashed, Foucault argued, by the same Enlightenment rationalism which gave rise to world war, genocide and famine, 'a rationalism of which one is entitled to ask what part it may have played in the effects of despotism in which this hope lost itself'.[16]

Disenchantment with revolution, however, is not to be equated with revolution's demise. On the one hand, the effects of revolution have been assimilated into both the exponential technological advances and the psychological, physiological, spiritual and moral battlefields of the Information Age. The constant revolutionizing of the means of production, foreseen by Marx and confirmed by Foucault, is now permanently transforming social life, from information overload through lifelong learning to enforced democratization. On the other hand, the theory of revolution has long been rationalized: people have become accustomed to revolution 'as interior to a history that is regarded as both rational and controllable', and in the process it has been legitimized and enervated.[17] In both these revised and refined forms, the hoary Enlightenment right to revolution lives on in today's increasingly interventionist human rights discourse.

Into the partial void left by the assimilation or displacement of revolutionary politics have stepped new forms of political practice. The original new social movements have over the past quarter-century been joined by numerous nationalist, ethnic, religious, community, business and even criminal and terrorist groups, many of which focus comparatively narrowly on specific and immediate issues. Fundamental social transformation, and the capture of state or economic power, is still a long-term aim for some, but is more likely to be achieved, if at all, in piecemeal and gradual ways; the search for meaning in everyday life, or the construction or preservation of identity, have become equally if not more important. Conventional labels, such as Right and Left, modern and traditional and even pro- and anti-globalization, tend to overlap and blur: elements of the establishment, including the state (once a primary target for many social movements), may often be allies, whereas groups advocating similar ideas might be considered to be competitors and even enemies. All seek to manage their changing environments and to reduce uncertainty, more so than trying to destroy or escape those forces which seek to monitor and normalize them.

Sensitive (if not always averse) to group tendencies towards authoritarianism, they often adopt looser coalition-based forms of organization, which aligns them more closely with local concerns but also permits them to link up with diverse groups or struggles across social and economic sectors and countries. While this discontinuous and more interdependent networking form of organization makes these new political practices more vulnerable to dissolution, especially once their initial objectives are achieved, it also renders them more flexible, reduces their susceptibility to hostile targeting and is well-suited for the appropriation of newly prevalent information technologies. In turn, the tendency for information technologies to converge into more integrated systems, and to process and distribute knowledge and skills in reconfigurable ways, gives more shape and unity even to coalition-based politics. Though imbued with informational logic and expertise, these political practices are nevertheless often antagonistic to the modern *régime du savoir*, forms of power/knowledge which tell us who we are collectively even as they examine who each of us is individually.[18]

Not only social movements but even the state itself, that alter ego of revolution, is transforming itself and developing alternative ways of acting politically. In today's interdependent world no less than in the early modern world, 'the principal difficulty faced is the mobilization of the forces and rational techniques which permit State intervention',[19] interventions intended to secure the state externally through alliances, military strength, colonial empires and, most recently, regional cooperation and integration, and to protect and encourage internal development, from seldom-realized *laissez-faire* through direct state control to, today, neoliberal interventions to facilitate international competitiveness. While conventional political science, obsessed with sovereignty, tends to ascribe such interventions largely to state initiatives, Foucault viewed the state more as effect than cause of political interaction, and summed up these 'forces and rational techniques' in his concept of 'governmentality':

> It is the tactics of government which make possible the continual definition and redefinition of what is within the competence of the State and what is not, the public versus the private, and so on; thus the State can only be understood in its survival and its limits on the basis of the general tactics of governmentality.[20]

The general tactics of governmentality, or the state's (trans)formation and (re)organization in terms of how its relation to itself (its own territory, population and economy) intersects with its relation to others (other states as well as all other entities which influence international affairs), are themselves mutating under the impact of globalization. In the context of new, network-based and issue-centred forms of political practice and the increasing permeability of institutions and borders to legal and illegal flows of people, money, goods, knowledge and information, the state needs to be rethought as an increasingly flexible and complex strategic system, in its collective, totalized, supernational guises as well as in its fragmented, individualized, subnational manifestations.

A system of initially autocratic, then increasingly nationalist and now, in addition, nominally democratic sovereign states arrayed in varying 'balances of power' has characterized international relations ever since the Treaty of Westphalia in 1648. One of the effects of globalization, arguably, is that, today, the states that constitute this system are 'in decline [,]...voluntarily or involuntarily...either combining into larger communities or falling apart'.[21] Beleaguered on all sides, from international and regional institutions above, corporations and NGOs on their flanks, and grassroots movements below, national states seem no longer to have complete authority or full capacity to make decisions regarding foreign policy, capital flows, the transmission of knowledge, population migration, labour politics and defence. At the very least, their decisions are now intertwined with and shaped by networks of super- and subordinate authorities: 'networks of capital, production, communication, crime, international institutions, supranational military apparatuses, non-governmental organizations, transnational religions...public opinion movements...communities, tribes, localities, cults, and gangs'.[22]

Despite this, national states, neither obsolete nor dispensable, still constitute the most essential components of all existing international institutions, are intimately involved in revitalizing regional and local government, and are in the forefront of creating new collective institutions in both more (European) and less (African) developed parts of the world. States still need to monitor, regulate and police themselves (not to mention other states), 'police' being understood here in its original broad sense, encompassing everything from economic development and trade through education and social control to group identity and human rights.[23] As international relations of interdependence multiply and tighten, states are being reorganized more as pragmatic managers or regulators, than absolute producers or final decision-makers, of economic development, social and political discourse, the transfer of knowledge and skills, and law and order.

First, precisely *because* of global interdependence and deregulation, extensive regulation and intervention by 'an effective state', 'not... a direct provider of growth but... a partner, catalyst, and facilitator', is seen as more essential than ever.[24] 'Effective' national states, and international agencies dominated by national states, intervene economically to foster growth, to protect against competition and even to swell the numbers of effective states (through structural adjustment or debt-reduction programmes). Moreover, it is often states in 'societies with strong national identities and group cohesiveness [which] provide the kind of stability'[25] required to effectively manage their political and economic environments. Second, amidst the burgeoning of home-schooling and private education, state-funded and -managed education systems still dominate the transmission, if not the definition and production, of knowledge,[26] and seek to sustain *both* local developmental needs and cultural values *and* international demand for adaptable and responsible workers with values (such as tolerance and empathy) appropriate to a growing cosmopolitan stratum. Third, individuals still give their primary allegiance to nation-states, which continue to be held responsible for guaranteeing a fair distribution of public goods and services and for assuring citizens' rights.

Lastly, states are still the most important means of disciplining their nationally-assigned portions of the world's population and also of regulating transnational flows of immigrants, refugees and criminals, assisted by private security firms and a vast array of 'non-lethal' weapons and techniques. Interdependence often means that more developed countries depend on the capacity of poorer states, whose poverty has long been recognized by the West as 'a handicap and a threat both to them and to more prosperous areas',[27] to feed, train and, most of all, restrain their own populations. Ironically, in a global context in which 'democratization' looms large, political stability is being preferred to democracy, and social control to human rights: 'often a state that abuses human rights remains a better option for its citizens and for the rest of us than anarchy or collapse into long-term civil war'.[28] For 'the rest of us', especially we denizens of stable liberal democracies, the capacity of other nation-states to retain enough sovereignty to maintain civil order indulges our hollow humane sensibilities.

Though it has been argued that 'nation-states have been transformed from sovereign subjects into strategic actors',[29] to a significant degree nation-states *have always been* 'strategic actors', with both their foreign and their domestic activities either facilitated or constrained by global events such as stock market crashes, epidemics, arms races, inventions and discoveries. Globalization has indeed accentuated this situation to the extent that certain traditional state functions are being radically transformed, precipitating a 'crisis of sovereignty'. Nevertheless, this crisis remains a crisis of *sovereignty*, a clear indication that for all their failings, self-determining if interdependent states are still the primary loci of legitimate political, economic and military decision-making in the world today. In political practice as much as '[i]n political thought and analysis, we still have not cut off the head of the king'.[30]

Sovereignty

State sovereignty is often assumed to be absolute, complete and evenly distributed, yet in practice it is always influenced by contextual factors – the perennial revival of much-partitioned Poland is a case in point – and dependent on capacity, such that stronger states can enforce a relatively greater degree of sovereignty. Sovereignty is a tactic in the arsenal of disciplinary technologies,[31] and the Westphalian nation-state and the individuals over which it came to preside are only two instances of several 'subjected sovereignties' invented during the Enlightenment and being transformed today. Other such 'subjected sovereignties', neither purely determined nor entirely untrammelled, include 'the soul (ruling the body, but subjected to God), consciousness (sovereign in a context of judgment, but subjected to the necessities of truth)...basic freedom (sovereign within, but accepting the demands of an outside world and "aligned with destiny")' and private property, where 'the proprietor is fully in control of his goods; he can use or abuse them, but he must nevertheless submit to the laws that support his claim to property'.[32]

Since their origins a few centuries ago, the sovereignty (or self-determining status) of nation-states has depended upon a prior determination or authorization by successive webs of interstate power relations within which they are enmeshed; conversely, the degree of stability or flexibility in this network of 'interdependencies' still depends upon the existence of nation-states capable of sovereign or free choice and action, as well as upon legitimating forms of knowledge (political rationalities such as nationalism, development and, increasingly, human rights).

In the face of globalization, national states persist to the extent to which they remain legitimate vehicles for global economic, political and cultural discipline, and national sovereignty, precisely because it is more diffused, helps to obscure and justify this disciplining process. On the one hand:

> [p]ower in the West is what displays itself the most, and thus what hides itself the best: what we have called 'political life' since the 19th century is the manner in which power presents its image (a little like the court in the monarchic era). Power is neither there, nor is that how it functions.[33]

Global power relations are not concentrated in states, international agencies or superpowers, though these remain very important for their operation, but are immanent in the individualizing and totalizing effects of disciplinary technologies. Sovereignty, however, is not merely an 'ideological' mystification; instead, it enjoys a regulative and strategic utility as a 'polymorphic' and recurrent,[34] though probably ultimately 'transitory',[35] instrument of criticism which, first levelled at declining absolutist monarchies, is equally applicable to the new democracies mushrooming the world over. In a world being made safe for liberal democracies, sovereignty constitutes a schema both 'for the regulation of governmental practice and...for sometimes radical opposition to such practice'.[36]

There are also distinct signs of a mutation in the tactic of sovereignty:

> Globalisation and international co-operation are changing our understanding of state sovereignty: states are now widely understood to be the servants of their peoples, and not vice versa. At the same time, individual sovereignty – and by this I mean the human rights and fundamental freedoms enshrined in our charter – has been enhanced by a renewed consciousness of the right of every individual to control his or her own destiny.[37]

Though 'sovereignty does still matter',[38] a certain 'necessary re-characterization' 'from *sovereignty as control* to *sovereignty as responsibility*' is required, such that national political authorities are responsible both to their citizens and to the international community for their actions and for their citizens' welfare.[39] States which, in addition to being stable and effective, 'more supple, less unitary and [less] intransigent',[40] are 'responsibly sovereign' are also 'likely to be those most respectful of human rights' and indispensable for the protection of human rights on a global scale.[41]

Human rights

Over the past half-millennium, the centralization of sovereign state power has been accompanied by:

> the increasing intervention of the state in the life of individuals, the increasing importance of life problems for political power, and the development of possible fields for social and human sciences insofar as they take into account those problems of individual behaviour inside the population and the relations between a living population and its environment.[42]

It is on the basis of thus sustaining and administering the lives of individual subjects, or bio-power, and not humanitarian feelings per se, that many individuals and states among the more developed countries feel it their duty to do something about the poverty and oppression of human beings in other parts of the world. Paradoxically, this sense of responsibility for the fate of distant foreign individuals is premised on a totalizing concern with group identity in its most encompassing sense, that of humanity as a whole.

Growing international legal recognition for the rights of individuals (and not just states), and a plethora of international groups which vigilantly monitor and will 'name and shame' both those who abuse human rights and those who fail to denounce or take appropriate action against abusers, has compelled widespread genuflection by all including the most oppressive states. While the intensifying ambit of watchdog organizations is another reason why national sovereignty is said to be under threat, states remain the only practicable instrument for defending human rights. Greater awareness of human rights issues, and greater willingness to act against perpetrators of abuse, first became feasible under the auspices of strong national authorities – the collective victors of 1945 – able to project their power internationally. However, in a postcolonial context where the Enlightenment-inspired claim to universality of Western rationality has been criticized as 'a mirage associated with economic domination and political hegemony',[43] the nascent rights-driven surveillance and disciplining of the globe is adopting a more pragmatic approach.[44] This has coincided with the realization that, in an interdependent world, even one overshadowed by a single pre-eminent military power, political instability – such as civil war or terrorism – is a far greater threat to human rights, and economic development, than authoritarian but stable states.

It is true that human rights discourse is not just a cudgel to beat non-Western others; it also facilitates the regulation of the same, as criticisms of Europe's immigration laws and America's prison standards attest. It is also true that a critique of human rights as bio-power runs the risk, paradoxically, of assuming the very rights it criticizes.[45] For Foucault, however, since both individuals and states, as 'subjected sovereignties', are the products of disciplinary technologies, to employ stark Manichaean oppositions which champion abused individuals, oppressed groups or marginalized states and denigrate their totalized or totalizing others,[46] or to claim that individual rights have been 'amputated, repressed, [or] altered by our social order',[47] is not to challenge but to expedite the spread of discipline.

While natural rights are neither modern nor exclusively Western, the current association of individual human beings with particular rights is a product of Enlightenment rationalism and Protestant reformism.[48] These rights are only 'natural' in the sense of being long-standing, the artificial products of centuries-long governmental interventions to normalize Western populations. Human rights emerged not from some apocryphal yearning for freedom derived from a state of nature, tribal spirit or town air, but were forged in the heat of modern state centralization.[49] Against the intolerance of an approach which circumscribes freedom by insisting on individualism, prescribing tolerance and limiting rights ('nobody is more humanist than the technocrats'),[50] Foucault believed that there are many more possible ways of inventing and freely determining ourselves than can be imagined by human rights.[51] By acknowledging the need to obtain victims' informed consent before intervening on their behalf, human rights discourse sets limits to itself; but by insisting that groups should be consensual, or 'respect an individual's right to exit when the constraints of the group become unbearable',[52] it heralds the limitation of all and offers not even cold comfort to states which have no recourse to 'exit' when the constraints of the evolving international framework, tolerant of everything except intolerance, 'become unbearable'.

It is on such theoretical premises that new conditions for the enforcement of human rights are being created, conditions which inevitably destabilize the values and structures of non-Western societies.[53] Should the disciplinary strategy of 'naming and shaming' fail, human rights discourse stands ready to 'assemble the reasons and the constituencies necessary for the use of force'.[54] Because 'norms alone will not stop a tyrant or an extremist faction bent on genocide', direct 'military intervention' becomes 'not only legitimate but also morally imperative'.[55] Here we recognize that the same venal conditions that first made rights, freedom and development possible within Western states, and which also fostered international war, will have to pertain if the entire world is to be rendered suitable for liberal democracy: 'bloody repression and forced cultural assimilation...projects of centralizing political power and state building...and...military conflicts within as well as between states'.[56] The global disciplinary consequences of human rights *militans* may be autocratic or democratic (after all, the United Nations itself is the outcome of victorious war); either way, they presage the pacification of the planet.

Conclusion

The technologies of discipline, which first bloomed as absolutist Leviathans imposed order on Europe's warring religious sects and determined that all individuals have a right to be free, are beginning to flourish on a global scale. Our world has already been rendered uniform by a comprehensive patchwork of sovereign nation-states; it is now poised to be further standardized in terms of coalitions of political practice, supple sovereignty and humanitarian intervention. As much as global citizens are being retooled for political networking, economic competence and cultural appreciation, states are being transformed to become more pliant (and compliant) and more pragmatic (and less principled), and the Kevlar-coated representatives of secular salvation no longer seek to disguise their efforts to save our rights and those of our planet from ourselves.

The globalization of discipline is not a fate which we can easily avoid, but we can seek to understand and shape its rationality. Since 'the deepest root of violence and its permanence come out of the form of rationality we use',[57] it follows that it is insufficient 'to denounce violence or to criticise an institution', to vail against globalization, censure imperialism, deplore terrorism, demand social justice or call for democratized institutions of global governance. Only by questioning 'the form of rationality at stake' can we 'avoid other institutions, with the same objectives and the same effects, from taking their stead'.[58] If we wish to explain, change and control globalization, we must first examine its Enlightenment rationality, not in order to reflect on the opportunities and liberties it bequeathed to us, but to interrogate the limits and effects of the disciplinary mechanisms which regulate who we are and how we relate to others: 'Reason as despotic enlightenment'.[59]

Notes

1 M. Foucault, 'Georges Canguilhem: Philosopher of Error', *Ideology and Consciousness*, 7 (1980), 53.
2 Ibid., p. 54.
3 M. Foucault, 'About the Beginning of the Hermeneutics of the Self: Two Lectures at Dartmouth', *Political Theory*, 21 (1993), 203.
4 M. Foucault, '*Omnes et Singulatim*: Towards a Criticism of "Political Reason"', in S. M. McMurrin (ed.), *The Tanner Lectures on Human Values II* (Cambridge: Cambridge University Press, 1981), p. 254.
5 Ibid., p. 227.
6 M. Foucault, *Discipline and Punish: The Birth of the Prison* (Harmondsworth: Peregrine, 1986), p. 168.
7 Ibid., pp. 222–4.
8 Foucault, '*Omnes et Singulatim*', pp. 227–30.
9 M. Foucault, 'Foucault at the Collège de France I: A Course Summary', *Philosophy and Social Criticism*, 8 (1981), 239.
10 M. Foucault, 'The Subject and Power', in H. Dreyfus and P. Rabinow, *Michel Foucault: Beyond Structuralism and Hermeneutics* (Brighton: Harvester, 1982), p. 212.
11 M. Foucault, 'Of Other Spaces', *Diacritics*, 16 (1986), 22.
12 M. Foucault, *Religion and Culture* (Manchester: Manchester University Press, 1999), p. 90.
13 R. Deacon, *Fabricating Foucault: Rationalising the Management of Individuals* (Milwaukee, WI: Marquette University Press, 2003), p. 148.
14 Foucault, *Discipline and Punish*, pp. 192–3.
15 M. Foucault, 'Power and Sex: An Interview with Michel Foucault', *Telos*, 32 (1977), 160.
16 Foucault, 'Georges Canguilhem', p. 54.
17 M. Foucault, 'Is it Useless to Revolt?', *Philosophy and Social Criticism*, 8 (1981), 6.
18 For details of this and the preceding paragraph, see: M. Foucault, *Language, Counter-Memory, Practice: Selected Essays and Interviews* (Oxford: Basil Blackwell, 1977), p. 215; Foucault, *Power/Knowledge: Selected Interviews and Other Writings 1972–1977* (New York: Pantheon, 1980), p. 81; Foucault, 'The Subject and Power', p. 212; Foucault, 'The Juridical Apparatus', in W. Connolly (ed.), *Legitimacy and the State* (Oxford: Basil Blackwell, 1987), p. 202.
19 Foucault, 'Foucault at the Collège de France I', p. 240.
20 M. Foucault, 'Governmentality', *Ideology and Consciousness*, 6 (1979), 21.
21 M. van Creveld, *The Rise and Decline of the State* (Cambridge: Cambridge University Press, 1999), p. vii.

22 M. Castells, *The Information Age: Economy, Society, Culture: Vol. 2: The Power of Identity* (Oxford: Basil Blackwell, 1997), pp. 303–4.
23 Foucault, *'Omnes et Singulatim'*, p. 249.
24 World Bank, 'World Development Report 1997', online at http://www.worldbank.org/html/extpb/wdr97/english/wdr97su1.htm.
25 M. Carnoy, 'Globalization and Educational Restructuring', seminar paper, University of Natal, September 1999, p. 7.
26 M. Carnoy and M. Castells, 'Globalization, the Knowledge Society, and the Network State: Poulantzas at the Millennium', Cape Town: Centre for Higher Education Transformation (1999), online at http://www.chet.org.za/castells/CastellsPapers.html.
27 Harry S. Truman, Inaugural Presidential Address, Washington, 20 January 1949, online at http://www.bartleby.com/124/pres53.html.
28 K. A. Appiah, 'Grounding Human Rights', in M. Ignatieff, *Human Rights as Politics and Idolatry* (Princeton, NJ: Princeton University Press, 2001), p. 101.
29 Castells, *The Information Age*, p. 307.
30 M. Foucault, *The History of Sexuality: An Introduction* (Harmondsworth: Penguin, 1981), pp. 88–9.
31 Foucault, *Discipline and Punish*, p. 222.
32 Foucault, *Language, Counter-Memory, Practice*, pp. 221–2.
33 Foucault, 'Power and Sex', p. 157.
34 M. Foucault, 'Foucault at the Collège de France II: A Course Summary', *Philosophy and Social Criticism*, 8 (1981), 356.
35 Foucault, *The History of Sexuality*, p. 89.
36 Foucault, 'Foucault at the Collège de France II', p. 356.
37 K. Annan, 'The Legitimacy to Intervene', *Financial Times*, 31 December 1999, online at http://www.globalpolicy.org/secgen/interven.htm.
38 ICISS, *The Responsibility to Protect* (Ottawa: International Commission on Intervention and State Sovereignty, 2001), pp. 7–8, online at http://www.globalpolicy.org/empire/humanint/2001/12responsibility.pdf.
39 Ibid., p. 13, emphasis in the original.
40 Ignatieff, *Human Rights as Politics and Idolatry*, pp. 32–3.
41 ICISS, *The Responsibility to Protect*, p. 7.
42 M. Foucault, *Technologies of the Self: A Seminar with Michel Foucault* (London: Tavistock, 1988), pp. 160–1.
43 Foucault, 'Georges Canguilhem', p. 54.
44 Ignatieff, *Human Rights as Politics and Idolatry*, pp. 19–20.
45 Foucault, *The History of Sexuality*, p. 145.
46 M. Foucault, *Michel Foucault: Politics, Philosophy, Culture. Interviews and Other Writings 1977–1984* (London: Routledge, 1988), p. 168.
47 Foucault, *Discipline and Punish*, p. 217.
48 M. Weber, *Economy and Society: An Outline of Interpretive Sociology* (New York: Bedminster, 1968), p. 868.
49 N. Elias, *The Civilizing Process* (Oxford: Basil Blackwell, 2000); I. Hunter, *Rethinking the School: Subjectivity, Bureaucracy, Criticism* (St. Leonard's: Allen & Unwin, 1994); M. Weber, *The Protestant Ethic and the Spirit of Capitalism* (London: George Allen & Unwin, 1930).
50 Foucault, *Religion and Culture*, p. 100.
51 Foucault, *Technologies of the Self*, p. 15.

52 Ignatieff, *Human Rights as Politics and Idolatry*, pp. 68–9.
53 D. Orentlicher, 'Relativism and Religion', in Ignatieff, *Human Rights as Politics and Idolatry*, pp. 145–50.
54 Ignatieff, *Human Rights as Politics and Idolatry*, p. 22.
55 R. Brody, 'Right Side Up: Reflections on the Last Twenty-Five Years of the Human Rights Movement', *Human Rights Watch World Report 2004*, online at http://www.hrw.org/wr2k4/17.htm; see also ICISS, *The Responsibility to Protect*, pp. 16, 57, 62.
56 C. Calhoun, *Critical Social Theory: Culture, History and the Challenge of Difference* (Oxford: Basil Blackwell, 1995), p. 234.
57 M. Foucault, 'M. Dillon: Conversation with Michel Foucault', *The Threepenny Review*, 1 (1980), p. 4.
58 Foucault, '*Omnes et Singulatim*', p. 254.
59 Foucault, 'Georges Canguilhem', p. 54.

4

Just Deconstruction? Derrida and Global Ethics

James Brassett and Federico Merke

Critical theory/practice has long held an ambiguous relationship with justice and questions of practical morality.[1] Marx characteristically eschewed morality as an instance of the liberal superstructure allowing for piecemeal administrative justice within society, while forgoing the question of changing that society. The equality in scientific socialism was an ideal to be *realized*, once the capitalist structures of power and domination were overthrown and a communist system erected. Similarly, Critical Theorists and writers from a postmodern perspective regard justice as an ideal to be *located in* the on-going overhaul of a diverse set of social structures. Their now relative establishment in International Relations (IR) has added to the discipline's previous concern with material state power, a focus on power dynamics operating through class, culture, gender, language discourse, and the media.

For reflective theorists the way we 'represent' reality informs the way we behave towards it. They distance their approaches from a modern positivist social science that has allegedly reified analytical notions such as the state. Instead, it is the binaries of inclusion/exclusion which pervade such concepts that serve as the target for realizing justice. On this view, ethics is not so much a tool to be applied to 'this' or 'that' moral question but an on-going approach that must be qualified by and *engaged with* contingent political practice.

The ambiguity in this position is related to contingency. If the analytical lenses we employ to theorize ethics – the state, community, market, and so forth – are tainted by the contingency of knowledge/power, then what possibility remains for a non-biased research agenda that regards particular issues or agendas as worthy? On what basis can a postmodern approach to ethics in IR assume any position of advocacy? These questions are more than the classic equation of relativism with nihilism – although this is worthy of consideration. There are fundamental tensions in post-positivist approaches that must be addressed if we are to realize a coherent and thoroughgoing ethical perspective from the reflective turn in IR.

In this chapter we deal with two questions. First: is deconstruction *just*? Or does the relativism in such a strategy risk undermining itself by the strength of its own critique? This is the more common charge levied by rationalist considerations of postmodernism. And second: is it *just* deconstruction? Should we accept a view of postmodernism as removed, scholastic and unable to offer substantive policy prescription? To invoke a common term: can postmodernism ever reconstruct? This we consider a more important question – often expressed by a mood of scepticism – for assessing post-positivist approaches to justice.

The third debate in International Relations

Positivism has had a profound impact within the social sciences. Underpinned by the knowledge structure of rationalism, positivist social scientists sought to understand and explain phenomena within the social world via the application of scientific principles which yielded the reward of both rigorously structuring research and simultaneously legitimating a newly professional discipline. Critical theory and postmodernism have in common a rejection of positivism. They seek to expose the processes whereby an empiricist epistemology can reify particular actors and issues at the expense of a greater sensitivity to contingency. But they fundamentally differ in their proposals.

From a critical perspective positivism can be criticized for taking 'the world as it finds it, with the prevailing social and power relationships and the institutions into which they are organized, as the given framework for action'.[2] Cox seeks to avoid such reification by proposing a critical theory that 'does not take institutions and social and power relations for granted but calls them into question by concerning itself with their origins and how and whether they might be in the process of changing'.[3] Indeed, a central theme of Critical Theory is the connection between knowledge and interest. As Cox affirms, 'theory is always *for* someone and *for* some purpose'.[4] Subjects are not separated from objects producing a value-free knowledge. Every theory has, implicitly or explicitly, a set of values and norms that tell us which facts are to be analysed. A second proposition is the critique of what Linklater calls the 'immutability thesis'.[5] This suggests that social and natural constraints eliminate the very possibility of a qualitative change producing a subject resigned to mere quantitative changes such as technology improvement and accumulation of capital at the domestic level and distribution of capabilities among states at the international level.

Critical Theory in IR has undermined the possibility of a value-free problem-solving theory. In particular Critical Theorists have attacked realism for its appropriation of the state as an analytical device whilst ignoring its sociohistorical contingency and possibly overlooking the potential for governance at levels above, below and regional to the state. Critical perspectives have also challenged neoliberalism for a methodological individualism, its underestimation of the social circumstances that structure economic activity and its potential to reify an ethnocentric conception of agency. On the former point economic circumstances such as inequality, commodification and credit systems serve to structure socioeconomic relations and therefore 'constitute' the limitations of agency. On the latter we might contest the universal applicability of the rational economic actor in microeconomic theory for reifying a logic pattern rooted in the behaviour of Western, white, Protestant males around the time of the Industrial Revolution.

Critical theory has criticized the scientific pretensions of dominant IR theories, demonstrating the intrinsic relationship between certain types of 'technical knowledge' and the contingent sociohistorical power relations which underpin them. In their place Critical Theorists seek to extract the emancipatory potentials of enlightenment thought via a reconstruction of method that emphasizes the political, economic, sociohistorical, ecological, racial and gender dimensions of IR. More pertinently, this 'next stage' of theory is intended to realize a cosmopolitan world order that will seek to universally apply principles of democracy, liberty and equality.[6] It is over this issue that the central point of contention with postmodernism arises.

Postmodern approaches challenge positivism by emphasizing the intrinsic relation between knowledge and power. Through discourse analysis postmodernism reaffirms the rhetorical quip, 'knowledge is power', to hyperbolic effect. As Foucault suggests: 'There is no power relation without the correlative constitution of a field of knowledge, nor any knowledge that does not presuppose and constitute at the same time power relations.'[7] Postmodernists are concerned with the way meanings constructed through language can serve to privilege a status quo. In this sense, discourse becomes more than a simple verbal representation of reality and its attendant social power relationships. Instead, discourse can be regarded as a rigorous set of signs, symbols and meanings that both reflect and engender *particular* conceptions of social reality with its attendant power relations. The positivist separation between observer and observed is undermined since language – the means for academic communication – is found to be a part of the 'problem' we seek to solve.

Postmodernism throws doubt upon the validity or even the implicit motivations of an inter-paradigm approach to IR, such as those of neo-realism, liberal institutionalism and Marxism. Each paradigm utilizes a core concern and makes assumptions about the principal actors in IR to form hypotheses about the nature of international society. Simple paradigmatic separations of fact and value, observer and observed, are open to question. If each paradigm tells us something different about reality then there will always be ample 'evidence' to fit within each framework. In essence, one's choice of paradigm can be reduced to a normative perception of what constitutes the 'core' concern or 'crucial facts' of IR. For instance, a realist might be concerned to justify American hegemony through appeals to the benefits of stability. Discursively, hegemonic stability is juxtaposed with the anarchy that would accompany a weakened American state. In the case of Marxism, universal considerations of the oppression of individuals within capitalism are emphasized. On this view, a teleological rendering of the individual's place in history permits the falsifications of 'real world' events such as the fall of communism, and sociological critiques of the concept of class, on the basis that they will be borne out in some future emancipation. Discursively, current questions of poverty, death, disease, marginalization and exclusion are juxtaposed with a teleological 'romance' for a historically determined future emancipation.

From a postmodern angle our understanding of IR has been presaged upon certain value-laden constructions of what constitutes the core of the subject and how its processes work themselves out. Following Steve Smith, a cautious rendering of the effect of this inter-paradigm debate is that it has acted as 'gatekeeper' to a view that the maintenance of state power in general, and US dominance in particular, *should be* the sole concern of IR.[8]

Collecting these ideas together, Critical Theory and postmodernism intersect on one crucial point that fundamentally undermines positivism in IR and opens the space for greater ethical reflection. Simply, the positivistic separation of epistemology from ontology, knowledge from 'reality', observer from subject, and analysis from values is not only argued to be demonstrably false, but accused of privileging a particular set of socioeconomic power relations. Thus a more complex post-positivist position requires reflexivity to the intrinsic relation between theory and practice. However, while Critical Theory highlights the 'progressive' potential of reflexivity via the reconstruction of emancipatory theory, postmodernists challenge this move for its potential to close the very theoretical space it celebrates. What if, by affirming the possibility of a universal good – no matter how reflexive and pluralistic – Critical Theorists achieve a theoretical hegemony that closes space to alternative discourses?

The attempt by Critical Theory to frame a next stage of theory, more sensitive to the contingency of social power relations, could be rendered as 'so many effects', as Foucault put it, of the existing power relations.[9] For instance, we might question the position of academia within power. Are not the successful universities from which Critical Theory emanates the product of Western bourgeois societies operating at the peak of the very social power matrix from which we require emancipation? A simple observation is that Critical Theory – like postmodernism – rarely emanates from the South. Such a claustrophobic tension has led some to doubt the possibility of any kind of postmodern ethic. As Habermas polemically questions:

> Why should we muster any resistance at all against this all pervasive power circulating in the bloodstream of the modern society, instead of just adapting ourselves to it?...It makes sense that a value-free analysis of the opponent is of use to one who wants to take up the fight – but *why fight at all*?[10]

It is in this context that something of an impasse has developed between Critical Theory and postmodernism. Critical Theorists have understood relativism to render postmodernism a disengaged and ultimately conservative force. Postmodernists have viewed any assault on their relativist position and requests for them to engage with the academy in less nuanced terms as acts to ensure the status quo dominance of mainstreamers.

We support the general conclusion of this debate, that – *contra* positivism – the way we think about global politics will shape the way we behave towards it. The realization of ethical agendas will be as much a function of our theoretical approach as it is our practical one. IR theorists should therefore engage these questions. We encourage the problematization of state power politics in IR and celebrate the recognition that, behind the *techne* of 'issues' in IR, there is a 'politics of reality' to be negotiated.[11] However, the pressing subtext to these discussions – namely, poverty, disease, alienation, subordination, social marginalization and ecological decay – are extant critical problems in their own right that require constant attention if they are to be overcome. Seductive as theoretical sophistication is, the way that we *reconstruct* our approaches to reality is just as important for the humans/nature we study.

This is not an argument for a 'back to basics mentality'; rather it is to remember with Marysia Zaleweski that 'International politics is *what we* make it to be, the contents of the "what" and the group that is the "we" are questions of vital theoretical and therefore political importance.'[12] In questioning the 'what' of international politics, critical theorists have, in general, been exemplary in developing the importance of non-state actors, new levels of analysis, and questions of identity in international relations. In questioning the 'we' the record is less impressive. There has been a tendency to caricature positions, to retreat into pockets of isolated dissidence, and ultimately – perhaps most regrettably for theorists claiming to open up discursive space – to talk past each other.

The idea that Critical Theory is a teleological approach insensitive to the politics of identity ignores Habermas's pursuit of a progressive approach that privileges 'neither unilinearity nor necessity, neither continuity nor irreversibility'.[13] And the proposition that postmodernism is a disengaged, aloof and apolitical force ignores the central aim of postmodern critique: to expose as political, to reveal as relations of power, those aspects of social life commonly assumed to be apolitical and undeserving of engagement. This is not to argue that there are no significant differences between Critical and postmodern approaches: rather, it is to agree with Chris Brown that much of the stand-off between Critical Theorists and postmodernists can be understood as Freud's 'narcissism of small differences' in action.[14] For this reason, it is in a mood of openness that we proceed. After elaborating upon the Derridean notion of deconstruction and its relation to justice, focus will turn to the international realm and discuss how – if at all – a postmodern approach can help us to think about global justice.

Deconstruction and justice

In this section, we outline some central themes in Derrida's thought before extrapolating them to the international realm. Employing Derrida's idea of deconstruction, we argue that modern conceptions of justice are silent upon the interrelation of justice, law and violence. Briefly, law – the means for administering justice – can be seen as a 'holding mechanism' that legitimizes a conception of justice as a technical affair, whilst ignoring the role of *force* in establishing that law. Modern conceptions of justice find legitimacy in their own *enforceability* as well as their ethical justifiability. Thus, the interrelation of violence and justice must act as a qualification to our ethical positions. On this view, justice should always be seen as a 'justice to come' – a perpetually sought yet postponed good – if we are to avoid reifying the violence inherent in legal administration. This is not to undermine the concept of justice (*pace* some realist accounts); rather it is to qualify the temporality of justice with a perpetual question: what violence made this justice possible?[15]

Drawing on psychoanalysis and linguistics, Derrida's approach to philosophy starts by problematizing the logic of identity. The laws of this logic can be traced back to Aristotle and presuppose an essential reality; an origin to which they refer. This origin must be (a) simple, (b) homogeneous, and (c) identical to itself. There must be no gaps between the origin and consciousness. According to these suppositions, subjects are either sensible or intelligible, internal or external, male or female, and the 'second term in each pair is considered the negative, corrupt, undesirable, version of the first'.[16] Complexity, difference and mediation are excluded conditions imposing the need to consider subjects in terms of binary opposites. Thus, Derrida demonstrates, Western philosophy has been constructed upon the premise of a clear, stable and transparent subject *who says what he means and means what he says.*

Texts, however, are mediated in their construction, in their communication, and in their reception. Texts cannot, by definition, simply transfer an author's ideas. If that were possible, we would have no need for questions such as: did Marx imply that the steam engine determines a particular stage of history, or was this simply a rhetorical metaphor that has been overemphasized by critics? Reading texts in a deconstructive mode is a matter of entering into the thoughtful play of contradiction, multiple references and the ceaseless questioning of conclusions and responses. Kearney points to Derrida's central notion of the 'irreducible structure of *différance* as it operates in human consciousness, temporality, history, and above all in the fundamental and overriding activity of writing'. And he follows:

> By means of this concept of *différance* – a neologism meaning both to 'defer' and to 'differ' – Derrida proposed to show how the major metaphysical definitions of Being as some timeless self-identity or presence... which dominated Western philosophy from Plato to the present day, could ultimately be 'deconstructed'.[17]

Derrida completes this idea by stating that the notion of *différance* is 'a non-concept in that it cannot be defined in terms of oppositional predicates; it is neither this nor that; but rather this *and* that (e.g., the act of differing and of deferring) without being reducible to a dialectical logic either'.[18]

These assumptions take us to Derrida's most well-known and debated concept of 'deconstruction'. It is said that deconstruction cannot be defined in a nutshell, especially when its very meaning or mission, as John Caputo states, is 'to crack nutshells'. Deconstruction cannot be described and stated as other positions can. Since deconstruction assumes the instability of any definition, as being non-identical to that to which it refers, a closed definition of deconstruction would be a contradiction. To paraphrase Brown, sentences which begin 'deconstruction is...' are very hard to complete as it is the very linearity of such sentences that is at issue in deconstructive thought.[19] Suspending such problems for the moment though, we offer here some central features of deconstruction.

The word 'deconstruction' is closely related not to the word 'destruction', but to the word 'analysis', which etymologically means 'to undo'. To undo does not mean to dissolve an entity into nothingness or a void: to undo is to resituate that entity in a broader perspective which commits itself to a permanent analysis of the difference forgotten within it. 'To undo' implies that the permanent consciousness of that which is being said is another way of naming the unspoken: a way that stabilizes what actually involves a working tension within. As Derrida affirms:

> to deconstruct the subject does not mean to deny its existence... Although there are 'subjects, 'operations' or 'effects' of subjectivity, this does not mean, however, that the subject is what it *says* it is. The subject is not some meta-linguistic substance or identity, some pure *cogito* of self-presence; it is always inscribed in a language.[20]

Deconstruction is not an absolute break with the past. As we will demonstrate in relation to Derrida's analysis of international politics, deconstruction is not trying to create everything anew out of the blue. Deconstruction tries to find a balance between the continuity of what is given and the discontinuity that *implies* an openness to 'the other'. And this openness to 'the other' entails an act of responsibility towards what is 'to come'. Deconstruction assumes that it is not a question of choosing between 'great white males' or 'black women' writers. A deconstructive practice is interested, at the same time, in the 'great canon' and in new cultures, new fields and perspectives.[21]

Deconstruction is not a methodology to be applied as something external to the object of analysis. To deconstruct something is to open up the *différance* enclosed in a self-supposed homogeneous work and uncover its destabilizing elements. Deconstruction is thus 'not a method or some tool that you apply to something from the outside. Deconstruction is something which happens and which happens inside.'[22] If we took this assumption to its extreme (and simplified) position, we could say that every text deconstructs itself. Any text provides the very 'seeds' to be deconstructed. In this way the student would be a sort of midwife who, in a Socratic sense, helps the text 'to give birth' to its internal contradictions.

Deconstruction is neither a nihilistic nor a relativistic posture that tries to 'undo' the achievements of Enlightenment and replace it with verbose but meaningless explanations. Deconstruction plays at the limit of the impossible and calls for an endless analysis of the present in order to affirm 'what is *to come*'.[23] And so, contrary to modernist accounts, deconstruction *can* be seen as a discourse of justice. If law is the tradition, the set of technical rules and the rights of any given judicial system, justice is beyond any definition and, hence, outside the very realm of deconstruction. Justice is always a justice 'to come'. It is 'what gives us the impulse, the drive, or the movement to improve the law, that is, to deconstruct the law'. As Derrida states: 'Without a call for justice, we would not have any interest in deconstructing the law. That is why I said that the condition of possibility of deconstruction is a call for justice.'[24]

The relation between justice and law is one of distance and difference. The 'to come' of justice ensures that it remains present in law and its institutions only as a possibility, and not as an explicit expectation. According to Derrida, there is an inevitable (and necessary) gap between justice and law. Deconstruction finds its place in that space or interval that tells us justice cannot be deconstructed to its very essence (if there is such a thing) but can only be grasped in the unstable and the 'always-to-be-improved-law'. On this view justice itself is not deconstructable: justice is merely an exhortation to *improve*. However, since law is a social construct it can be deconstructed.

For Derrida, law is the ultimate expression of an original violence that tries to establish a new order of things, a new social arrangement. When Derrida refers to the 'force of law', he points to the fact that law cannot be established without first claiming the ability to be 'enforced'. To deconstruct the law is to realize, as a first step, that law finds its source of legitimization not in some transcendental truth, but in its own 'enforceability'. As Derrida suggests, 'Applicability, "enforceability", is not an exterior or secondary possibility that may or may not be added as a supplement to law. It is the force essentially implied in the very concept of justice as law.'[25]

Derrida's arguments on justice and law are important for IR because many of its images rest upon a legalistic metaphor of rightful jurisdiction or sovereignty. Westphalia constitutes one of the first steps in the evolution of the war law, and then international law.

Deconstructing Westphalia

The Peace of Westphalia is taken as a foundational moment in the sovereign states system. Many IR textbooks reproduce this 'myth' in one way or another, claiming that 'With one stroke, virtually all the small states in central Europe attained sovereignty.'[26] Why should this account be taken as the 'official story', when history suggests it is an inaccurate description of events? Why did this particular historical narrative eventually become embedded in the IR discipline? A deconstructive understanding highlights the inevitability of such narrative.

Westphalia as a non-founded founding moment

A non-founded founding moment is analogous to a 'big bang' that *creates* a new order. Westphalia legalizes itself independently without the guarantor of a pre-existing law. For Derrida, the origin of law is an 'autobiographical fiction' that is forgotten over time. After decades or centuries, people start to believe that the foundation of the state is rooted in a higher order. The meaning of that order gets lost in the labyrinths of history: the myths and traditions that construct a nation-state. A deconstructive reading suggests that the constitution of a myth – *Westphalia as a founding moment* – was the necessary outcome of a process that tried to establish a primary origin for international law.

The main feature of this process is that law, in its instituting and founding moment, consists of a 'performative and therefore interpretative violence that is itself neither just nor unjust'.[27] Derrida regards this as law's 'mystical foundation'. To interpret the Peace of Westphalia as a founding moment is to acknowledge that the Peace – as an original violence – is beyond any justice discourse. It is an *ungrounded* violence: an authority that rests upon itself.[28] This moment, in which the founding violence is neither legal nor illegal, is the 'mystical' limit. The narrative of a clearly defined sovereign state – the bedrock assumption of IR – finds its limit in Westphalia, where a war established a new order of things. It is no coincidence that the Thirty Years War established a new law. This fact makes explicit the *implicit* relation between law and violence discussed above. As Derrida acknowledges: '[a]fter the ceremony of war, the ceremony of peace signifies that the victory establishes a new law.

And war, which passes for originary and archetypical violence in pursuit of natural ends, is in fact a violence that serves to found law or right.'[29]

In the Treaty then, a Derridean approach establishes a link between violence and writing. The very act of writing is reduced to a form of primogenial record, an arche-writing, or *arche-violence*. As Grosz explains, 'this arche-writing, the writing, or violence, inscription of trace, brings about the system of terms, differences that establish oppositions through which structures are made possible'.[30] The original violence of Westphalia establishes an inside/outside opposition: a supposedly stable and clear binary upon which international law finds its locus. The injunctions of modern justice are permitted inside, but only *marginally* outside, the nation-state. And thus IR (re)produces the order/justice dichotomy in its considerations of global justice.

Once the original violence has crystallized in a number of legal agreements, this original violence requires a second violence, 'a "reparatory" or compensatory violence, the violence whose function it is to erase the traces of the primordial violence, a kind of counter-violence whose force amounts to the denial of violence'.[31] International law guarantees the smooth functioning of the original violence. This second violence generates the illusory appearance of a given order as something natural, and thus non-violent. Any attempt to problematize that which appears to be 'natural' or 'logical' is delegitimized from the outset. If the first violence was called the 'founding moment', we will call the second violence the 'Westphalia effect'.

The 'Westphalia effect'

Beardsworth suggests that the 'repetition of the law implies at the same time another repetition of the originary violence which has "always already" accompanied the foundation and guarding of the law'.[32] The 'Westphalia effect' is, therefore, a permanent repetition of the supposedly non-violent Westphalian narrative. Its original violence is repeated via a twofold effect: the Westphalian understanding of identity and of community.

The Westphalia effect understands identity in terms of binary oppositions, which demand – at the same time as they *assume* – that every identity should be identical with itself. The Westphalia effect advances an idea of a unified, self-protecting and homogeneous identity which makes every effort to exclude difference: that which is not 'like me' and, hence, 'my threat'. The unknown becomes the unfamiliar, the strange, the foreign, the enemy. Such a concept of identity, says Caputo, 'does everything it can to prevent the "other" from crossing over "our" borders, from taking "our" jobs, from enjoying "our" benefits and going to "our" schools, from disturbing "our" language, culture, religion, and public institutions'.[33]

However, if we take a historical view, two ideas become clear. First, the 'we' of any community is rarely homogeneous. Far from being a story of ever maturing boxes, the history of most communities is one of migration, interpenetration and hybridization. It makes no sense to ask if an American Jew is a Jew or an American. They simply possess both identities in combination with other identities such as class, sexual identity, and political affiliation. And second, history tells us that fierce political conflicts are as likely to occur within communities – over issues of religion, language, wealth, and so on – as they are between communities. The rise of civil movements for blacks and women in the twentieth century, for instance, contested laws that were enshrined within communities. As Derrida explains, the identity of a culture 'is a way of being different from itself; a culture is different from itself; language is different from itself; the person is different from itself'.[34] Rather than being dissociable from an external other then, the concept of community is utterly, *and readily*, dissociable from itself.

This idea of dissociation can expose the possibilities that are closed off by accounts of community in IR. If we understand identity as a self-differentiating principle it can open new alternatives of social organization. Taking this view to the international level, the very idea of an international community excluding no one is a contradiction. As Beardsworth affirms, the 'very idea of sovereignty at the basis of our democratic understanding of law and subjectivity, is itself a violent decision which excludes as much as it promises'.[35] According to Caputo, a Derridean understanding of community should emphasize the instability of the word 'we'. The 'we' of any given community is always 'highly qualified and unsure, always running scared, a certain "we who cannot say we", a "we, if such a thing exists"'.[36]

Derrida has been associated with ethnic wars between groups who want their 'difference' recognized. But Derrida's concept of difference is far from being the same concept these groups claim to defend. The 'difference' they defend is the very 'effect' of a Westphalian conception of how community ought to be, and the violence they use is the consequence of an entire order (narrative) whose foundation is differential and, therefore, violent. Victims of the 'repetition of law', they fight for their rights against the 'injustice' of not being recognized as sovereign. It is the very 'rights' for which they fight that are constitutive of the injustice.

Our central problem has an endless difficulty: why and how should we overturn this narrative? Shall we do it only to replace it with another order, which, though potentially more just, instigates another founding violence? Derrida cannot think of this problem in any other way than as an *aporia*: a problem 'without a passage', a problem that demands a permanent analysis. As Derrida expresses in *The Other Heading*:

> when a responsibility is exercised in the order of the possible, it simply follows a direction and elaborates a program. It makes of action the applied consequence, the simple application of a knowledge or know-how. *It makes of ethics and politics a technology*.[37]

For example, in some Western countries, affirmative action policies have become an important policy tool in the prevention of social discrimination and attempts at rectifying the injustices of past social policy. However, in substance, they are short-term solutions that lack grounding in social realities. Affirmative action reinforces a spirit of victimization, by telling the excluded they can gain more by emphasizing their suffering, degradation and helplessness. Affirmative action, converted in technology, reinforces the very exclusion it tries to prevent. Instead, Derrida affirms that 'ethics, politics, and responsibility will only begin with the experience and experiment of the *aporia*' or the '*experience and experiment of the possibility of the impossible*'.[38]

Global democracy: towards a reconstruction?

When philosophers start invoking terms such as *aporia* and the *impossible justice*, IR theorists can be forgiven for ruffling their brows. Indeed, the *style* of postmodernism has often been a distinct problem for many in the IR community, and it has certainly figured in the impasse between Critical Theorists and postmodernists. But such stylistic difficulties can, indeed must, be overcome if we are to engage a constructive dialogue between post-positivist theorists. We thus propose a reconstruction. By this we mean to suggest that a Derridean approach can usefully converse with Critical approaches to global justice. The conversation itself is an act of justice that can in turn have far-reaching policy implications.

The experience of the *aporia*, the imagination of the impossible justice, are juxtaposed with critical reformism to suggest a postponement of justice – the ethical moment is that in which justice is sought but never found. The notion can be brought into public relevance via current debates over globalization and its meaning for democracy. By moving debates about justice in IR from interstate relations to supraterritorial or global governance, some interesting questions are raised about the possibility of decentring the state in IR. More importantly we can question how – if at all – we might mitigate further violence in new models of governance.

When approaching democracy, Derrida does not engage in the contemporary debates of political science. Going back to the canon, he deconstructs the works of Plato and Aristotle to analyse the concepts of friendship and democracy. Derrida – *like many Critical Theorists* – brings a global dimension to democracy that goes beyond the confines of the nation-state. As he expressed in an interview:

> Since no locality remains, democracy must be thought today globally, if it is to have a future. In the past one could always say that democracy was to be saved in this or that country. Today, however, if one claims to be a democrat, one cannot be a democrat 'at home' and wait to see what happens 'abroad'... Everything that is happening today, whether it be about Europe, the GATT [General Agreement on Tariffs and Trade], the Mafia, drugs, or arms – engages the future of democracy in the world in general.[39]

For writers such as Held and Linklater, this global dimension requires that democracy be rearticulated via institutional reform. Global governance must reflect the growing interpenetration of peoples and 'fate' that accompanies globalization. Global financial instability, global environmental degradation and global poverty are social 'bads' that can only be addressed by an overarching and overlapping system of regulation. From a Derridean perspective such reformism – valid and just as it may be – amounts to a geographical shift of democracy. Derrida argues that democracy must be 'decentred' from its central locus – the state – but also from its presupposed internal violence and inequality. For Derrida, democracy is a 'democracy to come'. But a 'democracy to come' is not simply a future-improved democracy, a more refined version of the supposed democracy that, according to Fukuyama, we already have. A 'democracy to come' is a permanent injunction, a permanent call for a democracy that is never fully present in any democratic regime. As Derrida states, in current 'democracies',

> all decisions made in the name of the Rights of Man are at the same time alibis for the continued inequality between singularities, and we need to invent other concepts than state, superstate, citizen, and

> so forth for this new International. The democracy to come obliges one to challenge instituted law in the name of an indefinitely unsatisfied justice, thereby revealing the injustice of calculating justice whether this be in the name of a particular form of democracy or of the concept of humanity.[40]

A 'democracy to come' poses the need to rethink the democratic relation beyond the borders of nation-states and their relation with non-citizens. It demands the invention of a new model of relationships, based upon a new international law and a transformed sovereignty. An imagination of the impossible justice is, on this view, a radical attempt to 'see', 'welcome', 'understand', 'love' the other *as other*.

This mood can be found in the work of Andrew Linklater. Taking seriously the limitations of social enquiry posited by the delegitimation of Marxism, and the assault of postmodernism, Linklater engages sociological binaries of inclusion/exclusion. He posits that the modern equation of freedom with citizenship rights implies that the sovereign states system may contain within it the seeds of its own demise. As he states:

> The anti-exclusionary dynamic is a trend of lowering the barriers which prevent excluded groups, such as subordinate classes, racial and national minorities, and women from enjoying the social and political rights monopolised by more powerful groups. To press this further is to recognise that the nation-state is one of the few bastions of exclusion which has not had its rights and claims against the rest of the world seriously questioned.[41]

For Linklater a praxeological dialectic, between freedom already actualized and the ability to further actualize freedom, will provoke a shift towards a morally inclusive post-Westphalian system. Such Critical scholarship is in line with Derrida's project to invent *new relationships*. There is much to recommend it in terms of concrete policy options. Developing the importance of actors and institutions above, below and regional to the state would certainly go some way towards reforming the exclusionary power of the state. But an important distinction must be drawn. Despite the sophistication of these approaches, from a Derridean perspective, they turn out as technical solutions to technical problems. They construct a theoretical system within which to subsume a plurality of communities. They neither undermine the system nor, more importantly, question the very concepts of community, justice or democracy.

How are we to judge between the claims of different members of different communities? If it is merely by a new institutional law, then at some level we are entering into a debate about which institution holds greater legitimacy/power/violence. This potential re-enactment of violence means that we must postpone any non-self-critical celebration of this 'justice-as-reform' approach. As Derrida notes, the violence of global justice is always already enshrined in the (international) organizations of global governance: 'we know today that even within international organisations and institutions, the sovereignty of the state is a rule, and that in the name of international law some nation-states more powerful than others make the law'.[42] But at the same time, he cautions,

> we shouldn't interrupt the work of these international institutions, the United Nations, the UNESCO, and so many others. It is something good and we have to improve them. This is an infinite process. But at the same time, it is not a continuous infinite process. We have to try and displace some concepts, which are absolutely essential to these constitutions.[43]

Such an attitude is a fitting complement to the argument of this chapter. Whereas some could interpret Derrida's ideas as a licence to 'resist' in favour of scholastic meditation, we see them as a healthy contribution to a broader conversation. As a normative ideal global democracy has much to recommend it. Thinking through the problems and possibilities of governance can be supplemented by the view of democracy as an *aporia*. Such a move could enhance the perception of fallibility in Critical Theory as well as make the conversation more inclined to the possibility of new, perhaps unimagined possibilities. With the assumption of system fallibility, the 'justice-as-reform' approach could thus take on a perpetual, 'infinite' quality. On our reading this postponement of the ethical moment is not nihilism; it is in fact a powerful call to arms, to translate into infinite meditation and effort the ethical impulse to reform/deconstruct.

Notes

1 In this chapter, we employ 'critical theory' as a generic term for theoretical approaches that go beyond and – in most cases – problematize dominant models of problem-solving theory. We use 'Critical Theory' to denote theory of, or following, the line set by the Frankfurt School.

2 R. Cox, 'Social Forces, States and World Orders: Beyond International Relations Theory', in R. O. Keohane (ed.), *Neorealism and its Critics* (New York: Columbia University Press, 1986), p. 208.

3 Ibid.

4 Ibid., p. 207.
5 See A. Linklater, *The Transformation of Political Community* (Cambridge: Polity, 1998).
6 See, for instance, A. Linklater, 'The Question of the Next Stage in International Relations Theory: A Critical-Theoretical Point of View', *Millennium*, 22 (1992), 77–98.
7 M. Foucault, cited in J. Edkins, *Poststructuralism and International Relations: Bringing the Political Back In* (London: Lynne Rienner, 1999), p. 53.
8 See S. Smith, 'The Forty Years Detour: The Resurgence of Normative Theory in International Relations', *Millennium*, 21 (1992), 494.
9 M. Foucault, cited in Edkins, *Poststructuralism and International Relations*, p. 53.
10 J. Habermas, *The Philosophical Discourses of Modernity* (Oxford: Basil Blackwell, 1987), pp. 283–4 (emphasis added).
11 See M. Zehfuss, *Constructivism in International Relations: The Politics of Reality* (Cambridge: Cambridge University Press, 2002).
12 M. Zalewski, '"All These Theories Yet the Bodies Keep Piling Up": Theory Theorists, Theorizing', in S. Smith, K. Booth and M. Zalewski (eds), *International Theory: Positivism and Beyond* (Cambridge: Cambridge University Press, 1996), p. 352.
13 J. Habermas, *Communication and the Evolution of Society* (London: Heinmann, 1979), p. 140.
14 C. Brown, 'Our Side? Critical Theory and International Relations', in R. W. Jones (ed.), *Critical Theory and World Politics* (London: Lynne Rienner, 2001), p. 199.
15 See J. Derrida, 'Force of Law: The "Mystical Foundation of Authority"', in D. G. Carlson, D. Cornell and M. Rosenfeld (eds), *Deconstruction and the Possibility of Justice* (New York: Routledge, 1992), pp. 3–67.
16 B. Johnson, 'Translator's Introduction', in J. Derrida, *Dissemination* (London: The Athlone Press, 1981), p. viii.
17 R. Kearney, *Dialogues with Contemporary Continental Thinkers* (Manchester: Manchester University Press, 1984), pp. 105–6.
18 J. Derrida, 'Deconstruction and the Other', in Kearney, *Dialogues with Contemporary Continental Thinkers*, pp. 110–11.
19 See C. Brown, *International Relations Theory: New Normative Approaches* (New York: Harvester Wheatsheaf, 1992), and '"Turtles All the Way Down": Anti-Foundationalism, Critical Theory and International Relations', *Millennium*, 23 (1994), 213–36.
20 Derrida, 'Deconstruction and the Other', p. 125.
21 See J. D. Caputo (ed.), *Deconstruction in a Nutshell: A Conversation with Jacques Derrida* (New York: Fordham University Press, 1997), p. 10.
22 Ibid., p. 9.
23 Ibid., p. 42 (emphasis added).
24 Ibid., p. 16.
25 Derrida, 'Force of Law: The "Mystical Foundation of Authority"', p. 5.
26 K. Mingst, *Essentials of International Relations* (New York: W. W. Norton, 1999), p. 28.
27 Derrida, 'Force of Law: The "Mystical Foundation of Authority"', p. 13.
28 Ibid., p. 14.
29 Ibid., p. 40.

30 E. Grosz, 'The Time of Violence: Deconstruction and Value', *Cultural Values*, 2 (1998), p. 193.
31 Ibid.
32 R. Beardsworth, *Derrida & the Political* (London: Routledge, 1996), p. 24.
33 Caputo, *Deconstruction in a Nutshell*, p. 106.
34 Ibid., p. 13.
35 Ibid., p. 68
36 Ibid., p. 108.
37 J. Derrida, *The Other Heading: Reflections on Today's Europe* (Indianapolis, IN: Indiana University Press, 1992), p. 45 (emphasis added).
38 Ibid., p. 41.
39 J. Derrida, 'Interview with Richard Beardsworth: "Nietzsche and the Machine"', *Journal of Nietzsche Studies*, 7 (1994), 7–66.
40 Ibid.
41 Linklater, 'The Question of the Next Stage in International Relations Theory', p. 93.
42 J. Derrida, 'Politics and Friendship. A Discussion with Jacques Derrida' (Centre for Modern French Thought, University of Sussex, 1 December 1997, online at http://www.sussex.ac.uk/Units/frenchthought/ derrida.htm.
43 J. Derrida, 'Of the Humanities and Philosophical Disciplines: Roundtable Discussion', *Surfaces*, 6 (1996), online at http://www.pum.umontreal.ca/revues/surfaces/vol6/derrida.html.

5

Empowering the Powerful, Enriching the Rich: On Neoliberalism, Economic Globalization and Social Criticism

Barry Smart

Encountering globalization

In so far as people, commercial corporations and the governments of nations are increasingly engaged in complex interconnected processes of interaction that reach around the world, there is now no escaping experiences of globalization. The ways in which people live, the communications to which they are exposed and in which they engage, the commodities that are consumed and the manner and locations in which they are produced and/or assembled, and the geopolitical forces that shape sociality and influence perceptions of lived existence are subject to processes of globalization that are powerfully driven by the development of international trade and investment, international relations and information technology. Every aspect of our existence – the environment, social and cultural forms, practices and values, politics and economic life – has been affected in some shape or form by what is now known as globalization.

While the notion of 'globalization' seems to have entered common parlance, questions concerning its precise meaning, origin and impact have remained matters of analytic debate and dispute. In one influential instance globalization has been defined as referring to both 'the compression of the world and the intensification of consciousness of the world as a whole'.[1] A related conception has emphasized the respects in which globalization signifies a 'stretching process' that has led to an 'intensification of worldwide social relations which link distant localities in such a way that local happenings are shaped by events occurring many miles away and vice versa'.[2] Although the term is of relatively recent origin, really only gaining currency in the late twentieth century, Robertson has argued that the germinal phase of the process of globalization began in Europe as early as the fifteenth century. It is worth adding that it was to a series of developments which took place around the turn of the fifteenth and sixteenth centuries among those living along the Atlantic seaboard of Europe that the beginning of the modern age of Western history has been traced.[3] Indeed globalization has been identified by Giddens as a 'fundamental consequence' of modernity, as the four institutional dimensions attributed to it, notably a world capitalist economy, international division of labour, nation-state system, and world military order, serve to indicate.[4]

While both Robertson and Giddens explore globalization as a multidimensional process and are inclined to place emphasis on social and cultural aspects, the focus of this chapter will fall on the *economic* dimension, specifically on the respects in which globalization has been identified as an economic phenomenon and has been equated with a neoliberal programme to cultivate a global free market capitalism. Particular consideration will be directed to critical analyses and responses to economic globalization, the liberalization of markets and the consequences that have followed closely in their wake.

Explaining globalization

Reference to globalization frequently leads on to issues associated with 'economic neoliberalism, deregulation, privatization, marketization' and the formation of a global capitalist economy.[5] This does not signify economic reductionism, for there is no dispute about the existence of other aspects or dimensions to globalization; rather it reflects a widely held view that it is primarily in economic terms and through economically driven transformations that globalization has had its most significant impact on contemporary social life.[6]

The closer integration of people and nations around the world, made possible 'by the enormous reduction of costs of transportation and communication, and the breaking down of artificial barriers to the flow of goods, services, capital, knowledge, and... people across borders', has been driven by the logic of an economic system that requires corporations to continually work to increase markets for their goods and services.[7] Distinguishing features of the capitalist economic system which has shaped production, consumption and circulation on a global scale were first identified in the course of the nineteenth century. In a series of notebooks drafted in 1857–8 Karl Marx drew attention to a tendency, intrinsic to the capitalist mode of production, to treat every 'limit . . . as a barrier to be overcome' as it sought to 'create the *world market*'.[8] Aspects of a process of globalization are anticipated in Marx's work, as are a number of the significant social and economic consequences that have become increasingly apparent with the formation of a global capitalist economy from the late twentieth century.

The distinguishing features of capitalism identified by Marx emphasize the significance of continual development, relentless expansion and the pursuit of free competition. As it has developed capitalism has continually sought to extend itself to new markets and to draw precapitalist forms of economic life into the system of capitalist commodity production. Formerly uncapitalized economies around the world have been exposed to the powerful influence of capital and have been compelled to organize their economies in a comparable manner. As productive forces have increased and developed there has been a commensurate requirement for the production of new consumption necessitating 'quantitative expansion of existing consumption' and cultivation of existing needs in new populations. But there has also been a requirement for the 'production of *new* needs and discovery and creation of new use values' which has made necessary 'exploration of the earth in all directions'. Increasing and extending existing markets and creating new markets are necessarily continual preoccupations in a capitalist economic system, preoccupations which have led to 'universal exchange of the products of all alien climates and lands', discovery of new 'useful qualities in things' and, through science and technology, the development of 'new branches of production'. In this way, Marx suggests, capitalism has a 'civilizing influence' in that it leads to a form of society that would now be described as cosmopolitan or global 'in comparison to which all earlier ones appear as mere *local developments* of humanity'.[9]

Although the concept is not employed, for Marx capitalism is necessarily globalizing in character. Capitalism constantly revolutionizes prevailing ways of life, and transforms both means of production and objects of consumption as it 'drives beyond national barriers'.[10] The continual need to expand the market for goods and services leads to the mode of production extending its reach 'over the whole surface of the globe' and, as the 'world market' has been established, it has 'given a cosmopolitan character to production and consumption in every country'.[11] Taking stock of developments in the late nineteenth century Marx and Engels describe some of the more significant consequences of the process of global commercial expansion unleashed, notably the erosion of 'national seclusion and self-sufficiency' and the growing 'inter-dependence of nations' in respect of both material and intellectual goods and services.[12]

In explaining the emergence of modern capitalism Marx and Engels describe how the barriers and fetters of feudal property relations were 'burst asunder' and 'free competition' was promoted. The subsequent history of the capitalist economic system has provided a series of further examples of the way in which prevailing conditions of production become a constraint, an obstacle or a barrier, and are themselves, in turn, 'periodically destroyed'. However, while social and economic forms of life have been subject to extensive processes of transformation since the nineteenth century, the central economic imperatives intrinsic to capitalism have remained prominent and their consequences have continued to preoccupy analysts.

Economic liberalism and the self-regulating market

One way of representing the history of capitalism from the end of the eighteenth century to the present is through a consideration of the parameters or limits within which economic rationality has been exercised. Reflecting on the historical development of capitalism towards the close of the Second World War Karl Polanyi identified two significant processes of transformation. The first, at the end of the eighteenth century, exemplified the influence of economic liberalism and involved a movement away from regulated to self-regulated markets. The second, early traces of which were evident towards the close of the nineteenth century, gathered momentum with the 1930s crisis in the market economy which called into question the claims of economic liberalism concerning the virtues of a market society based on the pursuit of self-interest and accelerated the cause of 'social protection' and the perceived necessity for a managed economy. This constituted a highly significant development, one (as Polanyi described it) 'under which the economic system ceases to lay down the law to society and the primacy of society over that system is secured'.[13]

At the end of the eighteenth century the liberal creed advocating a self-regulating market economy had promoted a transformation in the structure of society and brought about an institutional separation of economic and political spheres. Restraints on market practices designed to prevent damage to the fabric of social life were dismantled by the promotion of the institution of the free market. Social and cultural forms of life became increasingly subject to the control and direction of a market mechanism that turned virtually everything into a commodity and threatened 'the demolition of society'.[14]

Recognition towards the close of the nineteenth century of the 'pernicious effects' and social costs associated with the self-regulating industrial capitalist market economy led to moves to introduce various measures designed to restrict and regulate market forces. However, momentum remained behind the market mechanism through the 1920s as Europe and America experienced an economic boom and confidence in the market system appeared to be restored. The crisis of the market economy in the 1930s, the 'fascist solution of the impasse reached by liberal capitalism' and subsequent global conflicts in the 1940s served to further undermine the budgetary and monetary orthodoxy of economic liberalism and led Polanyi to conclude that his age would be 'credited with having seen the end of the self-regulating market', a conclusion that the benefits of hindsight have revealed to be premature.[15]

The relationship between society and economic system has not remained of the order anticipated by Polanyi. To the contrary, the re-imposition of limits on the deployment of capitalist economic rationality, exemplified by the Fordist–Keynesian economic and political formation that presided over a long-running boom in the capitalist economies of the West in the period 1945–73, was followed by a process of gradual abolition of constraints as the limitations of managed capitalism were exposed from the mid-1970s onwards. Interventionist Keynesian states and Fordist economic corporations were afflicted by a 'crisis of governability' and in response invoked a mechanism both 'invisible and anonymous . . . whose unauthored laws would be irresistibly imposed on everyone by force of circumstance as "laws of nature"'; that mechanism was 'the market'.[16]

The last quarter of the twentieth century was marked by three interrelated lines of argument and associated policy initiatives promoting the freedom of market forces, the freedom of individuals to pursue their own interests and be enterprising, and globalization as a seemingly autonomous (if not natural) process that affirmed the necessity to eliminate *national* regulations restraining companies productive and investment practices, respectively.[17] Market rhetoric has become a prominent feature of social and political discourse and associated policy initiatives and processes of deregulation of market forces now intrude into the everyday lives of people around the world.[18]

Neoliberalism, globalization and the political economy of insecurity

Central to neoliberalism is the notion that the 'competitive imperative', involving exposure to the free play of market forces, will produce a more effective allocation of resources, enhanced efficiency in the delivery of services, and greater economy in commodity production. The promotion of anonymous market 'laws' for 'laws state-societies lay down for themselves' prepared the way for capital to move beyond political regulation and become global.[19] The economic crisis of the mid-1970s forced corporations to restructure, become more flexible, and seek a radical reduction, if not an end, to state regulation over their activities through promotion of the notion of market supremacy. In pursuit of growth, multinational and subsequently transnational and global corporations sought to increase their share of world markets and to achieve this end liberalization (in respect of trade, capital flows, investment and borrowing) was identified as a necessary corollary.[20]

The transformation of economic life from organized, standardized and mass forms of production to more flexible, deregulated and globally extensive forms is to a substantial degree bound up with neoliberal policy initiatives. However, the globalization of economic life could not have developed as it has without the realization of potential benefits associated with innovations in information technology. As André Gorz observes, 'The information technology revolution made globalization possible. But, conversely, globalization enabled – then required – the accelerated development of the information technologies and their applications.'[21] What is indisputable is that the combination of global free markets and innovations in information technology that have significantly transformed production around the world have created instabilities and crises as territorially confined governments, trade unions and (to a substantial degree) workers have been left standing or have been out-manoeuvred by forms of capital, finance and commerce that are no longer territorially bound and are able to move wherever the logic of capital dictates.[22]

The globalization of economic life has provided economic corporations with a substantial degree of freedom from political power exercised by nation-states and is precipitating an end of economic nationalism. Supranational organizations, such as the WTO, International Monetary Fund (IMF), the Organisation for Economic Co-operation and Development (OECD) and the World Bank, have endorsed the neoliberal view of the importance of nurturing free competition and allowing what are described as 'the laws of the market' to operate unhindered. As corporations have become transnational 'global players' the policy emphasis has been placed increasingly on the virtues (and rights) of global free-market capitalism, and as these have been promoted employment has become increasingly subject to deregulation and flexibility and virtually all forms of work have become exposed to the growing risk of replacement as a consequence of the development of new information technologies.[23]

Capital is now deterritorial. It flows rapidly around the globe and exercises power and influence over nation-states and their territorially based forms of social and economic life. Nation-states compete against each other to attract capital to their territories by offering various inducements to corporations, including an appropriate climate for profitable investment, a relaxation of potentially costly standards in respect of protection of workers, consumers and the environment, and lucrative tax breaks.[24] The power of globalizing capital, in particular the influence of large institutions, pension funds and money markets in the dominant field of financial capital, has put pressure not only on states but also company managers. The pursuit of short-term profit, of ever higher returns on capital invested, has led to 'deregulated' and 'flexibilized' recruitment policies, and the 'downsizing' and 'casualization' of labour. As employment has become more precarious and the foundations of the social welfare state have been dismantled, so insecurity and uncertainty have grown.

The prevailing economic regime is one in which careers are increasingly being replaced by jobs, many of which are temporary and part-time. It constitutes a form of economic life in which the power of capital and the pursuit of short-term profit are of paramount importance. More than ever this capitalist mode of production 'entails a mode of domination based on the *institution of insecurity*, [or] domination through precariousness'; capitalist globalization constitutes a 'political economy of insecurity', and has created a condition of 'generalized insecurity'.[25] The association of capitalism with insecurity and precariousness is long-standing as the critical analyses of nineteenth-century liberal capitalism conducted by Marx and Engels established. Constant transformation of production and relentless pursuit of world markets and profitability continue, now as then, to lead to 'uninterrupted disturbance of all social conditions' and 'everlasting uncertainty and agitation'.[26] And how to confront the consequences of a globalizing free-market capitalism remains a pressing preoccupation for critical analysts.

For some analysts there seems to be little prospect of any significant alternative to the prevailing form of market economy and the only feasible option appears to be to try to curb market excesses and domesticate 'wild' capitalism; in short, to make it work better for people by 'modernizing social democracy'.[27] Others have adopted a more critical position and have sought to radically engage with the question of alternatives to neoliberal global capitalism and the culture of the market and relentless cultivation of consumption with which it is articulated.[28]

Interrogating globalization

Neoliberal economic discourse, espousing the virtues of the free market and the inescapable reality of globalization, has served to legitimate governmental decisions leading to 'deindustrialisation, growing inequality and retrenchment of social policies', decisions that reflect an accommodation to financial markets and their consequences.[29] The current geopolitical economy of globalization has developed through a process of de-politicization and disempowerment in which governments have effectively submitted control to economic forces. It is in this setting that the question of alternatives has been posed, it constitutes the context in which impoverishment of the political imagination, a corollary of the demoralization, insecurity and anxiety that has arisen with global 'marketization', can be openly addressed and countered.

Reflecting on the effects of economic globalization Bourdieu cautions that 'social laws, economic laws and so on only take effect to the extent that people let them do so'.[30] Noting the extent of political capitulation to the project for a global free market economy Bourdieu adds that 'the power of the dominant order is not just economic, but intellectual', and that it is necessary to speak out against it to restore a sense of other possibilities.[31] It is the responsibility of social analysts to counter the processes by which people come to regard prevailing social and economic forms of life with submission and fatalism.

The global free market has been described as an American project and, in turn, as *utopian* in the strictly etymological sense that it does not exist. But while a *universal* free market may not be a reality, the project to create a single global market endures. Indeed, as John Gray observes, 'Market utopianism has succeeded in appropriating the American faith that it is a unique country, the model for a universal civilization which all societies are fated to emulate.'[32] According to the fundamentalist rhetoric that has promoted the idea of market freedom, whereas alleged governmental inefficiencies and deficiencies are deemed to be relatively substantial and consequential, those of the market are conceived to be relatively minor and in a number of respects they are deemed to be self-correcting.[33]

In practice the freeing-up of markets has been a consequence of the exercise of corporate power and federal government policy, and the freedoms enjoyed by corporations in a deregulated global economy have led to rising inequality and social exclusion. The growth of an informational global capitalism and the promotion of free market policies has simultaneously produced forms of 'economic development and underdevelopment, social inclusion and social exclusion'.[34] This combination, of unrestricted market logic and an increasingly informational capitalism, has led to the emergence of a 'fourth world' of rising human suffering, inequality and exploitation, a world composed of 'multiple black holes of social exclusion'.[35] These circumstances are aggravated by the fact that the nation-state and the institutions of civil society appear to have lost, if not in some instances surrendered, the capacity to counter the consequences of a free market logic that is producing dramatic increases in social imbalances: an accelerating polarization of wealth and a growth in forms of 'individualized hyperconsumption', alongside overexploitation of workers, increasingly precarious labour relations, and rises in poverty and extreme poverty or deprivation.[36]

The increased integration of countries and peoples around the world through processes of globalization has not led to greater economic stability or to a reduction in poverty. As capital markets have been liberalized all countries, and developing countries especially, have been exposed to the possibility of volatile fluctuations in the movement of capital. Liberalization of capital markets 'has been pushed despite the fact that there is no evidence showing it spurs economic growth'.[37] Ironically 'market supremacy' has been promoted by the very public institution – the IMF – that was originally founded after the Second World War to provide a basis for collective action to counter the shortcomings of markets and the financial disruptions that adversely affected economies.

As things currently stand international market trading disproportionately benefits the stronger and more dominant parties, those entering exchanges already possessing the most assets. In short, it 'further empowers the already powerful and further enriches the already rich at the expense of the weak and the poor'.[38] Increasing manifestations of the dystopian consequences of market fundamentalism, or the global deployment of free market logic, have stimulated a number of critical responses.

One response has been to argue for greater recognition to be given to market systems other than the American neoliberal version, for greater consideration to be given to the ways in which governments in a number of countries – for example, Sweden, Germany and Japan – have continued to play a significant role in promoting social welfare and working to reduce levels of inequality and poverty. Given the evident deficiencies and discontents associated with economic globalization there is now a need for radical changes in international institutions such as the IMF, the WTO and the World Bank to counter the dominance enjoyed by trade, financial and commercial ministries and related corporate interests. Greater openness and transparency in public institutions with an involvement in forms of global governance is required, as are changes in voting rights at the IMF and World Bank. A widening of participation beyond trade ministers in each of the international economic institutions would allow those who have been without a voice to begin to express their views and contribute to the formation of more representative policies and alternative visions of the good economy.[39]

On a number of counts – growing disparities in wealth and access to resources, economic instability, environmental concerns, public health matters and humanitarian assistance – increased global interdependence has revealed the 'importance of global public goods' and in turn created 'a need for global collective action'.[40] The IMF and the global financial system, the World Bank and development assistance and the WTO and the trade agenda have each been identified as in need of radical reform if existing inequities and imbalances are to be corrected and a more economically just relationship is to be established between developed and developing countries. Drawing parallels between the Great Depression of the 1930s and the current form of economic life it has been argued that 'the system of capitalism is at a crossroads...[and] millions of people around the world are waiting to see whether globalization can be reformed'.[41]

Reform represents one response to the dilemmas and discontents associated with globalization and the liberalization of markets. Another critical response to the neoliberal 'free-market utopia' and development of a political economy of insecurity that is a corollary of globalization as an '*inter*-national, *inter*-state and *inter*-societal phenomenon' has been a proposal for transnational market regulation.[42] The proposal outlined is that the neoliberal project to reduce the state to a minimum must be countered by cosmopolitan national movements and political associations cultivating transnational institutions and transnational forms of recognition, regulation and management. With globalization the world has in effect grown smaller and more vulnerable to conflicts of interest in respect of trade, labour markets and the environment and it is in this context that 'transnational forums and forms of regulated (that is, recognized and non-violent) handling of mutually exclusive national, religious and cultural "egoisms"' become vital.[43]

The development of a neoliberal free market global capitalism has promoted increasing labour market flexibility and a deregulation of workplaces and these have led to employment in Western societies becoming increasingly precarious and insecure. Well remunerated, secure, full-time employment is fast diminishing and the foundations of the welfare state are being steadily eroded. Information technology has made possible the development of a global capitalist economy with the ability to dissolve spatial and temporal differences and organize 'a fragmented labor process into a planetary whole'.[44] The absence of any necessary fixed spatial location for production of commodities and services means that economic activities can be located at numerous sites around the world, which in the absence of effective global economic governance means that nation-states are driven to compete to attract capital investment and employment opportunities to sites within their territories.

The globalization of production has presented corporations with two distinctive strategic advantages. It has led to increasing competition between 'high-priced and low-priced labor' and it has meant that 'the fiscal conditions and controls of individual states can be played off against one another and undermined'.[45] Examples of the ways in which multinational corporations have taken advantage of the strategic possibilities opened up by globalization are well documented in a critical analysis of the shift of manufacturing production to export processing zones in countries providing the inducement of very low wage, non-unionized labour, deregulated factory production, and where, depending on location, a 'tax holiday' may mean corporations do not pay any income or property tax for a period ranging from five to ten years.[46]

The tyranny of capitalist globalization: Bourdieu's critique

A common theme that emerges from critical analyses of the consequences of a global neoliberal or free-market oriented capitalism is that to have any chance of being effective resistance or opposition needs must operate on comparable terms; that is to say, it must be transnational or cosmopolitan in scope. In the terms outlined by Bourdieu, to counter economic globalization it is necessary to lay the foundations for a 'new internationalism' and to this end two courses of action are proposed. First, as noted above, to help mobilize and organize effective opposition to neoliberalism it is vital to counter the 'fatalism of neoliberal thinking' by taking issue with representations of economic life that serve to naturalize prevailing forms of organization and associated relationships and assumptions that provide unquestioned grounds for social and economic conduct.[47] At stake here is the need to counter forms of demoralization that arise from the representation of neoliberal free-market economics as a 'great chain of Being'.[48] Analysis has to expose to criticism the idea that our destiny lies with 'transcendent, independent, indifferent powers, such as "financial markets" or the mechanisms of "globalization"'.[49]

Second, to promote the possibility of transnational state action it is necessary to act on and through existing national states, both to defend what remains of the 'social state' and public provision and also to help bring about forms of global governance that will rein in the free market project and accord priority to the 'implementation of . . . social measures designed to counter the . . . social consequences . . . [of] unbridled competition'.[50] In this instance what is required is recognition of the common ground shared by social movements with a variety of priorities in respect of social issues such as housing, health, employment, the environment, and so on. Social movements that have emerged to oppose different facets of globalization frequently share an antipathy towards conventional centralist forms of political mobilization, a predisposition towards direct action, and value solidarity as 'the tacit moving force behind the greater part of their activities'.[51]

The development of global free market capitalism has effectively made corporations 'the most powerful political forces of our time'.[52] The power of the multinational agencies and institutions which now exert global social and economic dominance derives from their capacity to be able to 'draw upon an extraordinary convergence of all forms of capital – economic, political, military, cultural, scientific, technological – amounting to a fundamental, unprecedented symbolic hegemony over all channels and means of communication'.[53]

In response connections have begun to be established across national boundaries and between various movements concerned about the global dominance exercised by multinational corporations. For example, culture jamming and ad-busting groups, environmental, labour and human rights activists, as well as others campaigning about ethical and moral matters in respect of corporate activity, and those involved in reclaiming the streets and fighting the corporate colonization of education, health and welfare, are contributing to 'a different agenda . . . that embraces globalization but seeks to wrest it from the grasp of the multinationals'.[54] It is an agenda that promotes the idea of 'citizen-centred' alternatives to what generally are represented as 'consumer-based', but are in actuality 'market-based' and predominantly corporate influenced forms of social and economic life. To confront capitalist globalization effectively resistance needs to be organized on a transnational basis, and to that end it is important to envision a different form of globalization, one in which the potential for common ground or solidarity between people is not perpetually disrupted (or worse, destroyed) by a relentless process of increasing intensification of competition.

Concluding remarks: critically engaging with globalization

The idea of globalization has served to conceal the way in which neoliberal free-market policies, according 'undisputed rule' to economic powers and installing an economizing mode of governance, have been 'imposed on the entire world'.[55] The current global economy is a product of policies of liberalization and deregulation, the destabilizing social and economic consequences of which have been compounded by the development and diffusion of market-driven technological innovations which have served to make temporary any competitive advantages gained from the deployment of new technologies. Disordered and disorganized by unregulated market competition and 'irrational capitalist management of technological rationalization', the global economic field has been exposed to criticism on a number of counts.[56]

Capitalist globalization promotes the interests of transnational corporations over nation-states and the populations under their jurisdiction; elevates self-interest over solidarity; 'swamps quality with quantity'; and is simultaneously undermining 'people's sense of self-worth in the marketplace while eroding traditional institutions which protected people against the market'.[57] With deregulation and the promotion of global free-trade the international mobility of capital has increased. Capital moves to countries possessing low labour costs and the capacity to produce consumer goods and services for those living in wealthier, high labour cost countries. Free-trade export processing zones located in countries such as Sri Lanka, China, the Philippines, Thailand and Vietnam exemplify the harsh consequences of the logic of neoliberal global capitalism: namely, that workers are paid as little as possible, are on temporary or short-term contracts, and work long hours in frequently unsafe and unhealthy conditions, while the companies involved in manufacturing in these low-wage zones are granted extensive tax breaks.[58]

The new informational global capitalist economy is a dual economy in a number of respects. It is an economy in which a growing number of people face the prospect of making do with temporary, part-time, unskilled, 'under-paid and low-productivity' forms of work while a shrinking and 'privileged minority' enjoy the benefits of secure and well rewarded employment.[59] It is a global economy in which the USA, representing a small proportion of the world's population, around 3 per cent, accounts for almost 50 per cent of the world's consumption. Within the USA itself a privileged minority of the population, approaching 2 per cent, owns the bulk of the national wealth, around 60 per cent of the total.[60] Since the 1970s growing disparities in income and wealth have become a feature of American society and a number of other countries around the world, including Britain, Brazil, Argentina, Venezuela, Bolivia, Peru, Thailand and Russia, and from the 1980s a similar pattern has been repeated in Japan, Canada, Sweden, Australia, Germany and Mexico.[61]

Increasing social inequality and polarization have been identified as intrinsic features of a global informational capitalist economic system in which financial markets have come to dominate the process of capital accumulation.[62] But capitalist globalization is not a natural force and the subordination of social life to the 'laws of the market' and the vagaries of global financial flows is not a necessity and should not be equated with 'modernization', as is frequently the case in political rhetoric seeking to extol the virtues of free market forces. The task of critical analysis is to confront the prevailing form of economic globalization, to expose the respects in which neoliberal capitalist globalization has promoted a wide-ranging decline in real wages, job security and working conditions, and has also contributed to a significant erosion of public services, while simultaneously exacerbating the risk of irreversible environmental damage as a consequence of an unregulated unrelenting pursuit of economic growth and short-term capital accumulation.

In such a context, to counter the neoliberal version of economic globalization, which represents itself as progressive, as promoting freedom and consumer choice, critical research needs to be directed towards the generation of alternative genuinely progressive 'visions of the future' and the production of 'realistic utopias' so that a different perspective can be gained on prevailing circumstances that will allow us 'to judge what we *are* doing in the light of what we *could* or *should* do'.[63]

Notes

1 R. Robertson, *Globalization, Social Theory and Global Culture* (London: Sage, 1992), p. 8.
2 A. Giddens, *The Consequences of Modernity* (Cambridge: Polity, 1990), p. 64.
3 A. Toynbee, *A Study of History, Vol. 8* (London: Oxford University Press, 1954).

4 Giddens, *The Consequences of Modernity*, p. 175. The institutional dimensions of modernity identified by Giddens are capitalism, industrialism, administrative coordination and surveillance of the nation-state and control of the means of violence (pp. 55–63).
5 R. Robertson, 'Globalization Theory 2000+ : Major Problematics', in G. Ritzer and B. Smart (eds), *Handbook of Social Theory* (London: Sage, 2001), p. 458.
6 See, for example, J. Stiglitz, *Globalization and its Discontents* (Harmondsworth: Penguin, 2002), and J. Gray, *False Dawn: The Delusions of Global Capitalism* (London: Granta 1999).
7 Stiglitz, *Globalization and its Discontents*, pp. 9–10.
8 K. Marx, *Grundrisse: Foundations of the Critique of Political Economy* (Harmondsworth: Penguin, 1973), p. 408. A world market or world economy pursuing capital accumulation around the globe has been developing for over five hundred years, but it is only with the late twentieth-century deployment of information technology that a truly integrated global economy has emerged.
9 Ibid., pp. 409–10.
10 Ibid., p. 410.
11 K. Marx and F. Engels, *The Communist Manifesto* (Harmondsworth: Penguin, 1968), p. 83.
12 Ibid., p. 84.
13 K. Polanyi, *The Great Transformation: The Social and Economic Origins of Our Time* (Boston, MA: Beacon Press, 1968), p. 251.
14 Ibid., p. 73.
15 Ibid., pp. 142, 237.
16 A. Gorz, *Reclaiming Work: Beyond the Wage-Based Society* (Cambridge: Polity, 1999), p. 11.
17 A. Gorz, *Critique of Economic Reason* (London: Verso, 1989); P. Bourdieu, *Firing Back: Against the Tyranny of the Market* (London: Verso, 2003).
18 B. Smart, *Economy, Culture and Society: A Sociological Critique of Neo-Liberalism* (Buckingham: Open University Press, 2003).
19 Gorz, *Reclaiming Work*, p. 5.
20 D. Harvey, *The Condition of Postmodernity* (Oxford: Basil Blackwell, 1989).
21 Gorz, *Reclaiming Work*, p. 14.
22 U. Beck, *The Brave New World of Work* (Cambridge: Polity, 2000).
23 Gorz, *Reclaiming Work*, p. 14; Beck, *The Brave New World of Work*, pp. 2–3.
24 G. Monbiot, *Captive State: The Corporate Takeover of Britain* (London: Pan Books, 2001); N. Klein, *No Logo* (London: Flamingo, 2001).
25 Bourdieu, *Firing Back*, p. 29; Beck, *The Brave New World of Work*, pp. 2–4; Gorz, *Reclaiming Work*, pp. 52–4.
26 Marx and Engels, *The Communist Manifesto*, pp. 83–4.
27 A. Giddens, *The Third Way and its Critics* (Cambridge: Polity, 2000), p. 29.
28 See, for example, Gorz, *Reclaiming Work*; Beck, *The Brave New World of Work*; Bourdieu, *Firing Back*; 'The Politics of Globalisation', *Le Monde*, 20 February 2002, and *Acts of Resistance: Against the New Myths of Our Time* (Cambridge: Polity, 1998); and M. Albert, *Parecon: Life After Capitalism* (London: Verso, 2003).
29 P. Bourdieu and L. Wacquant, 'Neoliberal Newspeak: Notes on the New Planetary Vulgate', *Radical Philosophy*, 108 (2001), p. 4.

30 Bourdieu, *Acts of Resistance*, p. 55.
31 G. Grass and P. Bourdieu, 'The "Progressive" Restoration', *New Left Review*, 14 (2002) p. 66.
32 Gray, *False Dawn*, p. 104.
33 D. O'Keefe (ed.), *Economy and Virtue: The Moral Case for the Market Economy* (London: Institute of Economic Affairs, 2004).
34 M. Castells, *The Rise of the Network Society*, Vol. I of *The Information Age: Economy, Society and Culture* (Oxford: Basil Blackwell, 1996), p. 82.
35 M. Castells, *End of Millennium*, Vol. III of *The Information Age: Economy, Society and Culture* (Oxford: Basil Blackwell, 1998), p. 164.
36 Ibid.
37 Stiglitz, *Globalization and its Discontents*, p. 16.
38 Albert, *Parecon*, p. 3.
39 Ibid.
40 Stiglitz, *Globalization and its Discontents*, p. 224.
41 Ibid., pp. 249–50.
42 Beck, *The Brave New World of Work*, pp. 25, 175.
43 Ibid., p. 175.
44 Ibid., p. 27.
45 Ibid., p. 28.
46 Klein, *No Logo*.
47 Bourdieu, *Acts of Resistance*, p. 68.
48 Ibid., p. 54.
49 Ibid., p. 69.
50 Ibid., p. 67.
51 Bourdieu, 'The Politics of Globalisation'.
52 Klein, *No Logo*, p. 339.
53 Bourdieu, 'The Politics of Globalisation'.
54 Klein, *No Logo*, p. 445.
55 Bourdieu, *Firing Back*, p. 9.
56 Gorz, *Reclaiming Work*, p. 145.
57 Albert, *Parecon*, pp. 3–4; R. Sennett, 'Growth and Failure: The New Political Economy and its Culture', in M. Featherstone and S. Lash (eds), *Spaces of Culture: City, Nation, World* (London: Sage 1999), pp. 14–15.
58 Klein, *No Logo*.
59 Bourdieu, *Firing Back*, pp. 30–1.
60 Albert, *Parecon*, p. 1.
61 M. Castells, *End of Millennium*, pp. 80–1; 'Pulling Apart: A State-by-State Analysis of Income Trends', April 2003, *Economic Policy Institute* and *Centre on Budget and Policy Priorities*, online at: http://www.cbpp.org/1-18-00sfp.htm; Gorz, *Reclaiming Work*, pp. 17–18.
62 Castells, *End of Millennium*, pp. 343–4.
63 Gorz, *Reclaiming Work*, p. 113.

6
Tricky Business: Challenging Risk Theory and its Vision of a Better Global Future

François Debrix

Introduction

Over the past ten years, risk theory has been one of the most fashionable theoretical models used to analyse the crises of late-modern society. Introduced by German sociologist Ulrich Beck in the early 1990s,[1] and later revisited by Anglo-Saxon constructionist and critical social theorists including Anthony Giddens, Scott Lash and Zygmunt Bauman,[2] risk theory has been deployed as a response to many destabilizing trends and fear-inducing phenomena of the 1990s. With the emergence of environmental disasters in the former Communist bloc countries, sweeping political changes in all of Europe, bloody ethnic rivalries from the Balkans to Africa, and growing social inequalities pretty much everywhere, risk theory has risen to academic prominence with its claims to be able to offer theoretical and practical guidelines that will help people to make sense of the inconsistencies of a globalized society (or what Beck often simply calls 'risk society'). While intimately associated with the problems of the Western world and the collapse of many of the West's political values (the state, sovereignty, democracy, welfare), risk society affects the entire world because the West has assiduously sought to 'globalize' its values and its political system for the past two centuries. Thus, risk theory purports to offer explanations for the social crises inherent in the era of globalization; but it also claims to be able to provide people the world over, not just in the West, with radical solutions for a better future. Basing itself on a social-democratic and, as Beck calls it, a 'new cosmopolitan' mode of political argumentation, risk theory maintains that a critical social utopia is an attainable goal. Risk theorists believe that recent popular and grass-root ecological challenges and some organized forms of opposition against economic globalization are clear signs that risk society is about to give rise to a global social democracy.[3] Accordingly, risk theorists such as Beck generally agree that a new global or 'cosmopolitan' manifesto is necessary.[4]

Risk theory's revival of critical engagement and of some social-democratic themes (although filtered through an analysis of issues that has no room for class-based understandings of social conflict[5]) is intriguing and at times compelling. Still, risk theory also reads as a desperate attempt at regaining a spirit of social criticism and engagement in an era when poststructuralist prophecies about the vanishing of the social into systems of objects and mediation seem to have been realized.[6] To revive a spirit of social action and to resurrect a sense of individuality and subjectivity at the heart of these new social critiques, risk theory has recourse to images of social unrest, political crisis and unpredictable dangers. Such images mobilize individual subjects and seek to reorganize social action by means of fear. And, despite the fact that those highlighted unrests, crises, uncertainties and dangers are not always obvious to all the populations in the world, risk theory claims that such fears are global. Clearly, risk theory's mobilization against a certain vision of globalized modernity by means of fear and the accompanying images of constant dangers and dramas (all derived from a certain vision of modernized technology) strike a chord with mostly Western populations living in highly industrialized and technology-dependent societies. Such societies are often taken over by all sorts of media-induced paranoias and popular psychoses that do not necessarily reflect the presence of material conditions of socioeconomic inequality. In fact, one could even argue that such popular scares today are often the privilege and prerogative of those individuals in Western societies who are relatively well-off and by and large benefit from the globalization of the economy, society, politics, culture and technology. Thus, by basing their critical engagement with (and their supposed opposition to) globalized systems and values on the presence of scares, dangers and risks mostly found in the West, risk theorists end up affirming yet another model of globalized modernization.

This chapter takes issue with risk theory on the grounds that its apparently strong critique of globalized modernity in the early twenty-first century is in fact a weak attempt at trying to recover a sense of individual subjectivity to be put to the service of an allegedly new (but traditionally 'cosmopolitan' and Western) form of social and collective engagement. Resorting to fear and brandishing the spectre of inevitable future dangers and crises reveal the pathos of a social theory that is necessarily involved in a love/hate relationship with the phenomenon of globalization and, as such, is much more conservative than it may appear at first glance. For, as much as risk theory claims that it has found a way out of the contemporary cynicism of today's globalized modernity that privileges the few to the detriment of the many, this new social theoretical critique also needs globalization and its technological excesses to remain intact and to continue to proliferate inequalities so that risk theory may continue to provide its vague, idealistic, and often ethnocentrically elitist appeal to a better cosmopolitan future. In short, risk theory (or, as Beck recently reformulated it, the theory of 'world risk society') needs globalization at the hands of corporate capital and Western nation-states to remain strong in order for its own global aspirations to continue to appear meaningful and useful to some.

Risk theory and late-modernity

In 1990, a few months after the collapse of the Berlin Wall and a couple of years before Beck's thesis about the notion of risk was finally translated and published in English,[7] Giddens anticipated much of risk theory's argument about late-modernity for English-speaking audiences by stating that:

> the world in which we live today is a fraught and dangerous one. This has served to do more than simply blunt or force us to qualify the assumption that the emergence of modernity would lead to the formation of a happier and more secure social order. Loss of belief in 'progress', of course, is one of the factors that underlies the dissolution of 'narratives' of history. Yet there is much more at stake here than the conclusion that history 'goes nowhere'. We have to develop an institutional analysis of the double-edged character of modernity.[8]

In this statement, Giddens did more than merely distance himself from poststructuralist analyses of modernity and the social which, as Giddens understood them, were mostly interested in emphasizing the discontinuities of modern history and unveiling the fact that such history, and its story of inevitable progress, was nothing more than a succession of narratives, multiple stories people and institutions told about themselves and others. Modernity and its history, Giddens suggested, could be reclaimed, at least partially. What needed to be realized for Giddens was that modernity had two dominant but contradictory histories or stories: one was the story of modernity's success, prowess, expansion and development; the other was the story of the inevitable, long-hidden, but increasingly visible consequences of modern development and modernized progress, with an emphasis in the late twentieth century on the dangers, insecurities and risks that modernity's tools, science and technology, were bringing to the modern world.

Beck's risk theory takes up Giddens' challenge. Away from the pluralized and proliferated narratives of and about the modern that most poststructuralist social analyses leave us with, Beck proposes a new but different story and history of modernity, one that is critical of the dominant line of analysis which, with few exceptions now forgotten since capitalism appears to have defeated communism, socialism and Marxism,[9] has repeatedly sung the praises of modern scientific progress and technological innovation. Not surprisingly as well, this other story about modernity must urgently be told since the negative and dangerous effects of scientific and technological modernization are running rampant and going global now that, as Beck previously stated, the 'bipolar world has faded away'.

Beck believes that modernity is characterized by two main eras and, currently, we are in a transition period from one modern stage to the next. Beck labels these two stages 'first modernity' and 'second modernity', or 'simple modernization' and 'reflexive modernization'.[10] The first modernity is characterized by the language and ideas of the Enlightenment, and scientific progress and technological advances are believed to be able to bring social, economic and political benefits to all those who take part in this modern, industrial society. The second modernity is 'advanced', as Beck sometimes mentions, because the technological and scientific abilities of first modernity seem to be limitless. But this other modernity is also dominated by the excesses, problems, crises and hazards that are part and parcel of simple modernization. This second modernity is, of course, the story/history that, as Giddens suggests, we are not supposed to be told. This story, however, is replete with examples of the inability of first modernity's institutions, and particularly the nation-state as the main structure of order and security, to control the inherent difficulties and tensions (bureaucratic, political, ecological, economic, and so on) of the modern project. For Beck, one of the underlying themes of modernity (first or second) is the logic of control: 'Politically and sociologically, modernity is a project of social and technological control by the nation-state.'[11]

Whereas first modernity is defined by industrial growth and state-assured control and security, second modernity is governed by the idea of risk. Risk, for Beck, is not to be confused with danger. Risk is an institutional calculation, an anticipation on the part of the institutions of second modernity (starting with the nation-state) of the future, based on the uncertainties produced by modern technologies. Both Giddens and Beck share the view that risk is the 'unintended consequence' of first modernity, an unplanned result of modern society's failure to control and protect, which nonetheless becomes the definitive mode of understanding and the main collective mood of the later stage of modernity. The notion of risk, which does not just dominate but more importantly captures the mode of living, being and planning of second modernity, is reflexive to the extent that risk emerges as a result of the loss of trust in modern social institutions. As Beck clarifies, 'the discourse of risk begins where our trust in security ends . . . The concept of risk thus characterizes a peculiar intermediate state between security and destruction, where the *perception* of threatening risks determines thought and action.'[12] Second modernity is a risk society because, at all times, individuals and institutions are asked to reflect upon the potentiality of threats, the perception of danger, and the virtuality of hazards that have yet to be unleashed on a globally destructive scale, but whose capacity for damage and drama is always assumed, suspected, anticipated, measured and, in a sense, expected.[13] Beck notes that 'the sociology of risk is a science of potentialities and judgments about probabilities'.[14]

Risk is not simply the dominant condition of second modernity for Beck; it is more importantly a 'paradigm shift, a new frame of reference' in the history of modernity.[15] It is a paradigm shift because risk replaces the idea of state-induced control and security as the main organizing model of social life. The calculus of risk gives rise to all sorts of institutions, agents, media and authorities whose job it is to prepare for potential future disasters and catastrophes. Still, as risk calculation at the hands of multiple authority and expert centres takes over social control and order, certainty and security become further eroded. And the hazards and dangers that the new calculus of risk was meant to buffer appear to be ever more present and real as risk society expands and becomes global.[16]

Thus, for Beck, due to the limitations of risk calculation, second modernity makes visible the problems of modernity and reveals the dangers of modernization theories that champion the global expansion of modern (Western) social and political institutions, commerce and culture, and technology and science. Yet this does not mean that modernity must be abandoned altogether, that modernity's grand narratives ought to be scrapped, or even that we can start to realize that modernity never even began to fulfil its promises.[17] Instead, Beck suggests, the crisis of modernity made visible by the phenomenon of risk in second modernity creates opportunities *within modernity* for individuals to take matters into their own hands and to reflect upon their place in the process of modernization. Put differently, another unintended consequence of risk society's expansion is the reclaiming of the political by individuals. As individuals the world over are faced with risks they cannot fully understand or control, what Beck calls a new subpolitics becomes the way out of structural apathy, uncertainty and fear. Beck uncovers a 'subjective backdrop of risk society' that turns into the next social-democratic ideology, the new hope mechanism of reflexive modernization.[18]

Risk theory and globalized modernity

As Elliott has remarked, Beck's announcement of the passage from simple to advanced modernity 'is not wholly about risk; it is also about an expansion of choice'.[19] Risk society's global spread is not to be interpreted as restrictive or confining; rather, risk society encourages the return of individualism, subjectivity and agency. When traditional areas of social life are liberated from communal or state-based institutional controls (because they are no longer effective in an era of risks), the individual subject is left to fend for himself/herself. 'The ethic of individual self-fulfillment and achievement is the most powerful current in modern Western society', Beck affirms.[20] And as risk society expands globally, individuality is bound to be the main characteristic of emerging globalization where 'choosing, deciding, shaping individuals who aspire to be the authors of their lives, the creators of their identities, are the central characters of our time'.[21]

For Beck, if the concept of globalization is meaningful today, it is not because it refers to a set of multinational structures and systems of production and control that are getting closer and closer to one another on a geographical scale and are functionally interrelated. Instead, what renders globalization meaningful is the degree to which the process of individualization developed through an awareness of risk is taking place across national borders. Beck believes that 'globality is an *unavoidable condition of human intercourse* at the close of the twentieth century'.[22]

What makes globalization, Beck intimates, is the fact that risks can no longer be local or even national. Conceived of in the aftermath of the Chernobyl scare, Beck's notion of risk has always been global and transnational. One of the main reasons why individuals are left to find their own strategies and solutions to deal with global risks is that territorial states have proved incompetent and inoperative in containing threats and hazards such as nuclear pollutions and ecological degradations. In an era of reflexive modernization, if risks are no longer local and, further, if risks inadvertently generate a new sense of individual responsibility, then, of necessity, global risks will also facilitate transnational links and relations between individuals who perceive the same dangers, are subject to the same types of fears, and are all left on their own, orphans of the nation-state security system, to devise new global political alternatives.[23] As Beck intimates, 'in order to speak of the world risk *society*, it is also necessary for the global hazards to begin to shape *actions* and facilitate the creations of *international institutions*'.[24]

Beck's individualization on a global scale (revealed through global risks) is not an end in itself. After all, it is always possible and, Beck admits, tempting for individuals who have allegedly regained a sense of choice and responsibility through their relationship to dangers, hazards and scares to use their renewed individualism for purely selfish motives.[25] While self-protection is a normal reaction and response to a prevailing culture of risk and uncertainty, it is also (according to Beck) a losing proposition in world risk society. Thus, individualization must be a tool for something else. And what individualization must be useful for, Beck continues, is the creation of a 'new cosmopolitanism' which is the only form of ideological engagement that can place 'globality at the heart of political imagination, action and organization'.[26]

Beck's new cosmopolitanism is the ideology of global risk society.[27] It is an ideology designed to make sense of and organize globalization, defined by Beck as a transnational condition characterized by unknowable dangers, impossible risk calculations, unreliable authorities and experts, and uncertain future prospects. It is also an ideology that is meant to give individuals a way of steering their agency and guiding their politics if they are to cope with global risks. Cosmopolitanism, Beck insists, is not antithetical to individualization or individualism. In fact, individualization in risk society is the necessary basis for this new version of cosmopolitan organization. Beck writes that 'individualization... implies, paradoxically, a collective lifestyle'.[28] Whereas first modernity subordinated the individual subject to structural and systemic collectives which ended up stifling individual choice and responsibility, second modernity is unburdened by these previous collective constructs since they have proved incapable of controlling risks. As such, Beck rationalizes, the new individualism that emerges as a result of the crisis of first modernity is able to view afresh collective, communitarian and altruistic endeavours. Thus, the 'I' of second modernity has no difficulty thinking in terms of 'we'. And if the 'I' can think as 'we', if the individual subject can see himself/herself as part of a collective, then, Beck concludes, 'I am convinced that a cosmopolitan democracy is a realistic, if utopian, project.'[29]

How this cosmopolitan democratic project is to take shape for Beck is not so clear. Once again, it is premised upon individualization. Only individualization at the service of the new cosmopolitan ideal can (re)politicize globalization.[30] And, Beck believes, globalization must be politicized, otherwise it will be left to the corporate world to run its course and, more urgently, a proliferation of global risks will leave no hope for change and social improvement to most individuals the world over. Beck attempts to make his utopian vision regarding the repoliticization of globalization more tangible by offering the spectre of global ecological dangers as prototypical examples of world risks that are capable of bringing in a cosmopolitan challenge. Claiming that powerful transnational environmental activist groups such as Greenpeace have been developing a 'globalization from below' for several decades, Beck argues that a 'New International' (cosmopolitan, not socialist) is being formed on the basis of a subpolitics.[31] This subpolitical mode of action/engagement unites individuals across the globe and irrespective of nationalities because it manages to bypass 'the representative institutions of the political system of nation-states'.[32] Furthermore, although starting from below, this subpolitics of transnational groups of individuals focuses its 'attention on signs of an (ultimately global) self-organization of politics... [encouraging] ad hoc individual participation in political decisions...and often even lacking the protection of the law'.[33] Finally, this cosmopolitan subpolitics is based on '"coalitions of opposites" (of parties, nations, regions, religions, governments, rebels, classes)' that use 'the methods of the media age to stage worldwide civil resistance' and thus set themselves up as 'enemyless democracy'.[34] All in all, what appears to give Beck's new cosmopolitan ideology of globalization its character is less its political content (references are made here and there to Kant, but only superficially) than its political form and mode of organization: 'It would be a global nexus of responsibility, in which individuals – and not their organizational representatives – could directly participate in political decisions.'[35]

Interestingly enough, while Beck hopes that this global mode of direct popular and pluralist democracy (every individual participates in decisions) will become the answer to world risks and dangers, Beck willingly admits as well, in a moment of excessive honesty perhaps, that this new global ideal, this 'politically strong cosmopolitan consciousness' as he calls it,[36] may not be so different from another cosmopolitan and democratic project implemented by Western states after the Cold War. After all, who could be better suited to provide the material boost needed to make the new cosmopolitan utopia a reality than the West, the cradle of modernity that, as Beck has taken great pains to remind us, has not yet run its course? As Beck puts it:

> today, for the first time, the West has *carte blanche* to define and promote universal values. With the removal of any challenge to the dominance of the world's major economic powers, these moral arguments too can be posited on uncontested grounds. The themes of global civil society and an ethical foreign policy have provided a new ideological cement for the project of Western power. Globalization implies the weakening of state structures... On the other hand, the idea of 'global responsibility' implies at least the possibility of a new Western *military humanism*, to enforce human rights across the globe... The striking feature here is that imperial power-play can coexist harmoniously with a cosmopolitan mission.[37]

Of course, Beck is presenting this possible scenario of a globalization filled with a vision of democratic cosmopolitanism supported by state-sponsored 'military humanism' to suggest that, as an idea at least, a global 'political republic of individuals' is preferable. Yet Beck's juxtaposition of his own cosmopolitan ideal with that of Western powers which, as he himself indicates, and despite their apparent imperialistic and militaristic tendencies, could be quite compatible with his own (since after all the ideas of democracy, direct participation and critical engagement in the face of risks are all derived from the same social and political ferment, first modernity or the Enlightenment) reveals the fragility of Beck's political designs. His cosmopolitan and subpolitical ideals, based on the belief of a return to individualization in modern societies dominated by risk preoccupations, may make sense to some individuals, in Western states mostly, and for whom a media-saturated and consumption-driven social environment that is likely to emphasize (if not exaggerate) risks, dangers and popular scares is an everyday reality. But whose society is this, and how global is it? Or, put differently, is this analysis of risk in Western late-modern (or advanced) societies suitable for the development of both a theory *and* an ideology of globalization as Beck proposes? It is to these questions and critiques that I now turn.

My critique of Beck's risk theory will be twofold. First, I will challenge his ethnocentric interpretation of the global whose main issues and problems (driven by risk) are derived almost exclusively from Western modern preoccupations. Second, building upon Anthony Elliott's and Scott Lash's respective critiques of Beck's theory, I will address some of Beck's premises about risk and modernity and I will suggest that, by presenting risk as a structurally and objectively given fact of second modernity, he is unable to consistently recognize and analyse the socially constructed and discursively mobilized texture of most fears and anxieties that are perceived today as one of the main outcomes of risk calculations. By failing to recognize this dimension of contemporary global risks, Beck is able to gain much conceptual and political leverage out of mobilizing concepts such as fears, dangers and hazards whose meanings and constructions are always placed beyond debate.

Risk theory and the inability to provide a critique of globalized modernity

In his earlier seminal study *Risk Society*, Beck chose to refer to the passage from first modernity to second modernity as a transition from 'class societies' to 'risk societies'.[38] Whereas class-based societies were organized around the logic of production and scarcity, risk-dominated societies were characterized by the fact that all individuals, irrespective of class and/or location, were potential targets of dangers (once again, the nuclear radioactivity and industrial pollution models greatly influenced Beck's thinking). Thus, Beck suggested, risk societies were not just individualizing (as seen above); they were also democratizing, both nationally and globally, because every individual was placed on an equal footing when it came to the distribution of and relation to risks. According to this perspective, risks were equalizing and globalizing factors. As Beck put it, 'risks display an equalizing effect within their scope and among those affected by them'.[39] The same risks and, more importantly, the same attitude *vis-à-vis* risk (calculation, anticipation, individualization, possible collective mobilization) were identified universally. Put differently, risks knew no class distinction, no national identity, and no local or global division of labour.

According to Engel and Strasser, though, an analysis of class is still crucial to an understanding of contemporary risks.[40] Even when risks or reflexive modernity appear to take hold of late modern society, class cannot be taken so easily out of the picture. Thus, Engel and Strasser note, 'the risk-society hypothesis fails to recognize the possibility that people are differentially exposed to modernization risks'.[41] More importantly, the reason why individuals (despite Beck's own thesis on individualization) are differentially exposed to risks has to do with class distinctions or, to broaden Engel and Strasser's critique, the not-so-equalizing nature of risk is directly related to the unequal distribution of resources globally and the division of tasks and labour in the global economy. Although the perception of risk and, as Mary Douglas famously argued, the fear of impurity and danger may be more heightened in Western developed societies where the presentation of the notion of risk to the public is filtered through a series of discourses (media discourses among others) that help shape its 'reality' to the populations in question,[42] the physical proximity to risk and the often corollary capacity of such risks to turn into actual dangers and disasters is much higher in the non-Western world. Lack of drinkable water in sub-Saharan Africa, the likelihood of being displaced, starving, raped or murdered in the Sudan, losing one's entire family as a result of mudslides in Nicaragua, flooding in Haiti, air raids in Gaza or suicide terrorist attacks in Jerusalem are, by and large, higher, more immediate, and for many people in the world more vivid risk potentials than contracting Creutzfeld–Jakob disease, suffering from Chernobyl's nuclear fallout, or committing suicide as a result of a stock-market collapse.[43]

The point is of course not to minimize the potentially destructive aspects for some individuals of these latter, mostly Western, forms of risk; the point is rather to suggest that Beck's notion of risk and, consequently, his passage from first to second modernity may not be meaningful at all to a large majority of people throughout the world (whom he would nonetheless want to be part of his cosmopolitan democratic project). The point is also to question what sorts of risk and, by extension, what sorts of risk calculation, are at the heart of Beck's risk sociology. As Engel and Strasser indirectly suggest, would his analysis of risk be the same, would the concept of risk lend itself to an understanding and ideological reorganization of globalization, if Beck had based his analysis on such 'global risks as unemployment, poverty, organized crime, aids, and migration' as opposed to the Chernobyl effect, the 'mad cow' crisis, and the Asian markets collapse of the late 1990s?[44] Additionally, one is also left to wonder whether those 'other' global risks from the non-Western world that Beck does not seem to take into account could still make possible the revival of individual consciousness and free choice Beck is so eager to champion.

There is no doubt that Beck's analysis of the global through an understanding of so-called world risks is, to use Arjun Appadurai's turn of phrase, a peculiar 'ethnoscape' within the broader spectrum of the global cultural economy.[45] World risk society is Beck's aesthetic and anthropological 'imaginary landscape' as seen mostly from his Western European perspective.[46] While his shifting of critical attention away from control and order and on to risk is intriguing, provocative, and at times may be useful in order to help us make sense of Western societies and their view of global economic, political and symbolic relations,[47] his risk theory may not have the global appeal that it claims to be able to offer. One of the main reasons why this is the case is because Beck, perhaps by removing any notion of class-conflict out of the analysis as Engel and Strasser suggest, has managed to provide a sociology of globalization that does not and cannot account for the concept of difference. Because the very possibility of social, cultural, and of course transnational difference has been excised from his sociology of risk, questions such as who bears the risks, who profits from risks,[48] what or whose risks are more valued in the global polity, and what dominant perceptions of risks are in charge of ordering and organizing globalization processes are questions which are left unanswered and, more importantly, cannot even be asked within Beck's allegedly global critical sociology.[49]

Furthermore, by developing a socially and politically idealistic analysis of the global from the perspective of what appear to be mostly Western risks (and possibly derived from Western European late twentieth-century anxieties too[50]), Beck's appeal to a new cosmopolitan democracy to form the ideological substance of globalization is yet another attempt at exporting Western modernization beyond its spatial and temporal confines. In fact, one may suggest that Beck's risk theory applied to the global society is not so different from previous efforts in the tradition of Western political sociology of modernization at postulating the Western model of social order as the prototypical model of organization, the master-example for all non-Western societies to follow. While Beck's theory gives the impression of being able to steer clear of this current through its critique of simple modernization, it nonetheless proposes to reorganize the world, and global economic, political and social relations, through a vague cosmopolitan democratic project premised upon the belief in direct popular participation (an Enlightenment dream) and the fear of risks and uncertainties mostly prevalent among Western European populations. Thus, far from offering a critique of globalized modernity, Beck's risk theory may well be guilty of trying to further impose Western modernity on a global scale. One might be tempted to say (paraphrasing Appadurai) that Beck's world risk society is yet another 'modernity at large'.

Although I have suggested above that Beck's analysis of risk may be partially useful (since at least it helps us to understand some of the contemporary anxieties found in Western societies), I now want to argue that its ability to make sense of the reality-constructing and meaning-making power of risk in late modern social relations, even if we were to limit those to the Western world, is hampered by the fact that Beck insists on treating risk as an all-encompassing objective and structural condition of global society. My critique here benefits from Elliott's and Lash's own challenges to Beck's risk theory, but it pushes their assessments further by bringing in the issue of fear and danger which, in Beck's work, are concepts that are taken for granted, rarely explained, and yet crucial in order for Beck's interpretation of risk to appear to be both intelligible and meaningful.

Elliott's problem with Beck's notion of risk is understandable. Risks, Elliott suggests, are always taken by Beck to be objective and structural phenomena. They are material realities that go without saying and are able to give Beck's envisioned new social reflexivity its shape and form.[51] What Beck ignores, Elliott rightly contends, is a large body of anthropological and cultural analysis of risk, spearheaded by Douglas and Wildavsky among others, which argues 'that advanced industrial risks are primarily constructed through a rhetoric of purity and pollution'.[52] Lash echoes Elliott's critical sentiment by adding that Beck's risk society 'presumes a determinate, institutional, normative, rule bound and necessarily hierarchical ordering' of social life, individual expectations, and utilitarian interests when, instead, risks are a matter of non-institutional, fluid, less hierarchical, indeterminate, and often symbolic expressions of social values, choices and preferences.[53] Thus, for Lash, the analytical emphasis should be placed not on the material and structural presence of one all-encompassing *world risk society*, but instead on the idea of the existence of *multiple risk cultures*.[54]

What both Elliott and Lash indicate is Beck's unwillingness to pay attention to the way meaning is attributed to objects and events (and accidents too) by agents in certain sociocultural and discursive contexts. Put differently, the possibility that risks may be socially and generally discursively constructed is not addressed by Beck who assumes that risks and the dangers, hazards and disasters they are supposed to anticipate are structurally given end-limits of second modernity. Placed in a global system where risks condition their everyday interactions and interests, individual subjects are only given a limited range of choices by Beck, one of which is to embark upon his new cosmopolitan project. But what if risks, instead of being structurally given, are constructed (even if unintentionally) by the many agents of global society through their own daily interactions, through their attempts at dealing with a social system and its institutions, starting with the nation-state, which often no longer seem to be able to provide control, order and certainty? What if risks are, as Beck himself mentioned (but failed to explain), a matter of perceptions, a way for social agents to make sense of what appear to be uncontrollable, uncertain, unstable and indeed indeterminate events and situations that the social agents themselves, through their reliance on late modern technologies, machineries and ecologies, have helped to produce and reproduce (as Lash suggests)?

According to both Elliott and Lash, this is precisely the point where Beck's analysis of risk could have benefited from the kind of conceptual and critical approach introduced by Douglas and Wildavsky.[55] What Douglas and Wildavsky have shown is that some agents in society (and the agents that matter vary as social contexts change) have an interest and a capacity, at key junctures, to create discourses about certain dangers, potential disasters, fears and future anxieties which help to substantiate a social reality that is often apprehended by other social actors as risk. Furthermore, as constructionist social theory championed by scholars such as Giddens has taught us,[56] the fact that some agents at some point in time have a distinct interest and capacity to construct such discursive social realities does not mean that these agents (the 'risk constructors' as Lash calls them[57]) are able to retain control over their constructs. Rather, in an era when reflexivity is supposedly encouraged and unintentional consequences of actions can always produce new meaning effects, agents who may not have had control over the production of a given risk as this risk was being discursively constructed and propagated can nonetheless reclaim mastery over it and manipulate it later on, even if only temporarily, in order to produce additional meanings and possibly construct new social realities out of it. As some scholars have argued, the 'mad cow' crisis in Great Britain and France primarily may be seen as a case in point. Even though some social agents such as national and European political elites and scientific experts sought to construct the 'mad cow' risk in the mid-to-late 1990s in a specific fashion (mostly by trying to de-emphasize the link between the mad cow pathology and its human variant of Creutzfeld–Jakob disease), other agents – including the media and, later on, consumers – did not feel limited by the perception of risk that had been presented by the supposedly original 'risk constructors'. Instead, for better or worse, they chose to recapture the 'mad cow' risk. They discursively redesigned it. And they re-presented it, often in a way that, in the end, probably produced more fear and uncertainty.[58]

By ignoring or at times simply dismissing the argument about risk as a social construct,[59] Beck ends up reifying the concept of risk. Risk, for Beck, is not just a material phenomenon that structures every individual's life-choices in the global society. More importantly, it becomes an all-encompassing, all-transforming and all-constructing conceptual category that is beyond question. All sociological truths (Beck's own, anyway) are supposed to emanate from it. There is no doubt that, from many other late modern sociological perspectives, Beck's risk theory appears to be universalistic.[60] What is equally problematic is that, in the process of establishing risk as a universal sociological truth, Beck also imposes some of the most common contemporary cultural, psychological and symbolic responses to risk – fear, anxiety, belief in inevitable catastrophes, public paranoia, and so forth – as normal, expected and necessary reactions to a structural reality that is meant to be terrifying.[61] Because the reign of global fear and danger that comes with risk analysis is supposedly as objective, material and physical as risk itself, there is really no room for manoeuvre, no possibility for change, and no place for political creativity and/or playfulness with the notion of risk. Once again, the only apparently remaining alternative is for individuals to channel their own capacity of choice and responsibility into Beck's preferred collective cosmopolitan ideal. In many ways, for the contemporary and future global polity, and in total contrast to what Beck actually claims, this is the most de-politicized alternative that could ever be provided.

Instead of this de-politicized perspective on globalization, I suggest that if risk is not ignored but rather pluralized, one may be able to examine how risk is differentially mobilized in globalized modernity. One may question who or what, in different parts of the global polity and at different moments in time, is in a position to develop dominant discourses and perceptions of risk.[62] Moreover, as Elliott and Lash have started to argue, if one is allowed to see risk as a matter of social and discursive construction, one may also be afforded the possibility of re-politicizing risk because, instead of being what is placed beyond debate, risk now becomes what needs to be contested and negotiated. Contrary to what Beck might fear, this move does not reduce the relevance of risk in contemporary analyses of global society. Rather, it enriches the notion of risk by trivializing it, bringing it down from its structural heights, and placing it at the heart of popular cultural debates and representations of danger and fear. Finally, looking at risk as a social construction – always redefined, always remobilized, and always in the making – may allow social agents not just to pluralize the concept of risk, but also to question the social meaning and reality-producing effects of a whole range of global constructions of fear (from food contamination scares to cyber-crime panics, from anxieties about new animal-transmitted diseases to paranoias over sudden climatic changes) which today often appear to be valued more highly than a wide array of more mundane risks (poverty, starvation, human rights abuses, migration, sex slavery, and so on) that are part and parcel of our globalized modernity.

Notes

1 See U. Beck, *Risk Society: Towards a New Modernity* (London: Sage, 1992).

2 See, for example, A. Giddens, 'Living in a Post-Traditional Society', in U. Beck, A. Giddens and S. Lash, *Reflexive Modernization: Politics, Tradition and Aesthetics in the Modern Social Order* (Stanford, CA: Stanford University Press, 1994), pp. 56–109; S. Lash, 'Risk Culture', in B. Adam, U. Beck and J. Van Loon (eds), *The Risk Society and Beyond: Critical Issues for Social Theory* (London: Sage, 2000), pp. 47–62; and Z. Bauman, *In Search of Public Space* (Cambridge: Polity, 1999). It is worth noting, though, that scholars such as Lash and Bauman have also been critical of some of Beck's analyses.

3 See in particular Beck's argument about democracy in *Democracy without Enemies* (Cambridge: Polity, 1998).

4 U. Beck, *World Risk Society* (Cambridge: Polity, 1999), pp. 1–18.

5 For a critique of risk theory for its lack of class analysis, see U. Engel and H. Strasser, 'Global Risks and Social Inequality: Critical Remarks on the Risk-Society Hypothesis', *Canadian Journal of Sociology*, 23 (1998), 91–103.

6 See, for example, J. Baudrillard, *In the Shadow of the Silent Majorities* (New York: Semiotext(e), 1983) and J.-F. Lyotard, *The Postmodern Condition: A Report on Knowledge* (Minneapolis, MN: University of Minnesota Press, 1984).

7 Beck's *Risk Society* was first published in German in 1986, a few months after the Chernobyl accident.

8 A. Giddens, *The Consequences of Modernity* (Stanford, CA: Stanford University Press, 1990), p. 10.

9 As Fukuyama alleged in the aftermath of the Cold War: see F. Fukuyama, *The End of History and the Last Man* (New York: Perennial Press, 1993).

10 On this distinction, see A. Elliott, 'Beck's Sociology of Risk: A Critical Assessment', *Sociology*, 36 (2002), 297.

11 Beck, *World Risk Society*, p. 139.

12 Ibid., p. 135.

13 A recent case in point is the colour-coded terrorism risk scale invented by the newly created US Department of Homeland Security in the aftermath of the 9/11 attacks.

14 Ibid., p. 136.

15 Ibid., p. 2.

16 Elliott, 'Beck's Sociology of Risk', p. 296. For more on the failure of risk calculations, see D. Lupton, *Risk* (New York: Routledge, 1999), pp. 63–5.

17 For more on Beck's rejection of the postmodern argument or the perspective of scholars such as Bruno Latour or Donna Haraway, see Beck, *World Risk Society*, pp. 25–31 and 150–2.
18 See Elliott, 'Beck's Sociology of Risk', p. 298.
19 Ibid., p. 298.
20 Beck, *World Risk Society*, p. 9.
21 Ibid., p. 9.
22 See U. Beck, *What Is Globalization?* (Cambridge: Polity Press, 2000), p. 15; my emphasis.
23 Ibid., pp. 98–101.
24 Beck, *World Risk Society*, p. 142.
25 For Beck, this is exactly what happens when individuals are simply interested in protecting themselves in the short term and relinquish any action to already apathetic, indifferent and incompetent social institutions. Beck refers to this phenomenon as 'organized irresponsibility'. See Elliott, 'Beck's Sociology of Risk', p. 296.
26 Beck, *World Risk Society*, p. 9.
27 See U. Beck, 'Rooted Cosmopolitanism: Emerging from a Rivalry of Distinctions', in U. Beck, N. Sznaider and R. Winter (eds), *Global America? The Cultural Consequences of Globalization* (Liverpool: University of Liverpool Press, 2003), pp. 16–17.
28 Beck, *World Risk Society*, p. 9.
29 Ibid., p. 9.
30 See also Beck, *What Is Globalization?*, p. 99.
31 Beck, *World Risk Society*, p. 38.
32 Ibid., p. 39.
33 Ibid., p. 39.
34 Ibid., p. 40 and p. 46.
35 Ibid., p. 43.
36 Ibid., p. 14.
37 Ibid., pp. 13–14.
38 Beck, *Risk Society*, pp. 20–2.
39 Ibid., p. 36.
40 See Engel and Strasser, 'Global Risks and Social Inequality', pp. 91–103.
41 Ibid., p. 94.
42 See M. Douglas, *Purity and Danger* (New York: Routledge, 2002) and M. Douglas and A. Wildavsky, *Risk and Culture: An Essay on the Selection of Technological and Environmental Dangers* (Berkeley, CA: University of California Press, 1982).
43 Many studies, including Beck's, have argued that risk theory is particularly well suited as an explanation of late-1990s Western 'luxury and comfort' crises, such as food contamination scares, agricultural and genetically modified organism-related panics, financial turmoils, retirement systems collapses, and so forth. See R. Almas, 'Food Trust, Ethics and Safety in Risk Society', *Sociological Research Online*, 4 (1999), online at http://www.socresonline.org.uk/4/3/almas.html.
44 Engel and Strasser, 'Global Risks and Social Inequality', p. 94.
45 See A. Appadurai, *Modernity at Large: Cultural Dimensions of Globalization* (Minneapolis, MN: University of Minnesota Press, 1998).

46 The term 'imaginary landscape' is derived from Appadurai's understanding of the power of images and imagination in global cultural representations. See ibid., pp. 31–3.
47 For example, the notion of risk may help us to begin to understand the attitudes and perceptions of Western European populations *vis-à-vis* the many food scares of the 1990s.
48 These last two questions are asked directly by Engel and Strasser, 'Global Risks and Social Inequality', p. 95.
49 For a critical analysis of global economic and cultural relations that seeks to restore and maintain the concept of difference, see N. Inayatullah and D. Blaney, *International Relations and the Problem of Difference* (New York: Routledge, 2003).
50 Some have noted that it is also possible that many of the perceived risks (ecological and alimentary in particular) in Western Europe in the past decade have something to do with a general sense of uneasiness with regard to greater and faster European Union integration. See, for example, E. Dupin, 'L'Europe Roulée dans la Farine Animale', *Libération*, 29 November 2000. If this is the case, this could also indicate that Beck's risk theory is not just spatially limited (or 'ethnoscapic', to use Appadurai's language) but that it is also time-specific, that is to say, dependent upon a certain temporal context that Beck seems to be willing to extend to all of second modernity.
51 See Elliott, 'Beck's Sociology of Risk', p. 301.
52 Ibid., p. 301.
53 See Lash, 'Risk Culture', p. 47.
54 On this point, see also S. Lash, 'Reflexivity and its Doubles: Structure, Aesthetics, Community', in Beck, Giddens and Lash, *Reflexive Modernization*, pp. 110–73.
55 See again Douglas, *Purity and Danger*, and Douglas and Wildavsky, *Risk and Culture*.
56 See in particular A. Giddens, *The Constitution of Society: Outline of the Theory of Structuration* (Berkeley, CA: University of California Press, 1984).
57 Lash, 'Risk Culture', pp. 48–9.
58 On the social construction of fear and risk in the mad cow crisis, see Almas, 'Food Trust, Ethics, and Safety in Risk Society'. See also F. Debrix, 'Don't Have a Cow Man! Food Contamination, Popular Paranoia, and the Aesthetics of Madness', mimeo, paper presented at the 'Security Bytes' Colloquium, Lancaster University, Lancaster, United Kingdom, 18 July 2004.
59 In a section of his *World Risk Society*, Beck largely rejects the constructivist argument. Unfortunately, even as he does so, he does not make an effort to seriously engage Douglas and Wildavsky's perspective. See *World Risk Society*, pp. 23–6.
60 Such is the critique that Beck has often received from postmodern and poststructuralist approaches. See also Elliott, 'Beck's Sociology of Risk', p. 310.
61 As Lupton notes (*Risk*, p. 60), Beck 'demonstrates anger at the ever-hazardous nature of life in late modernity, presenting an apocalyptic vision of how hazards and dangers may destroy humankind and other living creatures'.

62 I would like to suggest that a Foucauldian archeology of risk in specific social contexts, by paying close attention to how a certain idea or form of risk develops, is distributed by certain agents and institutions, may be recuperated by other social actors, and may come to form new institutional and discursive positivities of action, expectation and interpretation, might be a more satisfactory and probably much less universalistic epistemological approach to the phenomenon of risk. On some epistemological directions for this kind of approach, see M. Foucault, *The Archeology of Knowledge* (New York: Pantheon, 1972).

Part II

Reconceptualizing Citizenship, Democracy and Human Rights under Globalization

7

Between Empires: Rethinking Identity and Citizenship in the Context of Globalization

Michael A. Peters

Introduction

This chapter addresses the question of rethinking citizenship within the context of globalization. It accepts the proposition that we are between two different historical periods characterized by forms of empire: essentially the nineteenth-century imperialism of the European powers and the American decentred system of global rule of the twenty-first century. This chapter focuses on the latter by contrasting two competing and influential conceptions of the 'new imperialism' that have emerged recently to focus on questions of international security, world order and the evolving system of states. Questions of globalization, national identity and citizenship are transformed when raised in this new geopolitical context.

Robert Cooper, Deputy Secretary of the Defence and Overseas Secretariat in the British Cabinet Office, posits the development of a postmodern European state system based on transparency, interdependence and mutual surveillance. He calls for a 'new imperialism' – one compatible with human rights and cosmopolitan values – in order to sort out the problems of rogue states and the chaos of premodern states. By contrast, Hardt and Negri use the combined resources of Marx and Deleuze to chart the emergence of a new form of sovereignty they call *Empire*. They narrate a history of the passage from imperialism to Empire: that is, from a modernity dominated by the sovereignty of nation-states and the imperialisms of European powers, to a postmodernity characterized by a single though new decentred logic of global rule.

In a strong sense Hardt and Negri's *Empire* and Cooper's 'new imperialism' are both geopolitical and juridical forms of globalization that are dependent on emergent forms of global sovereignty. The difference between the two views is that, whereas the former focuses on American Empire as the dominant form, the latter concentrates on an emergent European postmodern state system. They both entertain extranational forms of citizenship based on these supranational systems and problematize the concept of citizenship based on the bounded system of the sovereign state.

Perhaps, more than ever before, the question of globalization and citizenship revolves around the free movement of peoples. By this I mean not only the modern diaspora, or the planned colonial migrations or the more recent global mobility of highly skilled labour that is rewarded by citizenship; but more importantly, I mean refugees of all kinds and asylum-seekers and all that that entails – enforced border crossings, ethnic cleansing policies, the huge illegal movement of so-called 'aliens', detention camps such as Woomera and even Guantanamo Bay, where the concept of rights is fragile or has entirely disappeared.[1]

Globalization and citizenship

At the beginning of the twenty-first century the world is experiencing processes of both integration and disintegration. The expansion of world markets, as a form of economic globalization, can be understood as a process of integration composed of international flows of capital, goods, information and people. The same process is both a form of economic integration and a polarization of wealth that exacerbates existing tendencies towards greater global inequalities between rich and poor countries and regions. It also accentuates the need for reviewing the templates of the global system of governance that emerged from the Bretton Woods agreement, founding many of the institutions that now comprise the architecture of the world system. Now, more than at any time in the past, with the end of the Cold War, the collapse of the Soviet system, the consolidation of the EU and the entry of China into the WTO, we are witnessing an accelerated set of changes – economic, cultural, technological and political – that impinge on one another in novel ways and create new possibilities and dangers, both for the democratic state and the notions of citizenship and national identity that underpin it.

The modern concept of citizenship implies the existence of a civil or political community, a set of rights and obligations ascribed to citizens by virtue of their membership in that community, and an ethic of participation and solidarity needed to sustain it. Most traditional accounts of citizenship begin with the assertion of basic civil, political and social rights of individuals and note the way in which the modern concept, as inherently egalitarian, took on a universal appeal with the development of the liberal tradition, which is often understood as synonymous with modernity. Yet the concept has appealed to both conservatives and radical democrats: the former emphasize individual freedom at the expense of equality and see state intervention as an intolerable and unwarranted violation of the freedom of the individual, while the latter stress the democratic potential of citizenship. Increasingly, on the Left the concept has been seen as a means to control the injustices of capitalism. For the Left, the most pressing question has been the status of citizenship in the modern state and what kind of political community best promotes it.

The classic theorization of democratic citizenship is to be found in Marshall's famous modelling of three forms of citizenship: civil, political and social. In this conception, civil citizenship referred to personal liberty and a regime of individual rights; political citizenship referred to both political participation and democratic representation; and social citizenship referred to intervention by the state to reduce economic inequalities and promote social justice. It is now possible to chart the significant shifts in the definitions of citizenship that have accompanied globalization, including the breakdown of the historic compromise between capitalism, democracy and the welfare state, and the rise of neoliberalism (and, with it, the expansion of world markets). In the United Kingdom under Third Way politics there has been a shift from the concept of *rights* to *responsibilities*, a move away from state intervention towards community involvement in civic networks with a corresponding emphasis on promoting forms of social capital, and a shift from active political citizenship to passive political literacy.[2]

These shifts are emblematic of what Faulks[3] calls the 'ten dualisms of liberal citizenship'. The abstract individualism of the liberal tradition, dating back to Locke, tends to view 'the individual and community as being in opposition and... in part this explains their ambivalence towards responsibilities, democracy and social rights'.[4] In particular, the emphasis placed on individual autonomy makes liberals suspicious of notions of community and tends to result in what Faulks describes as 'thin' and 'thick' citizenship.[5] Neoliberalism – and, some would argue also, Third Way politics – tends to entertain versions of 'thin' citizenship, which are largely compatible with the diminished role of the state following the rise of globalization and multinational capitalism.

The two terms 'globalization' and 'citizenship' are not normally juxtaposed in social and political analysis. They appear as contradictory or, at least, conflicting: the former points to an economic and cultural process of world integration, based on the unregulated flows of capital and underwritten by developments in new information and communications technologies, while the latter serves as a metaphor for political community. Globalization seems to threaten the sovereignty of the nation-state and with it the notion of citizenship that developed during the modern era. Within the context of globalization, the pressing political question is how people can create and protect a sense of community and local identity in order to protect and bolster the institutions that provide them with social protection.

On one influential interpretation, globalization represents the historical culmination of a set of world processes that began much earlier in the age of colonization leading to the now dominant system of late world capitalism, based on the form of the multinational corporation. It is this multinational form of the corporation which many theorists see as threatening the sovereignty of the nation-state and also diminishing the prospect for community, civil society and citizenship. On this view, economic liberalization and restructuring have eroded the economic and social rights of people in many countries, while at the same time developments in international communications have expanded the international awareness of rights and created conditions for the emergence of international networks that may come to comprise civil society on a global scale. The processes of globalization, on this view, undermine both the modern notion of citizenship and the sovereignty of the nation-state on which it depends. More importantly, some theorists argue that the logic of globalization increases inequalities and weakens the basis and ideological underpinnings of social protection and partnership.[6]

Yet so far most of the debate on citizenship has occurred within national boundaries without much regard for the impact of globalization. As the United Nations Research Institute for Social Development (UNRISD) indicated at its international conference on the theme of globalization and citizenship held in 1996, 'globalization' serves as a synonym for contemporary forms of rapid structural change, and 'citizenship' serves as a metaphor for social protection and the reconstruction of solidarity:

> Until recently, they were not systematically juxtaposed in social analysis. 'Citizenship studies' have traditionally been more likely to focus on debates over civil and political rights, immigration law or

> forms of political participation in particular countries than on global economic and social trends. And analysis of 'globalization' has been the terrain of macro-economists and sociologists not usually well trained in the intricacies of individual rights. But as the pace of change quickens, the relevance of the two concepts for each other becomes clearer... In consequence, it becomes increasingly important for national citizenship debates to incorporate international elements, and for students of globalization to understand the changing parameters of citizenship.[7]

Not only is it important for national citizenship debates to incorporate international elements, but it is also important to rethink questions of citizenship and national identity within the context of globalization. In what follows I offer a synopsis and analysis of two competing versions of the 'new imperialism', both of which question forms of citizenship tied to the nation-state and to national sovereignty.

Two versions of empire: Cooper's 'new imperialism'

In two influential publications – *The Postmodern State and the World Order*,[8] and 'The Postmodern State'[9] – Robert Cooper has helped to shape Tony Blair's foreign policy outlook. The *New Republic* describes Cooper as the foremost commentator on strategic issues of our age, and Cooper's diagnosis of the era we live in has taken on the power of prophecy after the events of 9/11. His analysis is terrifyingly simple and, I would argue, also alarmingly Eurocentric. Cooper argues that the year 1989 marked a turning point in European history, not only being the end of the Cold War but, perhaps, more fundamentally a change in the European state system: it marked the end of the balance-of-power system in Europe. What emerged after 1989 was not a rearrangement of the old system but an entirely new system based on a new form of statehood, which Cooper calls the postmodern state.

With the emergence of the postmodern state, we now live in an international system made up of three parts: the premodern world (of, for example, Somalia, Afghanistan or Liberia) where the state has lost its legitimate monopoly on the use of force and chaos reigns; the modern world where the classical state system remains intact; and the postmodern world where the state system is collapsing and a new system is being born. The new postmodern system of states is best characterized by the EU. It exhibits the following characteristics.

1 The breakdown of the distinction between domestic and foreign affairs.
2 Mutual interference in (traditional) domestic affairs and mutual surveillance.
3 The rejection of force for resolving disputes and the consequent codification of rules of behaviour, rules that are self-enforced because all EC states have an interest in maintaining the rule of law.
4 The growing irrelevance of borders.
5 Security is based on transparency, mutual openness, interdependence and mutual vulnerability.[10]

The postmodern system of states – the so-called decentred state – originates in the postmodern world. The old imperialism is dead, at least among Western states. Member states no longer want to go to war against each other to acquire territory or subject populations. The postmodern state is 'more pluralist, more complex, less centralised than the bureaucratic modern state'. In this postmodern system that state becomes less dominating and state interest becomes less determining in foreign policy. With the deconstruction of the state, the media, popular sentiment, public opinion and the interests of particular groups and regions come into play. As the deconstruction of the state proceeds – a process not yet complete – so the processes of individualization, regionalization and privatization become more important.

On Cooper's analysis Europe is postmodern, and so are, possibly, Japan and Canada, but what of the USA? He writes:

> The USA is the more doubtful case since it is not clear that the US government or Congress accepts either the necessity and desirability of interdependence, or its corollaries of openness, mutual surveillance to the same extent as most European governments now do. The United States' unwillingness to accept the jurisdiction of the International Criminal Court and its relative reluctance about challenge inspections in the CWC [Chemical Weapons Convention] are examples of US caution about postmodern concepts.[11]

He characterizes the USA in terms of a 'defensive modernism'. There is a certain force to his analysis on this point. After 9/11, the US created the Department of Homeland Security, perhaps the biggest change in government departments in the USA since the Second World War. It is a superdepartment combining departments of immigration, customs and domestic security, with an $80 billion budget and some 175,000 employees. With this new office and the prevailing ethos, the USA has turned in upon itself, policing its borders and monitoring the flows of people, information, and goods in and out of its territory. As well as greater internal surveillance, the USA has shifted its historic policy of containment to one of 'pre-emptive first strike' and 'regime change' in the name of national security.

What are the implications for security? In the postmodern zone there is a new transparent and interdependent security order. 'Our task', Cooper says, 'must be to preserve and extend it'.[12] Yet dealing with the modern world requires a different approach, as evidenced by the Gulf War and wars in the former Yugoslavia. In the first case, he suggests the Western response to Saddam Hussein's attack on Kuwait was exactly what it should have been: 'Build the most powerful coalition possible, reverse the aggression, punish the aggressor, deal with the weapons programme.'[13]

The initial support for the notion of a New World Order following the Gulf War was based on the hope that the UN was going to function as a world authority policing international law – that is, as an organization of collective security – but 'the Gulf War was fought to protect an old order, not to create a new one'.[14] Thus, for the postmodern system or state, there is a difficulty in dealing with militant, rogue modernist states, as Cooper writes:

> We need to get used to the idea of double standards. Among ourselves, we operate on the basis of laws and open cooperative security. But when dealing with more old-fashioned kinds of state outside the postmodern continent of Europe, we need to revert to the rougher methods of an earlier era – force.[15]

In his second essay,[16] Cooper openly advocates a new kind of imperialism: 'What is needed is a new kind of imperialism, one compatible with human rights and cosmopolitan values: an imperialism which aims to bring order and organisation.' He distinguishes between two kinds of 'new colonialism' that can 'save the world': 'voluntary' imperialism, such as the IMF and the World Bank, which 'provide help for states wishing to find their way back on to the global economy', and the 'imperialism of neighbours', when states intervene to sort out 'instability in their neighbourhood'.

While Cooper has nothing directly to say about citizenship or rethinking this concept within the context of globalization his analysis provides at least a three-pronged approach: premodern, modern and postmodern. In premodern states, the concept of citizenship is hazy, fragile and volatile. The notion of rights in premodern states often is not recognized at all, and, if it is, the weak state is often unable to enforce or uphold those rights. The notion of citizenship in modern states is straightforward and conforms to the pattern of rights and responsibilities previously discussed. The important addition from Cooper might be the notion of citizenship in the postmodern state, and while he does not discuss this we can draw some inferences from his analysis. The notion of citizenship is still modern in that rights are ascribed first on the basis of national sovereignty and only second in terms of the greater EU. So we have a kind of two-tiered or layered structure that has both a national and an international community component, where the latter covers the right to work, to move freely, and to make use of the developing judicial and legal infrastructure such as the European Court. While Cooper's analysis might have something to say about citizenship in the postmodern state, he has nothing to say about stateless peoples or the vexed question concerning the rights of stateless peoples.

Two versions of empire: Hardt and Negri's *Empire*

Nothing could be further from Cooper's conception than the picture Hardt and Negri present in their path-breaking *Empire*.[17] This book has been variously hailed as 'the first great new theoretical synthesis of the new millennium' by Fredric Jameson, and 'nothing less than a rewriting of *The Communist Manifesto* for our time' by Slavoj Žižek.[18] At the same time it has been vilified as 'the profoundly silly book that has set the academic left aflutter',[19] and a 'new anti-Americanism' by the likes of Kimball.[20]

Writing in the spirit of Marx and in combination with Deleuze and Guattari, Hardt and Negri provide the poststructuralist basis for a renewal of materialist thought, charting the emergence of a new form of sovereignty they call *Empire*. As they indicate in a footnote, 'Two interdisciplinary texts serve as models for us throughout the writing of this book: Marx's *Capital* and Deleuze and Guattari's *A Thousand Plateaus*.'[21] Hardt and Negri narrate a history of the passage from imperialism to Empire: that is, from a modernity dominated by the sovereignty of nation-states and the imperialisms of European powers, to a postmodernity characterized by a single (though decentred) new logic of global rule. They write: 'Our basic hypothesis is that sovereignty has taken a new form, composed of a series of national and supranational organisms united under a single logic of rule. This new global form of sovereignty is what we call Empire.'[22] They use *Empire* not as a metaphor but as a concept that calls for a theoretical approach:

> The concept of Empire is characterized fundamentally by a lack of boundaries: Empire's rule has no limits. First and foremost, then, the concept of Empire posits a regime that effectively compasses the spatial totality . . . that rules over the entire 'civilized' world. No territorial boundaries limit its reign. Second, the concept of Empire presents itself not as a historical regime originating in conquest, but rather as an order that effectively suspends history and thereby fixes the existing state of affairs for eternity . . . Third, the rule of empire operates on all registers of the social order extending down to the depths of the social world. Empire not only manages a territory and a population but also creates the very world it inhabits. It not only regulates human interactions but also seeks directly to rule over human nature. The object of its rule is social life in its entirety, and thus Empire presents the paradigmatic form of biopower. Finally, although the practice of Empire is continually bathed in blood, the concept of Empire is always dedicated to peace – a perpetual and universal peace outside history.[23]

They go on to suggest that the passage to Empire, with its processes of globalization, will 'offer new possibilities to the forces of liberation', arguing that our political future will be determined by our capacity 'not simply to resist these processes but to reorganize them and redirect them toward new ends'.[24]

Imperialism, in its heyday, was simply the extension of the sovereignty of European nation-states beyond their own boundaries.[25] Imperialism or colonialism in this sense, they seem to agree with Cooper, is now dead. But so are all forms of imperialism in so far as they represent restraints on the homogenizing force of the world market. Empire is, thus, both 'postcolonial and postimperialist'. Drawing on the Deleuzo-Guattarian concepts of (de/re)territorialization,[26] they argue:

> Imperialism is a machine of global striation, channelling, coding, and territorializing the flows of capital, blocking certain flows and facilitating others. The world market, in contrast, requires a smooth space of uncoded and deterritorialized flows . . . imperialism would have been the death of capital had it not been overcome. The full realization of the world market is necessarily the end of imperialism.[27]

Writing before the impending Iraq invasion, Hardt and Negri argue that the US 'does not, indeed no nation-state can today, form the centre of an imperialist project. Imperialism is over. No nation will be world leader in the way modern European nations were.'[28] In retrospect, it is interesting to focus on their assessment of the USA. The Vietnam War, Hardt and Negri suggest, 'might be seen as the final moment of the imperialist tendency and thus a point of passage to a new regime of the Constitution'.[29] This passage to a new global constitutional regime is shown by the Gulf War, during which the USA emerged:

> as the only power able to manage international justice, not as a function of its own national motives but in the name of global right... The U.S. world police acts not in imperialist interest but in imperial interest. In this sense the Gulf War did indeed, as George Bush claimed, announce the birth of a New World order.[30]

As Forster proposes, reading Hardt and Negri, 'the struggle now is simply over the form that globalization will take'.[31] As Bruce Lindsay makes clear, the new axiom of geopolitical power implies a spatial totality that differs:

> from the system of nation-states, linked contractually (i.e., by treaty), centered on a form of 'the people' (whatever the specific form of regime) and containing a particular ordering of space (the internal and the foreign, or 'outside'). Empire tends to supersede this basis of sovereignty, posing imperial authority as an overarching framework without a centre, embodied in networks of institutions, states, military forces and corporate powers.[32]

Without necessarily endorsing Hardt and Negri's view, it is easy to see the connections to the pressing themes of globalization, identity and citizenship, and particularly to a form of global rule based on the globalization of communications. There is a form of global government rationality that we might refer to as *communicative governmentality*. It is a concept-marriage that recognizes the need for new terms to critically discuss forms of global rule that depend upon spaces of subjectivity more than ever linked to media and other forms of communication. The mouthful *communicative governmentality* also refers to the relations between modernist nation-state conceptions of 'the people' as a basis for democracy and postmodern forms of subjectivity that may form the basis for alternative conceptions of globalization: a sort of antagonistic or anti-globalization and anti-Empire.[33]

Anti-globalization, anti-empire

Hardt and Negri have coined the term 'multitude' to refer to the new spaces for subjectivity within globalization and its democratic impulses. In the nation-state the multitude was reduced to 'the people'. The first element of a political programme for the global multitude is global citizenship: a political demand 'that the juridical status of the population be reformed in step with the real economic transformations of recent years'.[34] Hardt and Negri proceed to argue:

> This demand can also be configured in a more general and more radical way with respect to the postmodern conditions of Empire. If in the first movement the multitude demands that each state recognize juridically the migrations that are necessary to capital, in the second movement it must demand control over the movements themselves. The multitude must be able to decide if, when, and where it moves. It must have the right also to stay still and enjoy one place rather than being forced constantly to be on the move. The general right to control its own movement is the multitude's ultimate demand for global citizenship... Global citizenship is the multitude's power to reappropriate control over space and thus to design the new cartography.[35]

Hardt and Negri have applied their analysis to recent events surrounding the so-called anti-globalization protests. Writing in *The New York Times*, they recognize that the rainbow protests at the Genoa G-8 'world' summit are united in the belief 'that a fundamentally new global system is being formed' and that '[t]he world can no longer be understood in terms of British, French, Russian or even American imperialism'.[36] They maintain that no longer can national power control or order the present global system and that, while the protests often appear anti-American, they are really directed at the larger power structures.

The protestors must win the same kind of battle for democracy at the global level that ordinary people – citizens – won at the level of the nation-state over three hundred years ago. And since those first democratic revolutions, movements of various kinds – civil rights, anti-racism, anti-war, women's rights, children's rights, animal rights, environmental protests – have progressively enfranchised ever larger groups of the world's populations, although not inevitably or without struggle or reversals.[37] Hardt and Negri point out the salient fact that 'this new order has no democratic institutional mechanisms for representation, as nation-states do: no elections, no public forum for debate'.[38] And they go on to describe the anti-globalization protestors as a coalition united against the present form of capitalist globalization, but not against the forces or currents of globalization per se. Neither are these protestors isolationalists, separatists or nationalists. Rather, as Hardt and Negri claim, the protestors want to *democratize globalization*: to eliminate the growing inequalities between nations and to expand the possibilities for self-determination. Thus 'anti-globalization' is a false description of this movement.[39]

Against all odds, against the power of supranational forces, people on the streets in Genoa – and earlier in a series of locations at Gothenburg, Quebec, Prague, and Seattle – still believe in a form of resistance in the name of a better future. They believe, against all propagandizing and media control, in the story of democracy and in the seeds that were sown for emancipation and self-determination over three centuries ago. Hardt and Negri believe that a new species of political activism has been born, reminiscent of the 'paradoxical idealism of the 1960s'. Such protest movements are part of democratic society even though they are unlikely to provide the practical blueprint for the future. Yet they create political desires for a better future and, remarkably, unify disparate interests and groups – unionists, ecologists, priests and Communists – in openness towards defining the future anew in democratic terms.[40]

Hardt and Negri are not the only ones to have asserted a connection between the so-called anti-globalization protestors and those who demonstrated during the 1960s. Todd Gitlin also clearly considers the present-day movement evident at Genoa as a successor movement to the student movements of the 1960s and 1970s – one that he claims has already engaged more activists over a longer period of time and one he predicts will be longer-lived.[41] Gitlin, similarly, pictures the protestors as 'creating a way of life', although he profiles the protestors as engaging in the debate about the meaning of Europe, seemingly truncating its obviously more global aspects outside Europe. He also questions the anti-globalization label, drawing attention to anti-capitalist revolutionaries, reformists who demand to 'Drop the Debt', and anarchists bent upon violence. The new face of protests is a *composite* of different types: anarchists and Marxists, 'kinder, gentler globalists', health-issue advocates, environmentalists, consumer advocates. The protest groups have been named from violent to non-violent in the following order: Black Blocs (anarchist and Marxists who wear black masks); those who claim to be non-violent but often provoke retaliation such as Globalize

Resistance, Reclaim the Streets, Tute Bianche (Luca Casarini), and *Ya Basta!*; decidedly non-violent groups ranging from celebrities to religious leaders, including AIDS activists, ATTAC (Bernard Cassen and Susan George), CAFOD, Christian Aid, Cobas, Confédération Paysanne (José Bové), various consumer groups, Drop the Debt (Bono), Greenpeace, La Via Campesina, Oxfam, Rainforest Action Network, Roman Catholic Church, War on Want and the World Wildlife Fund.[42]

The multitude against Empire is best represented in spatial movements which cannot be subjugated to the laws of capitalist accumulation. These movements reappropriate space to reconstitute themselves as active subjects. The political action of the multitude is expressed in its ultimate demand for global citizenship and in the constitutional principle that links right and labour.[43] Further, in their discussion of 'postmodernization' or what they also call 'the informatization of production',[44] Hardt and Negri provide an analysis of what I have called 'knowledge capitalism'.[45] They argue, for instance:

> The first aspect of the *telos* of the multitude has to do with the senses of language and communication. If communication has increasingly become the fabric of production, and if linguistic cooperation has increasingly become the structure of productive corporeality, then the control over linguistic sense and meaning and the networks of communication becomes a more central issue for political struggle.[46]

Later they ask:

> How can sense and meaning be oriented differently or organized in alternative, coherent communicative apparatuses? How can we discover and direct the performative lines of linguistic sets and communicative networks that create the fabric of life and production? Knowledge has to become linguistic action and philosophy has to become real *reappropriation of knowledge*.[47]

Reappropriation, in this context, 'means having free access to and control over knowledge, information, communication, and affects – because these are some of the primary means of biopolitical production'.[48] For Hardt and Negri, it is the figure of the militant which best expresses the life of the multitude, as they say *'the agent of biopolitical production and resistance against Empire'*, yet a militancy that is constitutive not representative and based upon a form of resistance that is at once positive, constructive and innovative.

Conclusion and postscript[49]

Both Hardt and Negri and Cooper entertain extranational forms of citizenship based on supranational systems that to some degree problematize the concept of citizenship based on the bounded system of the sovereign state. Yet in the form of empire identified by Hardt and Negri and in the form of the postmodern state system identified by Cooper, it is clear both that the traditional concept of citizenship based on the state remains, and that the traditional Left concern for nation-building and developing a sense of community and local identity necessary to sustain and defend social rights must also remain as part of the political agenda against the undermining effects of globalization on social and welfare policy. Yet we might argue that questions of identity and citizenship, at least in the EU, have a layered complexity that arises from the effort to build extranational, indeed universal, 'Kantian' judicial structures and systems (such as the International Criminal Court) which are seen by Europeans as prototype world institutions. Indeed, the EU is behind the promulgation of a Kantian philosophy of universalization of world institutions that attempt to determine rights per se, springing from earlier attempts going back to the Nuremberg Trials and the human rights and genocide conventions developed and adopted in 1948 by the United Nations, and to the constitutions of the League of Nations and United Nations (with its impetus to carry forward the project of human rights).

In this process of Europeanization with ten new members joining the EU in 2004, local identity – especially that based on ethnicity and language – is still significant for recognizing social and linguistic rights and may well become even more important, for example, in the realm of education. States still ascribe rights, yet EU membership enhances and legitimates those rights in some respects, especially in relation to the free movement of people. I remarked at the beginning of this chapter that more than ever before the question of globalization and citizenship revolves around the free movement of peoples, and its opposite: the curtailment of cross-national and cross-regional mobility, especially for Third World peoples and refugees of all kinds. Yet members of the EU both nationally and internationally have not tackled the question of illegal immigration and refugees with any distinctiveness that distinguishes the UN ethos on human rights.

What Hardt and Negri on the one hand, and Cooper on the other hand, demonstrate is that citizenship now has other dimensions. Cooper's analysis of the imperatives of the new imperialism has directly contributed to a policy outlook in Britain that identified Blair's Labour government – against his own backbenchers, affiliated trade unions, and people in the party machinery – with a conservative, Republican, US oil-President. Cooper's foreign policy stance, which deliberately embraces 'double standards', may well have provided the analysis and 'moral vision' that Blair acted on, but it has embarrassed the EU, splitting 'old' Europe (France, Germany and Belgium) from 'new' Europe (basically the former Soviet satellites, including Poland, the Czech Republic and Hungary), as well as risking a longer term stand-off or uneasiness between the EU and American foreign policy. One of the consequences of the protection of the special Anglo–American relationship and the split with so-called 'old' Europe is a historic distancing between the USA and EU with potentially enormous political fallout not only for NATO but also for US ratification of treaties and conventions struck by the EU and UN.[50]

Hardt and Negri anticipate a form of extranational and extraparliamentary protest – 'anti-globalization' – that, in part, is also aimed at a form of global citizenship or, at least, world democracy. This is the counternarrative and countermovement to the US hegemon and export of American juridical forms as the value basis and ethos for world governmental organizations.

The recent Iraq War – an illegal war if we are to judge by the Nuremberg principles adopted by the International Law Commission of the UN – is clearly an extension of the neoliberal/neoconservative project of globalization. The postwar reconstruction is driven by the same principles that underwrote the 'Washington consensus' and, in particular, the privatization of public services, which is entirely unsuitable for a country that has such a poorly developed public sector. Moreover, Halliburton, one of the world's largest oil and gas companies, of which Cheney was Chief Executive Officer from 1995 to 2000, has been granted contracts to resurrect Iraqi oilfields, along with other US companies (including Bechtel, the Fluor Corporation, and the Louis Berger Group, which also have strong links to the present US administration).

It is also clear that the export and transplant of American democracy is a project likely to fail in the sense that, it could be argued, democracy is not something that can be imposed or easily transplanted at will but requires generations of development as well as a commitment to the public sphere and public institutions to sustain it – to a local sense of identity. There is no way that the present US administration will allow an Iran-style religious government even if it is freely elected by the people. The question of citizenship and democracy cannot ignore local history and local identity. For Iraq, as for other states where democracy has been imposed, the issue of culture and of local identity is paramount. A pressing question for the coming years is whether Iraq (and other Islamic states) can embrace modernity and democracy in a way that reflects its own values, culture and sense of identity. This would be to begin the process of rethinking citizenship and identity within the context of globalization.

Notes

1 See J. Derrida, *On Cosmopolitanism and Forgiveness* (London: Routledge, 2001); and M. Dummett, *On Immigration and Refugees* (New York: Routledge, 2001). Derrida argues for a form of cosmopolitanism that entails the right to asylum, while Dummett discusses refugee and immigration policy in Great Britain.
2 See E. Gamarnikow and A. Green, 'Social Capital and the Educated Citizen', *The School Field*, 10 (1999), 103–26.
3 K. Faulks, *Citizenship* (London: Routledge, 2000).
4 Ibid., p. 57.
5 Ibid., p.11.
6 For example, R. Mishra, *Globalisation and the Welfare State* (Cheltenham: Edward Elgar, 1999).
7 The United Nations Research Institute for Social Development, *Globalization and Citizenship*, Geneva, 9–11 December 1996, online at http://www.unrisd.org, pp. 5–6.
8 R. Cooper, *The Postmodern State and the World Order* (London: The Foreign Policy Centre, 2000).
9 Published in M. Leonard, *Re-ordering the World: The Long-term Implications of September 11* (London: The Foreign Policy Centre, 2002), pp. 11–20.
10 Cooper, *The Postmodern State and the World Order*, pp. 19–20.
11 Ibid., p. 27.
12 Ibid., p. 34.
13 Ibid., p. 36.
14 Ibid., p. 37.
15 Ibid., p. 39.
16 R. Cooper, 'Why We Still Need Empires', *The Observer*, 7 April 2002.
17 M. Hardt and A. Negri, *Empire* (Cambridge, MA: Harvard University Press, 2000).
18 Cited in R. Kimball, 'The New Anti-Americanism', *New Criterion*, 20 (2001), pp. 17–25.
19 T. Peyser, 'Empire Burlesque: The Profoundly Silly Book that has Set the Academic Left Aflutter', *Reason*, 33 (2002), 51–7.
20 Kimball, 'The New Anti-Americanism'.
21 Hardt and Negri, *Empire*, p. 415. See also M. A. Peters, *Poststructuralism, Marxism and Neoliberalism: Between Politics and Theory* (Lanham, MD, and Oxford: Rowman & Littlefield, 2001), ch. 5.
22 Hardt and Negri, *Empire*, p. xii.
23 Ibid., pp. xiv–xv.
24 Ibid., p. xv.
25 Ibid., p. xii.

26 For a discussion of these concepts see M. A. Peters, 'Geophilosophy, Education and the Pedagogy of the Concept', Paper presented at the Deleuze and Education Conference, University of Dundee, 27 November 2002.
27 Hardt and Negri, *Empire*, p. 333.
28 Ibid., pp. xiii–xiv.
29 Ibid., pp. 178–9.
30 Ibid., p. 180.
31 J. B. Forster, 'Imperialism and "Empire"', *Monthly Review*, 53 (2001), 1–9. Forster champions the 'decidedly unfashionable' view of Istvan Meszaros' book, *Socialism or Barbarism* (New York: Monthly Review Press, 2002).
32 B. Lindsay, 'Toni Negri's Empire', *Arena Magazine*, December 2000. Hardt and Negri refer to Samir Amin's *Empire of Chaos* (New York: Monthly Review Press, 1992) as the leading *centre/periphery* alternative view to their own.
33 In this regard, see M. A. Peters, 'Anti-globalization and Guattari's *The Three Ecologies*', *Globalization* (2002), online at http://www.icaap.org/iuicode?193.2.1.2.
34 Hardt and Negri, *Empire*, p. 400.
35 Ibid., p. 400.
36 M. Hardt and A. Negri, 'The New Faces in Genoa Want a Different Future', *The New York Times*, 25 July 2001, p. 6.
37 In *The Age of Rights* (Cambridge: Polity, 1994), Norberto Bobbio provides a useful description of these generational rights, although his Hegelian philosophy of history appears to me wrong-headed, especially in light of the reversal of so-called social rights that occurred in the 1980s under the combined forces of the neoconservative Thatcher–Reagan administrations. There are no real signs that Third Way governments in the West have attempted to restore these social rights. If the second-term Blair government is anything to go by, the privatization of public services and, thereby, the continued erosion of citizen rights is pursued with a renewed vigour.
38 Hardt and Negri, 'The New Faces in Genoa Want a Different Future'.
39 Klaus Schwab, founder and chairman of the World Economic Forum, also points to the 'systemic failure' of the present institutions that provide a measure of world governance (UN, IMF, World Bank, WTO) and embraces the need for global institutions that more effectively and democratically deal with the problems we face. He suggests that the G-8 be replaced with the broader Group of 20. The Foreign Office minister in the Blair Government, Peter Hain, like a number of other commentators, criticized the 'ruling elite' in Europe talking to itself and becoming remote from ordinary people. K. Schwab, 'The World's New Actors Need a Bigger Stage', *Newsweek*, 30 July 2001, p. 18.
40 Susan George, by contrast, provides a graphic account of the anti-democratic strategies and tactics adopted by the opponents of the protestors at Genoa, detailing the use of force and manipulation and reporting on the ideological backlash. George suggests that there is evidence of complicity between authorities and gangs of the Black Bloc *agents provocateurs*. See her web page at http://www.tni.org/george/index.htm.
41 T. Gitlin, 'Having a Riot', *Newsweek*, 23 July 2001, pp. 48–9.
42 M. Brant and B. Nadeau, 'First Blood', *Newsweek*, 30 July 2001, pp. 14–18.

43 Basically, Hardt and Negri call for *a social and a guaranteed income for all* (a citizenship income) and *the right to reappropriate the means of production* (i.e., the right to self-control and autonomous self-production). On the knowledge economy, see M. A. Peters, 'Poststructuralism and Marxism: Education as Knowledge Capitalism', *Journal of Education Policy*, 18 (2003), 115–29; and Peters, *Poststructuralism, Marxism and Neoliberalism.*

44 See Negri and Hardt, *Empire*, pp. 280ff.

45 Peters, *Poststructuralism, Marxism and Neoliberalism*; Peters, 'Poststructuralism and Marxism'.

46 Hardt and Negri, *Empire*, p. 404.

47 Ibid.

48 Ibid., p. 407.

49 This chapter was written before the Iraq war; hence this postscript.

50 On this very matter, see the recent book *Of Paradise and Power* (New York: Knopf, 2003) by Robert Kagan who now speaks of the US hegemon and Americanization of world institutions – a kind of Right-wing interpretation of Empire based upon the export of American democracy and juridical forms. This split, Kagan claims, now problematizes the concept of 'the West' and recognizes a divergence based upon the level of investment in military technology during the 1990s which has given the USA unrivalled power.

8

Human Rights, Moral Articulacy and Democratic Dynamism: In Defence of Normative Philosophy

Mark Evans

Introduction

Today, the idea of human rights dominates the discourse on the morality of globalization. As boundaries erode and connexions multiply, it no longer seems naïvely utopian to hope that humanity may at last be embarked on the road to an international order in which basic human rights could in practice matter more than the cynicism of state-centric *realpolitik* and the avarice of multinationalized capitalism. If we still have a long way to go in this regard, the supreme relevance to us all of the human rights agenda nowadays seems starkly evident in the fact that those whose suffer violence, repression, degradation and destitution, no matter where they are, give voice to their plight in the common language of human rights which thereby resonates around the world.

It is thus disturbing to encounter theoretical arguments which seem sympathetic to the aspirations of the human rights concept but yet which contend that it is irredeemably flawed, such that we may do better without it. Given the concept's power, perhaps it would be understandable if some chose to treat such arguments with dismissive contempt. Certainly, I would find it hard to condemn anyone who simply ignored them in advancing the human rights agenda, but some of these arguments provocatively contend that the extreme difficulties faced by this agenda do not all arise in spite of the concept. Some of them emerge, they claim, precisely *because* of the concept's unfortunate properties, and that is a possibility that should not be so insouciantly dismissed.

To be sure, no great philosophical exertion is required to deal with some of the more commonly heard complaints about human-rights talk. For example, it is sometimes said that, far from being genuinely 'human', human rights are in fact only codifications of 'Western' values which are too frequently prejudicial against non-Western interests and prone to hypocritically selective deployment by Western powers. But it is difficult to think that these claims constitute effective attacks on the very concept of human rights as opposed to certain mere instances of its (mis)application. It is true that some of what have been formulated even in international treaties as 'human rights' look to be too culturally specific to warrant the name, but (as I hope will become clear in what follows) I suspect that even the most diversity-sensitive individual would be hard-pressed to deny universal domain to some iteration of, for example, the right to life. And, invariably, when we level charges of hypocrisy in this regard we implicitly affirm, rather than reject, commitment to human rights: we are saying that the hypocrites should practise what they preach. The human-rights abuser who does not hypocritically pretend to be respecting them can hardly be regarded, by virtue of such sincerity, as a morally better person than the hypocritical abuser. Indeed, in so far as hypocrisy might betray an implicit recognition of the moral force of human rights, the hypocrite could be a (very) small step nearer the realm of morality than the non-hypocrite.[1]

The more perturbing criticisms cut much closer to the heart of the concept. Ever since it emerged, originally in its precursor form of 'natural rights', thinkers from both sides of the political spectrum have assailed it. Though they naturally diverge, these attacks have often proceeded from some version of the claim that the concept is damagingly abstract in both form and content, deliberately but in fact perversely lifted out of people's actual social circumstances and hence ill-equipped to characterize and address the moral problems that beset them.

Given the profound ubiquity nowadays of what has been called the 'human rights culture' as a concretely 'lived' phenomenon, this charge of 'abstraction' may seem curious. But particularly in some of the theoretically rigorous Leftist responses to what has been called 'human rights interventionism' – the upsurge in usually US-led military action in the name of human rights – we find it going well beyond the conceptually superficial problems of cynical selectivity and hypocrisy to cast serious doubt on the utility of the human rights idea. In this chapter, I examine a representative statement of this critique: David Chandler's *From Kosovo to Kabul*.[2] This text sympathetically acknowledges the moral passion with which the idea of human rights is to be deployed. But it develops the 'abstraction' charge to contend that in some respects it is crucially indeterminate conceptually in terms of its content and political ramifications and that, to the extent that we can elaborate some of its assumptions and implications, it degrades rather than dignifies the human being in a manner which militates against democratic politics. Hence the concept haplessly apologizes for an oppressive world order, quite contrary to the cosmopolitan utopia it promises.

Some might think that, coming from the Left, this critique is nothing but the sigh of a politically spent force. But quite apart from the grievous error in assuming that the dominant ideas of today are necessarily adequate to the challenges which they confront, it is a myopic view which occludes perception of the Leftist-inspired resistance to the ways in which globalization is proceeding. Its challenge, therefore, is highly pertinent.[3] I will, however, present considerations to show how a commitment to the concept of human rights may ride through its objections. Focusing upon Chandler hardly exhausts the kinds of challenge that may be launched against the human-rights concept, of course, and space prevents a full elaboration even of his position, let alone the responses it may elicit. But the chapter will succeed if enough is said to cement what I believe to be much-needed confidence in the idea of human rights.

Chandler's critique of human rights discourse

Chandler proceeds from a distinction between two conceptions of rights, derived from two different conceptions of the rights-bearing agent. First is what I shall call democratic political rights, in which the agent is conceptualized as a rights-bearing member of a self-determining (and in that sense democratic) political society. Chandler contends that this concept of 'the rights-bearing individual with the capacity for self-government' lies at the heart of all democratic systems of rights and laws: '[t]he framework of regulation of the modern democratic system is historically and logically derived from the formal assumption of equal self-governing individuals, responsible and accountable for their actions and capable of rational decision-making'.[4]

He suggests that, prior to the 1990s, Western states tended to privilege such rights – narrowly conceptualized as formal political and civil liberties – and, in effect, identified 'human rights' (placed at the heart of international law after the Second World War) exclusively with them. This was partly a manifestation of the ideational struggle with the communist bloc, and partly a reluctance to formulate broader economic and social demands (which would require material redistribution on a large scale) as *rights*.[5]

In Chandler's narrative, the distinctiveness of the second conception has become much clearer in the post-Cold War era. No longer so tied to the propagandistic trumpeting of Western political systems, a more distinctive conception of human rights has emerged as a broader moral idea of what all human beings, simply by virtue of being human, are rightfully owed and can claim from each other. The human rights conception of the agent is abstracted from all concrete and particular social contexts and, specifically, from any conception of membership of a political society. Its main intention is to make up for what are perceived to be the deficiencies of political rights:

> [t]here is a human rights consensus that traditional democratic rights to civil and political freedoms are no longer, or never have been, adequate to safeguard the public or individual 'good'. The essence of human rights is the ring-fencing or protection of certain 'rights' that are too important to be left without guarantee.[6]

Radicals have long pointed out that the equality of political rights is purely formal, derivable only by their separation from unjust inequalities in the social and economic domains. Supporters of HR claim that 'human rights' make good this deficiency, treating these injustices as fundamental rights-violations and thereby demanding their rectification.

For Chandler, HR predetermine certain substantive moral *outcomes* in advance of any deliberation by a political community beyond whatever must logically follow from the commitment to the (mere) *process* on which DPR rest – and this is a problem, not a virtue. He urges that HR fail to deliver their radical promise for reasons which can be summarized as follows:

1 In substantiating their content, HR proceed from a conception of universal human 'evils' or 'wrongs'.[7] So whereas DPR are based on the 'positive' capacity of the agent for self-government, HR are demeaningly premised upon the vulnerability and hence *incapacity* of the rights-bearing agent.[8]
2 The non-proceduralist distrust of democratic politics at the heart of human rights leaves them at least tacitly supporting non-democratic, elitist and (pseudo-)paternalist institutions acting 'on behalf' of incapacitated moral agents.[9]
3 The anti-democratic impulse behind HR is exacerbated by the fact that it basically 'writes off' the nation-state in its disdain for the latter's ability to underwrite its own moral basis. Yet the abstractive character of human rights means it cannot specify in any concrete and realistic

details what alternative bodies should be entrusted with the ultimate responsibility for human rights.[10]

4 Even when proceeding from the 'universal evils' angle, the abstractiveness of human rights can lead to insuperable problems in agreeing content to 'human rights', making its usage vulnerable to the culturally specific 'wish-listism' of those who nominate themselves to speak on behalf of the (incapacitated and degraded) bearers of human rights.[11]

5 The 'normative philosophy' by which HR are formulated must therefore be regarded as 'impoverished', degrading the human subject 'to the lowest level, in need of paternalist guidance from the "great and good" who can establish a moral agenda of human rights to guide, educate and "empower" the people'.[12]

The critique summarized

Deliberately conceptualized in abstraction from concrete political contexts in order that one may have at hand an independent radical critique of them, Chandler comments that HR thereby mount what 'is in many ways a stunningly confident attack on the political sphere under the cover of ethics and morality'.[13] Circumventing 'existing society' and hence 'serious consideration of the real and profane',[14] he thinks that HR consequently disrespect the democratic autonomy of individuals, dismissing the moral significance of the political realm in which the real problems they face are actually confronted. Now, one might immediately retort that Chandler's argument itself constitutes a stunningly brusque attack on what I have already stressed is at the core of 'real-world' political struggle for millions of people. Of course, it may be possible that they are all wrong to invest so much faith in HR; or perhaps it could be patronizingly suggested that the language of HR is fine for polemical purposes but that, unfortunately, it does not withstand intellectual scrutiny. Whatever, it is difficult to escape the impression that Chandler's argument does not itself avoid some belittling of real moral agents. But perhaps this is merely a trivial *tu quoque* point: more compelling would be a counterargument which disarms the direct assault on HR themselves. And a very effective way of mounting such a case would be to depict HR in terms that DPR would feel compelled to adopt as an appropriate conceptual framework.

Rights proliferation and Thin Universalism

One way in which HR are said to by-pass democracy is by stipulating a whole range of moral, political and socioeconomic guarantees that are supposedly 'prepolitically' – certainly 'predemocratically' – determined and thereafter not up for debate in (what is left for) democratic politics.

Now I believe there is indeed something about human-rights talk that lends itself to potentially unwise extension. As Chandler notes, Milan Kundera puts this point particularly eloquently:

> the more the fight for human rights gains in popularity, the more it loses any concrete content, becoming a kind of universal stance towards everything, a kind of energy that turns all human desires into rights. The world has become man's right and everything in it has become a right.[15]

It certainly seems congenial for claimants, and rhetorically powerful for their audience (especially one which is itself immersed in a rights-culture) to frame as rights whatever it is they wish to demand. But is this expansionist tendency a devastating intrinsic flaw of HR?

In responding to the value-pluralism which some think impugns the possibility of any universal morality, normative philosophers nowadays often reject 'thick' in favour of 'thin' universalism (hereafter 'TU'). TU proceeds from the belief that what, morally speaking, is universally applicable to human beings is sparse, for diversity runs deep through humanity, but is nevertheless determinate and fundamental. We can still say that certain liberties and resources, for example, are necessary for any recognizably 'human' life. And some thin universalists, such as myself, are happy to frame these still in the terms of 'human rights'.[16] But the precise form and content of this universal morality is substantiated in full only by particular social contexts, which may vary in how they might legitimately do so. Furthermore, TU says nothing about a whole range of moral and political matters which it regards as appropriate only for local, not universal, specification. Thus it is much less comprehensive than most of the standard human rights covenants and declarations one finds in international law, and it underdetermines the full content of particular moralities and political ideologies. It is obvious, then, that TU posits a morality whose content cannot be said necessarily to foreclose on democratic deliberation.

Admittedly, Chandler's nominated representatives of HR, such as Ken Booth and Mary Kaldor, are not explicitly associated with TU in normative philosophy. But leaving aside the point, which some might think would unfortunately reinforce somewhat arbitrary boundaries between academic disciplines, that these people are not generally thought of as normative *philosophers* (the group specifically identified as the object of his critique), Chandler's argument conspicuously fails to engage with the most importantly relevant strand of current normative-philosophical thinking – at best, a serious omission in his case.

The pertinence of Thin Universalism

The reasons why TU is relevant here are twofold. First, recalling Chandler's concern to criticize the 'humanitarian interventionism' of the West in the post-Cold War era, it is immediately apparent that the normative issues at stake need only TU to characterize them. This is not to deny that the West interferes in other states' affairs in the name of thicker, more culturally specific rights (for example, certain characterizations of property rights which just so happen ideologically to support neoliberal economic regimes); but direct *military* intervention is what preoccupies Chandler and the moral issues raised by HR with respect to it are much thinner, even perhaps reducible to the singular right to life, whose violation on a specific scale constitutes the internationally recognized category of 'genocide'.

The second reason points out that DPR – at least in Chandler's hands – are best conceptualized as themselves premised on TU: their idea of human rights is entirely congenial for their intentions. Democratic political rights turn the factual assumption that agents are capable of self-government into the normative claim that they should be allowed to govern themselves in some meaningful way. For Chandler this generates a set of 'political rights' to guarantee the equal political liberties by which the deliberative democratic order implied by this commitment is instantiated.[17] He argues that we need not look beyond the realm of existing nation-states and their own legal orders, into any abstracted realm of 'humanity', to yield the appropriate concepts for this practice. But it is perfectly clear that he intends this to be a *universal* conceptual model: we disrespect *human* beings and *human* communities if we do not recognize these rights to self-government. So how, then, do DPR talk of those regimes – past, present and future (and they are many) – that in no conceivable way conform to preferred democratic norms? On what might rest democratic political rights' own possibility for radical critique if not something like the abstractive basis of HR?

We can reflect on this question using the thought of Hannah Arendt, which Chandler seems to think supports his position.

Defending Human Rights discourse

Chandler argues that the 'transcendental moral values' of HR are 'portrayed as the progressive solution to the problems of the narrow political sphere' and that (quoting Booth) '[t]his is the hope of progressively leaving behind the politics of the concentration camp – the ultimate sovereign space – for a cosmopolitan democracy aimed at reinventing the global human being – being human globally . . . and badged with a common humanity'.[18] He goes on claim that this point is the 'exact opposite' of a central theme in Arendt's *The Origins of Totalitarianism*:

> in fact it is the loss of political and legal rights that were the crucial precondition for the horrors of the concentration camp. [Arendt] . . . demonstrated, that for those lucky enough to escape, the stateless refugees, 'the only practical substitute for a non-existent homeland was an internment camp'; in reality the only guarantor of rights was the nation-state.[19]

'For the founders of political and civil rights theory', he continues, 'rights could only be guaranteed by the subjects of the rights themselves. If a right could not be protected, or exercised, by its bearers, then it could no longer be a right, an expression of self-government.'[20] Human rights are said by Chandler to sever the link between 'rights' and subjects capable of exercising them: people need actual political institutions to be rights-bearers, but the human-rights bearer is conceptually abstracted from any such context. He claims that HR consequently render democracy meaningless, though in fact the upshot of his position also seems to be that HR render *rights* meaningless, too.[21]

Now it would be foolish to deny that human rights require certain specific institutions to put them into effect, but they are not 'meaningless' when such institutions are lacking. Democratic political rights veer dangerously close to a Hobbesian equation of 'having a right' and 'having the power to enjoy that right'. Human rights insist instead on the crucial importance of the distinction between 'having a right' and 'having a right respected'. It is precisely because people have a right to *X* that it is wrong when they are denied *X*: the possession of the right is what establishes the wrongness of the denial. And that is profoundly meaningful. Hence the claim that DPR in Chandler's hands are morally inarticulate: resisting the discourse of human rights, they deprive themselves of a means by which they can furnish their commitment to democracy with an account of why democracy *matters*, and what else must matter as a result of such a commitment. In this regard, it is pertinent that Arendt does not in fact utter the 'exact' opposite of Booth's cosmopolitan humanitarianism. *The Origins of Totalitarianism* is passionately fired by the belief that:

> human dignity needs a new guarantee which can be found only in a new political principle, in a new law on earth, whose validity this time must comprehend the whole of humanity while its power must remain strictly limited, rooted in and controlled by newly defined territorial entities.[22]

She is obviously right that classical Enlightenment talk of the 'rights of man' drastically failed to materialize in appropriate practice, but she emphatically does not regard that as a reason to abandon talk of a human morality – which she is sometimes quite happy to conceptualize in terms of rights. All human beings are indeed owed substantive moral respect, and totalitarianism's rise showed just how poor have been the means devised thus far to concretize it. Significantly for Chandler's argument, the nation-state thus has in Arendt's eyes a particularly lamentable balance-sheet in this regard. Her insistence that rights must be made 'actionable' leads her to focus far more on the political means to do so and away from reflection on what human rights we may be said to have. And on this score, she has no doubt that cosmopolitan moral commitments require supranational institutions to make good the limitations of sovereign national states.[23]

In an eloquently critical discussion of Richard Rorty's moral particularism, Norman Geras compellingly reinforces the cosmopolitan view by illustrating the centrality of universalized 'humanity-based' judgements of those non-Jews who helped the Jews during the years of Nazi persecution.[24] His discussion helps to confirm it surely to be the case that an equally crucial precondition of the horrors of the concentration camp is the absence within the perpetrators of a sufficiently empathetic moral commitment to the victims *expressed in the form of a generalized moral commitment to fellow humans simply because, whatever particular identity they bear, they are also human beings and hence part of our moral community and concern.*

In sum: we should ask of DPR 'What is so special about self-government? Aren't you in effect saying that all human beings have a right to self-government? But to be effective wouldn't that also assume that each citizen has a certain set of liberties and resources? Should you not therefore say that humans have a right to these determinate items *as well*, precisely because they are logical corollaries of the right to self-government? And on what basis would you condemn any political system – and there are, and have been, many – which would withhold these rights? What would you say to a state which abolished democracy and initiated genocide against its citizens?' If it wishes to avoid complete moral vacuity, DPR must rely upon some such universal normative conception of the human being. The concept wants to say that people must be allowed to govern themselves, and to have at least the basic essentials of life which enable them to do so – and what better way is there to frame these demands other than the language of people having *rights* to such things?

Defending normative philosophy

Arendt is critical of those philosophers who tried to justify the 'rights of man' in terms of the supposed universal, ahistorical properties of human nature or reason, for these substituted illusion and fantasy for the recognition that human rights are artifices, social conventions.[25] It is not altogether clear whether Chandler thinks that normative philosophy, in defending HR, must fall foul of this particular criticism, but it emphatically does not necessarily do so and is nowadays dominated by what is at least an attempted avoidance of this. To see how it might do so, let me briefly sketch one way of doing it.[26]

We start with widely entertained and hence important moral intuitions which arise from reactions to particular situations that move us emotionally to make judgements about what is right and wrong, good and bad. We then infer from these judgements certain general principles, stepping back abstractively to identify them. For example, we can infer from our horror at the particular famines in Sudan and Zimbabwe a commitment to the general principle that no human should be allowed to starve. Philosophy can not only articulate these principles, but can also test their candidacy for inclusion in a universal morality by, for example, considering how well they fit with other principles we might wish to entertain, or whether we are prepared to accept the practical consequences of their application which we might hypothesize. This is how we construct a moral perspective which, by virtue of its generality, helps us to avoid – for example – accusations of inconsistency, cynical selectivity or hypocrisy in our judgements.

Nothing in this procedure commits us to any particular view about the meta-ethical status of human rights, for looking at such matters *sub specie aeternitatis* (if this is understood as the metaphysical point of view of the 'universe', the real nature of things) is not the same as looking at them *sub specie humanitatis* (the 'human', or 'humane' judgemental perspective).[27] Indeed, normative philosophy need not address the question of morality's nature at all, particularly when TU is at issue. For although we might believe it prudently sceptical to look for some independent justifying reason as to why we should embrace a TU principle, which may well require us to consider what sort of 'thing' the principle is, I would contend that such an exercise may well be redundant. When dealing, as TU does, with universal moral fundamentals – such as the rights not to be murdered or raped – we typically do *not* suspend our belief in them in advance of formulating what we would regard as satisfactory justificatory reasons. We still regard them as justified moral beliefs even though we have yet to work out *why* they are justified.

Further evidence that we tend to assume as our starting-point that certain moral beliefs are justified lies in the fact that our reason for judging a supposedly independent justificatory theory to be successful is often whether it generates the fundamental principles which we are taking as given. If it does not do so, that is taken as reason enough to reject *not* the principles but the justificatory theory. (The most popular reason for rejecting act-utilitarianism, for example, is that it does not guarantee fundamental rights.) If one regards respect for a principle as criterial of a justificatory theory's success, one is logically committed already to regarding that principle as justified.[28]

Given that this raises obvious questions about justificatory theory's utility, perhaps normative philosophy's most useful function is *critical-expository*: rather than asking for independent good reason to accept a belief in a particular human right before putting it to work, one may take its justification for granted and then, through philosophical reflection, try to articulate it clearly and clarify what other beliefs and practical consequences follow. In working out properly where we stand given our fundamental moral beliefs, we may simply end up affirming all that we already believed (the 'exposition' in the method). But this process can also cause a fundamental revision of our beliefs when we find that philosophy has uncovered gaps or inconsistencies in our thinking or has shown how our beliefs unfold in unwelcome ways (the 'criticism').

TU's normative philosophy is abstractive only in the sense that it conceptualizes our moral judgements about a particular situation as based upon general principles that can thus be formulated in abstraction from that, or any other, situation. So, for example, we ultimately make the particular judgement that 'the rape of X was wrong' on the basis of commitment to the general principle that 'rape is wrong', which we also judge to apply in all relevantly similar cases. Thus Chandler's abandonment of the abstractive 'theoretical realm' for the empirical one of the 'real world' is misconceived,[29] for if one aspires to a critique which is cogent, consistent, robust and *principled* it is necessary to work out what principles hold in themselves, in general, before we can properly approve of, or condemn, what is going on in any one time or place. Normative philosophy and empirical critique are thus not opposites in this regard: they are necessary complements in practical judgements of what ought and ought not to be the case.

Human rights and democracy

We have already established that TU cannot sensibly be accused of substantially pre-empting the contingencies of democratic deliberation: it is too thin for that. We may go further in suggesting that a right to self-determination (which is, after all, part of that to which supporters of HR appeal in justification of certain military interventions) is a likely component of a defensible TU, which would therefore have an inbuilt mechanism biasing it in favour of democratic politics. I make the point no more strongly than that, for the internal political implications of a people's right to self-determination in practice can well be left by TU for local interpretation. One can see, however, the prima facie oddity of entertaining both this right and the idea that the people in question could be justifiably governed non-democratically. Whatever, we have good reason to believe that TU could support a democratically dynamic (instead of straitjacketed) political order, in which critical normative-philosophical deliberation helps to drive the conversation of the citizenry.

For Chandler, to enshrine human rights in law as constitutional constraints on the democratic process is to 'juridicalize' politics, turning it over in effect to non-elected jurists and other 'experts' to speak and act on behalf of the politically helpless citizenry – or, more pertinently when talking of international politics, to those who have the power to claim to be the (self-appointed) 'world's policemen'. A global order in which HR-based international law constrains state sovereignty is therefore structured to favour undemocratic practices. In this disdain for constitutional limitations on the prerogatives of the demos, he is at one with many contemporary thinkers who believe it is a matter of appropriate trust in people not to ring-fence certain issues in democratic deliberation. As we have already seen, however, and as is urged by many constitutionalists, the 'mere' commitment to democracy implies commitment to a set of quite distinguishable principles and 'outcomes'; procedure can never be 'pure' in that sense. So it is mysterious why a constitutional protection of that which is necessitated by a commitment to democracy, lifting it somehow out of the vagaries of everyday politics, should be thought to be such a debilitating incubus on the demos. Indeed, if constitutional provisions *frame* the democratic process, it is inappropriate to think of them as *limitations*. Certainly, there is no *conceptual* problem with the possibility of a democratic political society collectively agreeing to be bound by extrademocratic constitutional strictures: embodiments of, not restrictions on, the will of self-governing agents. To make the point directly relevant, there is nothing necessarily undemocratic in principle – compromising of state sovereignty – if states accept that their sovereignty is premised on HR-respecting international law, for the very commitment to 'sovereignty', the right to self-determination, implies respect for that which such law codifies.

The specific problem with Chandler's opinion on the nature of democracy on which I want to dwell illuminates the final problem we shall consider with his account. Of HR-based constitutionalism, he comments that '[i]t is a deeply negative perspective on human collective experience where governments can no longer be trusted not to engage in genocide against their own people'.[30] The sad truth is, of course, that it is just naïve to dismiss the experiences of human history – and, indeed, present-day society – and place such unqualified trust in the state.[31] And the well-placed fears about the potential for badness in politics need not be based, as Chandler mistakenly holds, on the idea that *all* human beings are to be regarded as untrustworthy and incapacitated in this regard. All that the case for constitutionalism requires is the claim that *some* who find themselves in the vicinity of power are corruptible by it.[32] HR's cosmopolitanism, therefore, proposes that there can and should be a legally structured and morally motivated international order to which member states are accountable in the sense that significant moral failings on their part become the concern of that order, which has the right and perhaps even the duty to rectify them if the states in question do not.

Theorising the ideal and non-ideal

It is not necessarily a fault of HR that their view of what the ideal, fully rights-respecting world order would look like remains so radically incomplete. In part, at least, it is a mark of how far we still have to travel to construct that order: the destination remains obscure from view for the obstacles in our way are substantial and perplexing. But, in identifying the principles of HR as those whose full realization would underpin the ideal world order, normative philosophy has also identified those principles which should inform *as far as they possibly can at present* how we cope with the current, non-ideal globalizing world. Non-ideal theory proposes courses of action within the context of practices and possibilities in the here and now, but always informed by ideal theory's account of what ought to be the case.

In failing to grasp this ideal/non-ideal theory distinction, Chandler is thus simply mistaken to think that HR theory 'argues for a rejection of the existing framework of international society and the political sphere of the states which compose it'.[33] Non-ideally, it typically assumes that we must still work within the society of states for the foreseeable future. (In fact much HR ideal theory thinks that some kind of state system will survive, as well,[34] so Chandler doubly exaggerates.) But in conjoining this empirically rooted pragmatism and its vision of an ideal world order, HR can identify *in principle* what is wrong with the present and illuminate the road we should try to take to improve it.

Of course, 'being non-ideal' there are likely to be reservations aplenty about the steps HR currently recommend: they may have little quibble with many of Chandler's negative comments about the actual politics of human rights today yet, in abjuring an explicit ideal-theory vision, Chandler ends up idealizing the present, romanticizing the existing system of nation-states in the faith he invests in it to cope with the problems of the non-ideal world. In itself, this point does not rule out the possibility of a non-ideal level argument that Chandler's preferred arrangements move us closer to what ideally should be the case than human rights' conception of supranational organizations and law, and of humanitarian intervention as a moral option. But to conduct this argument we need an account of general principles to postulate what ought to be the case for human emancipation, and in HR this is what normative philosophy yields. Attuned to the myriad of deficiencies of today's world order – and most importantly those attendant on the state-centric system – it is the vehicle by which we can identify and articulate what matters most to us. It furnishes us with a moral vision that can inspire, rather than enervate, democratic politics in our struggles to build what we feasibly can of that ideal world.

Notes

1 It is important to note, however, that selective application of human-rights concerns is not itself necessarily evidence of a moral flaw, for selectivity of moral concern is often unavoidable. See my 'Selectivity, Imperfect Obligations and the Character of Humanitarian Morality' in A. Moseley and R. Norman (eds), *Human Rights and Military Intervention* (Aldershot: Ashgate, 2002), pp. 139–52.

2 D. Chandler, *From Kosovo to Kabul: Human Rights and International Intervention* (London: Pluto Press, 2002). Published before the 2003 invasion of Iraq, that event nevertheless would not appear to give Chandler any cause to alter his argument as he wishes to present it.
3 It should be stressed that not all Leftists attack the idea of human rights.
4 Ibid., p. 104.
5 Ibid., pp. 91–4.
6 Ibid., p. 97.
7 Ibid., p. 96.
8 Ibid., pp. 100–2.
9 Ibid., pp. 109–10, 116–18.
10 Ibid., pp. 113–14.
11 Ibid., pp. 97–8, 118.
12 Ibid., p. 119.
13 Ibid., p. 107.
14 Ibid.
15 M. Kundera, *Immortality* (London: Faber & Faber, 1991), p. 153.
16 Some other thin universalists may be reluctant to go *as far* as saying that these essentials constitute the specific norm of 'rights'.
17 I use the word 'deliberative' here to acknowledge Chandler's desire that this democracy is in some way genuinely participatory for the citizens. As I shall suggest later, though, he provides us with little guidance as to what form such a polity might take.
18 Chandler, *From Kosovo to Kabul*, pp. 107–8.
19 Ibid., p. 108. The quotation comes from H. Arendt, *The Origins of Totalitarianism* (New York: Harvest, 1979), p. 284; cf. Arendt, *Origins of Totalitarianism* pp. 296–7.
20 Chandler, *From Kosovo to Kabul*, p. 109.
21 Ibid., p. 114.
22 Arendt, *Origins of Totalitarianism*, p. ix.
23 The key text here is H. Arendt, 'Karl Jaspers: Citizen of the World', in P. Schilpp (ed.), *The Philosophy of Karl Jaspers* (La Salle, IL: Open Court, 1957), pp. 539–49. For an extended defence of Arendt as a human-rights thinker, see J. C. Isaac, 'A New Guarantee on Earth: Hannah Arendt on Human Dignity and the Politics of Human Rights', *American Political Science Review*, 90 (1996), 61–73.
24 N. Geras, *Solidarity in the Conversation of Humankind* (London: Verso, 1995).
25 See Isaac, 'A New Guarantee on Earth', p. 64.
26 Those familiar with moral philosophy will recognize 'reflective equilibrium' as one variant of the approach sketched here.
27 Many critiques of abstractive universal moral theories misleadingly conflate these two perspectives in their account of what such theories supposedly depict.
28 Space permits no further elaboration of this argument and its nuances, qualifications and implications; this is provided in my forthcoming piece on 'Thin Universalism and the Limits of Justification'.
29 Chandler, *From Kosovo to Kabul*, p. 119.
30 Ibid., p. 236.

31 Once again, Arendt's position actually favours HR over Chandler; see Isaac, 'A New Guarantee on Earth', pp. 67–8.
32 Often, it is rightly pointed out that constitutional provisions are not enough to thwart concerted attempts to undermine a political order. But this argument applies, *mutatis mutandis*, to the mere commitment to democratic procedure – and perhaps even more strongly, such that Chandler's position can draw no succour from it.
33 Chandler, *From Kosovo to Kabul*, p. 108.
34 See, for example, D. Held, *Democracy and the Global Order* (Cambridge: Polity Press, 1995).

9

The Other Side of Obligation: Cosmopolitan Distributive Justice and Duties of the Less Affluent

Luis Cabrera

Cosmopolitan theorists of distributive justice have rightly given most of their attention to the obligations owed by those in affluent states to those in less-affluent states. Whether calling for direct transfers of resources across borders or, more recently, for some limited transformation of the Westphalian system, cosmopolitan theorists have focused on actions that individuals in rich states should feel compelled to take. In this chapter, I argue in part that strong critical emphasis also should be given to the duties of the global poor. Just as we are concerned with what the relatively fortunate should be asked to surrender of their resources, time and personal energies, we should avoid treating those in recipient states as mere objects of charity by failing to ask what contributions they might make to help improve their own circumstances. An approach is advocated here in which individuals in less-affluent states are viewed as global co-citizens working jointly with those in affluent states to improve economic and political conditions worldwide. Such an approach, I will argue, is consonant with a strong institutional cosmopolitanism, where the duties of all individuals include the promotion of democratically accountable economic and political integration between states in order to improve the life chances of the less-affluent globally.

Obligations of the affluent

Cosmopolitanism will be somewhat narrowly understood here as an approach to the distribution of benefits and burdens that accords the interests of all individuals equal weight.[1] State memberships are not presumed to have intrinsic moral significance, and obligations to distribute to co-citizens may be no stronger than to those overseas. I will not discuss 'mild' or moderate cosmopolitanism, a distributive approach presuming that we do owe some few stronger or unique obligations to co-citizens.[2] Also, I will bracket for now the distinction between institutional cosmopolitanism and the moral variant, which does not prescribe specific institutional changes to achieve broader distributions. The key point here is that, within a cosmopolitan approach to distributive justice, questions naturally arise about the fairness of a global system in which birthplace continues to do so much to determine life chances. To illustrate, some 2.5 billion persons in developing states – around 40 per cent of the global population – continue to subsist on $2 per day or less, measured in purchasing power parity (ppp).[3] Mostly within this group, some six million children under the age of five continue to die each year of hunger-related causes.[4] About 2.4 billion persons live on $8 per day PPP or less, and fewer than one in six, or 965 million worldwide, live in states designated high income, where PPP is $25 per day, or slightly more than $9,000 per year.[5]

Cosmopolitans have responded to the existence of such stark poverty alongside relative affluence by calling for global redistribution of material resources and, in some cases, opportunities in the form of freer immigration.[6] Specific distributive proposals have ranged from the application of a global Rawlsian difference principle[7] to the collection and distribution of taxes on the use of natural resources or global commerce.[8] Some have emphasized direct charitable transfers that those in richer states should make, without necessarily prescribing dollar amounts or income percentages.[9] Others, especially consequentialists, have attempted to determine with precision exactly where the cut-off should be for individuals. Brad Hooker, for example, would require international charitable transfers of between 1 and 10 per cent of income, depending on the individual's affluence.[10] Peter Singer recently has suggested that households in affluent states may be obliged to transfer all annual income above $30,000.[11]

Obligations of the impoverished

Few cosmopolitans, however, have emphasized the question of what also should be asked of the global impoverished. The question has been addressed somewhat obliquely in the discussion of issues surrounding global overpopulation, including whether the Earth should be viewed as an overloaded 'lifeboat' where some must be allowed to drown so that others may live.[12] A considerable number of others have explored the question, raised by Derek Parfit, of whether in a consequentialist frame we would have to concede that overpopulation might even be choiceworthy, since it could increase overall welfare even if all persons in a population were leading virtually joyless lives.[13] But there has been little direct attention given to what the less affluent may be expected or required to do *themselves* in order to improve their own situations.

Singer is a notable exception.[14] He has argued that those in less-affluent states may have to be willing to accept intrusive population controls as one condition of their receiving aid. Measures could include offering payment to those with several children in exchange for sterilization. Such a policy would be justified, he suggests, because 'if the people we save have several children, and so contribute to a situation in which their children, along with many others in the country, are starving in 20 years' time, we have not, on balance, prevented starvation'.[15] Singer's general approach has, of course, generated much controversy. In the sterilization scenario, bargaining power between the contracting parties would probably be highly asymmetrical.[16] Also, the potential for oppressive policy measures, similar to those imposed under China's one-child policy, would seem strong in an act-utilitarian frame where reducing population is the overriding concern.[17] That said, Singer's discussion is useful because it can prompt us to look at the now-widespread conditions, or 'conditionalities', to which less-affluent states must conform to receive aid transfers. Aid conditionalities can be viewed as indirectly imposing obligations on ordinary citizens of recipient states. An examination of how they have been applied will provide the context for an alternative way of approaching the conception and distribution of duties, one that I will argue is more consistent with the emphasis in cosmopolitanism on giving the interests of all individuals equal weight.

Conditionalities on international aid

Large-scale development aid has been a fixture in the global system at least since the Marshall Plan of 1948–51, when the USA transferred some $13 billion to European states to aid in postwar rebuilding.[18] In the Cold War context of the 1960s, donor states, especially the USA and Soviet Union, commonly linked aid to the recipient-state's support for their geopolitical aims. Strictly economic conditionalities became more prevalent in the 1970s and especially 1980s, as the IMF and World Bank began requiring extensive liberalizing changes in recipient states. Reforms included cuts in public spending, currency devaluation, privatization of state industries, wage controls and a lifting of restrictions on foreign investments.[19] Individual donor states and the European Union also have increasingly been insisting on such economic conditionalities. And, since the 1990s, some donor states have been requiring recipients to commit to straightforward political conditionalities.[20] The European Union, for example, has required recipients to follow principles of democracy, human rights, the rule of law and good governance, the latter including principles of transparency and public accountability.[21] In the USA, the Bush administration proposed designating $8.5 billion in development aid from 2004 to 2006 specifically for states that agreed to 'rule justly, invest in their people, and encourage economic freedom'.[22]

The most common rationale given by donor states and institutions for attaching both economic and political conditionalities to aid is that they want to ensure that transfers will achieve their intended purposes. The scholarship on aid effectiveness is extensive, and there is considerable debate about how much difference political conditionalities can make in the relatively short term towards achieving development aims. However, a number of studies have found that transparent, accountable and democratically responsive institutions are a significant component of ensuring that aid does its intended work, and increasingly of determining which states will even be considered for some transfers.[23] In this context, we can return to the question of which obligations the globally less-affluent might owe. Let us presume first that those within affluent states are meeting at least some of their own global distributive obligations, as seen in a cosmopolitan frame. That is, some of the $58 billion in development aid transferred in 2002, the latest year for which figures were available,[24] was given to improve the lives of ordinary citizens of recipient states, rather than simply to reward less-needy states that supported donors' strategic aims.[25] In addition, private charitable giving by individuals to programmes operating in developing states – some $5.7 billion from the USA in 2002, compared to $13.3 billion in US government aid – further fulfilled some cosmopolitan distributive obligations. What might be the obligations on the other side, of those receiving such aid?

I will note first that there are important differences between official development assistance and private aid, which is delivered mostly by non-governmental organizations.[26] However, both can be classed as overseas transfers, and it seems plausible that the same sorts of duties could be asked of individuals benefiting from aid disbursed to their government and that disbursed perhaps more locally, in a regional or village project sponsored by a private organization. In the most general terms, those duties might be seen as ones to support the creation of conditions in which both government and private aid can be best assured of having its intended effect. Ordinary citizens in recipient states might be expected to adopt an attitude of willingness to endure the dislocation pressures inevitable in a liberalizing economy, one whose production sectors are being opened to competition with producers elsewhere in the world. Similarly, they might be expected to support or at least endure the pressures accompanying the privatizing of state industries, cutting of state spending, wage controls, currency devaluations and other changes, rather than staging mass demonstrations against economic conditionalities. Where political conditionalities are concerned, they could be asked to become more fully involved as citizens, to vote, attend public meetings and otherwise engage where possible in the political process in ways that would contribute to success in the reforms required of their governments. They also could be expected to demonstrate respect for the rights of women and minority groups as outlined in aid agreements, especially with the European Union.[27]

What, in such an approach, might be considered objectionable, or in tension with a cosmopolitan approach to distributive justice? First, we should note the criticisms of economic conditionalities as too often being 'one size fits all' policies dictated by the neoliberal Washington Consensus. Critics of the International Monetary Fund, for example, charge that IMF officials have routinely ignored legitimate local variations in economic needs and applied virtually the same sweeping prescriptions in state after state, with sometimes tragic results.[28] It is well beyond the scope of this chapter to attempt to settle whether the IMF approach to structural economic reform has been misconceived; however, there is an important underlying issue, which is that economic conditionalities have been so controversial in part because they have been perceived as forced upon those within less-affluent states, with little genuine input from them. Especially in the case of states in fiscal crisis that must approach the IMF for emergency loans, negotiating power is often very weak. At a deeper level, it is significant also to note that, in the current global system of (presumably independent), sovereign states, development aid is viewed as a charitable contribution. It may be given by affluent states from enlightened self-interest, or from more fundamental ethical reasons,[29] but it is understood that aid is given at the pleasure and prerogative of donor states. They may set the levels of aid they deem appropriate, direct it to the states or programmes they choose, and ultimately set the conditions they prefer on the use of the aid, even if they do negotiate with or take some input from recipients.[30]

Conditionalities in a global citizenship frame

Here I want to introduce an alternative approach to thinking about development aid and obligations. Rather than asking which actions by the less affluent would do most to achieve the economic and political aims set primarily by affluent states, this approach would view the distributive obligations of all persons within a world citizenship frame grounded in an institutional cosmopolitan approach to distributive justice. Under such an approach, specific duties would be determined with the understanding that recipients are potential co-citizens who ultimately would have the same formal opportunity to give input on policy choices as those in current donor states.

We can return now to the distinctions between the moral and institutional approaches to cosmopolitan distributive justice. The main difference is one of prescription. That is, unlike institutional cosmopolitans, moral cosmopolitans do not advocate large-scale institutional changes in the global order to effect the distributive changes they seek.[31] In general, they advocate holding existing state and global institutions to account according to cosmopolitan principles, for example, assessing the justice of common practices in the global economic system. Institutional cosmopolitanism directly advocates the creation of strong supranational institutions – those with the ability to obtain compliance from states – to facilitate global transfers. Changes prescribed could include the creation of extensive networks of supranational regional and global institutions, up to some fully elaborated form of global government. There are of course many shadings between plain moral and institutional cosmopolitanism, with a number of theorists arguing for the creation of limited, specific supranational institutions.[32] Here, however, the main distinction should suffice.

I have argued at some length elsewhere that the moral cosmopolitan also should be an institutional cosmopolitan, promoting democratically accountable economic and political integration wherever possible in service of bettering the life chances of the global poor.[33] In brief, the argument asserts that the current global system gives rise to three powerful, mutually reinforcing biases within states that tend to discourage the kinds of routine, large-scale international distributions the cosmopolitan seeks. A 'foundational' bias springs from the foundations of the sovereign states system, where such norms as non-intervention and formal legal equality are grounded in the presumption that the state's primary role is to protect and promote the interests of its own citizenry. State leaders would be subverting their own mandates if they followed instead the dictates of a cosmopolitan ethic, which would see the interests of all persons as equally worth promoting. A second 'electoral' bias is concerned with how states' leaders, in both democratic and more hierarchical states, have strong incentives to distribute resources domestically rather than overseas in order to continue in office or ensure the success of their favoured policy programmes. Finally, and probably most importantly, a kind of Lockean 'own-case' bias is reinforced by the structure of the sovereign states system. Those in affluent states essentially are judges in their own cases about the appropriate levels of transfers they should make, and their perceptions of their own obligations may be skewed, in much the same way Locke argued that the perceptions of those in the state of nature can be skewed when they are judges in their own cases.[34]

Due to the biases inherent in the Westphalian system, I have argued, the cosmopolitan should advocate the transformation of that system into one which is more integrated, roughly along the evolving institutional lines of the European Union. In the context of the duties of the globally less affluent, an institutional approach can help to highlight important issues of paternalism and ways in which the interests of all persons might be most plausibly said to be given due weight. I will not suggest that any sort of requirement that could be construed as paternalistic is necessarily unjust or inconsistent with a cosmopolitan approach. As Martha Nussbaum notes, the reason that forms of paternalism may seem so offensive is that they represent illegitimate restrictions on an individual's ability to choose. However, many initiatives opposed on grounds that they are paternalistic actually are aimed at broadening the classes of people able to exercise meaningful choice. 'The Indian Constitution, for example, is in that sense paternalistic when it tells people that it is from now on illegal to use caste or sex as grounds of discrimination. But that is hardly a good argument . . . against opposing the attempts of some people to tyrannize others.'[35] In a similar way, adopting an institutional cosmopolitan approach can be viewed as a way of expanding the global class of persons who ultimately will be empowered to have some input on the determination of duties, as well as on the distributions of duties among all persons.

To illustrate the alternative, we can turn first to the European Union's aid relations with prospective member states. In 2004, the EU formally admitted 10 new member states. All acceding states – Cyprus, the Czech Republic, Estonia, Hungary, Latvia, Lithuania, Poland, Slovakia, Slovenia and Malta – were required to follow extensive economic and political conditionalities before being approved. However, the conditionalities framework was significantly different from those imposed on non-associated recipient states. The differences lay not primarily in the requirements imposed, though acceding states did have significant leeway to negotiate individual compliance timetables, but in the framework's fundamental 'partnership' construction and ultimate aims. Conditionalities agreements for acceding states were guided by the understanding that reforms were needed to ensure full movement to EU partnership, rather than to ensure effective use of the charitable donations that could be spared. As the European Commission, the EU executive body, noted in the context of human rights conditionalities placed on other potential members in the region, such requirements 'should not be seen as imposing conditions, but in the spirit of joint undertaking to respect and promote universal values'.[36] That spirit of joint undertaking extends to the obligations assumed by the 15 core EU states, which are formally held to the same body of treaty law and general sorts of economic, political and human rights standards they have imposed on acceding and associated states. They also have faced sanctions for failures to comply with their own standards.[37] Further, and unlike in charitable agreements with distant third-party states, they have had to make a substantial number of changes themselves as part of the accession process. Those have included changes in the size and procedures to be followed by the European Parliament and other institutions, and continuing changes in agricultural and other common policies.[38]

Perhaps most importantly, the 15 member states were making a commitment to formally incorporate the acceding states into trans-state distributions of both resources and opportunities. Material distributions are formalized in the EU system through structural- and cohesion-fund initiatives aimed at stimulating development and lessening the impacts of integration, mainly within less affluent states.[39] Those in most member states have also seen the distribution of life opportunities expand in the form of free movement, granted first to workers and gradually to all citizens.[40] Acceding states were negotiating free movement schedules for their own citizens, leading to an ultimate guarantee that they would be able to pursue life and work opportunities as formal citizen equals throughout the union.[41] Finally, those in acceding states were to be represented in the EU governing bodies, enabling them to have a say in the distribution of citizen obligations, as well as in a range of other policy areas, as formal equals. So, while the initial economic and political conditionalities required of potential new members may appear similar to those that have been imposed on, for example, recipient states in the EU's Africa, Caribbean and Pacific initiatives,[42] the ultimate approach adopted is that of a partnership of expected co-equals.

Mexican President Vicente Fox has pressed over several years for a similar partnership approach in North America. Fox has proposed that the North American Free Trade Agreement (NAFTA) be revised to include freer movement of workers and material distributions to directly support road and other infrastructure projects.[43] The USA did agree in 2002 to enter with Mexico into a 'Partnership for Prosperity' that would provide mostly technical assistance and encouragement to US firms to help improve Mexico's infrastructure, home mortgage availability, and access to US business franchising opportunities.[44] Also, by early 2004, the Bush administration had proposed a broad guest worker plan that would allow many undocumented workers to obtain legal-resident status.[45] However, both initiatives were much more limited than the large-scale transfer of development resources and freer movement of workers sought by Fox and advocated by an institutional cosmopolitan approach.

In an institutional approach, exemplified by a formal partnership frame where equal membership in a larger union is the long-term expectation or aim, those within less-affluent states are to be viewed not as passive subjects of charitable contributions, seeing their duties dictated primarily by those in donor states; rather, they are morally co-equal actors, shouldering those burdens necessary to become full partners in a joint political and economic project. In such a frame, it will be more difficult for donors to ask recipients to assume duties they would not themselves be prepared to discharge, or to otherwise dictate unfavourable terms. That is not to suggest, of course, that 'domesticating' the obligations of the less affluent will automatically erase concerns about potentially unjust paternalism. Such concerns have generated a substantial literature on the appropriate structure of domestic social-support programmes,[46] as well as on the kinds of government or societal paternalism highlighted by Mill.[47] Space constraints prevent a detailed exploration of issues surrounding paternalism here. However, we can note a key difference between the kinds of obligations expected of those in domestic social programmes and those receiving overseas charity: that is, domestic support is given at least in part to enable individuals to function more fully as co-citizens. Unlike overseas aid recipients, those in a democratic domestic context have some ability or at the least a recognized right to bring their concerns to the table. Such a right can help to ensure that the affluent in their own societies are not merely judging in their own cases about their own distributive obligations, or about the appropriate level of supervision and direction accompanying direct aid.

Obligations of the less affluent in an institutional approach

I will suggest here that the primary obligations owed by the less affluent in a co-citizen, institutional cosmopolitan frame would be to promote the kind of democratically accountable economic and political integration that could make lasting, concrete improvements in their lives and the lives of the similarly situated worldwide. Those in less-affluent states should advocate accountable integration wherever possible, while demanding the access to suprastate governance bodies which could better ensure that their distributive and other justifiable demands are recognized. For example, in the NAFTA context, that could mean that ordinary citizens of Mexico would, while continuing to protest about provisions that have allowed damaging imbalances in agriculture and other areas, demand with full voice a deepening of the organization in the broad direction advocated by Fox, Robert Pastor and others.[48] They could demand appropriate access to more autonomous and more broadly empowered NAFTA institutions, as well as routinized input on regional environmental, labour and other vital issues. Such efforts do have precedents. In the months leading to the launch of NAFTA in 1994, a number of civil society groups in Mexico worked with like-minded groups in the USA to press for changes in the agreement.[49] Similar campaigns could be launched, or current protest efforts modified, towards making NAFTA a genuine partnership and broad polity, one where those within member states could increasingly be viewed as regional co-citizens with equally important interests and concerns. Further, as regards the proposed 34-member Free Trade Area of the Americas (FTAA), those NGOs and ordinary citizens of Latin American states who have been demanding a rejection of the agreement could reconsider its potential for beneficial integration. Instead of advocating a region-wide popular vote against FTAA,[50] they might demand equally vigorously that any organization created provide for equitable economic and political integration, including access and accountability to them, even if only in relatively limited ways in the near term.[51]

Similar duties can be envisioned in relation to other projects of suprastate economic integration, including the Asia-Pacific Economic Cooperation forum, the Association of South-East Asian Nations (ASEAN), the Southern African Development Community, and especially in the global trade regime overseen by the World Trade Organization. The

WTO is significant because of its ability to obtain compliance with its rules through the threat of trade penalties, and its potential for linking the observance of labour, environmental and human rights to trade privileges. Some controversy has been generated by proposals for such linkages, including one made by then-US President Bill Clinton at the 1999 WTO ministerial summit in Seattle.[52] Some economists and leaders of less-affluent states have viewed labour linkages as potential disguised assaults on their states' comparative advantage in wages.[53] However, linking the privileges of WTO membership to such standards on collective bargaining and working conditions as those promoted by the International Labour Organization[54] could mean significant gains for the ordinary citizens of less-affluent states. Further, those within less-affluent states could provide significant additional pressure for greater openness and accountability from the WTO. Such pressure could open the way initially to increased NGO access to dispute panel proceedings, and ultimately to the creation of some formal representation for ordinary citizens similar to the WTO advisory parliament proposed by European Union Trade Commissioner, Pascal Lamy.[55]

I am not suggesting, of course, that the primary activities of those in less affluent states, especially those subsisting on $2 per day or less, should be global political engagement. But in fact, even the lives of those in impoverished rural areas are being affected in dramatic ways by the processes of economic integration and trade liberalization associated with globalization. Their responses increasingly are being prompted or provoked.[56] The argument here suggests that the most appropriate response from the less affluent is to press their leaders and supranational actors for more accountable integration. Consonantly, some of the most prominent obligations of those within affluent states may be to help empower the less affluent to press their own interests with their own governments, within and via global non-governmental organizations, and within global trade and other forums.

In sum, both those in affluent and less-affluent states should be viewed as global co-citizens tasked with undertaking efforts that will better enable all persons to have access to the resources and opportunities needed to lead a decent life. Promoting accountability and social linkages in the processes and agents of global economic integration is the most promising route to ensuring such access. Such efforts can make more possible the creation of joint supranational projects where the biases inherent in the Westphalian system are mitigated and the interests of broader sets of persons are protected and promoted in common. Further, and probably most importantly for the purposes of this chapter, viewing the less affluent as global co-citizens and potential partners is most consistent with the equal respect for all persons that lies at the foundations of a cosmopolitan approach to distributive justice. It establishes a framework in which the less affluent are treated as moral agents fully capable of contributing to their own well-being, and one in which they can become actual partners in determining and governing the distributions of burdens and benefits in societies, however ultimately large.

Notes

1 For detailed definitions of moral and institutional cosmopolitanism, see C. Beitz, 'Social and Cosmopolitan Liberalism', *International Affairs*, 75 (1999), 125–40, especially p. 129.

2 For a critique of mild cosmopolitanism, see my *Political Theory of Global Justice: A Cosmopolitan Case for the World State* (London: Routledge, 2004), ch. 2; See also D. Miller, 'Debate. Caney's "International Distributive Justice: A Response"', *Political Studies*, 50 (2002), 974–7.

3 World Bank, *World Development Report 2004* (New York: Oxford University Press, 2004), p. 253. Purchasing Power Parity is a measure used to try to capture the buying power that local incomes have in local economies: see also p. 265.

4 Food and Agricultural Organization of the United Nations, *The State of Food Insecurity in the World* (2002), online at http://www.fao.org/sof/sofi/index_en.htm.

5 World Bank, *World Development Report 2004*, p. 254.

6 J. Carens, 'Migration and Morality: A Liberal Egalitarian Perspective', in B. Barry and R. Goodin (eds), *Free Movement: Ethical Issues in the Transnational Migration of People and Money* (University Park, PA: The Pennsylvania State University Press, 1992), pp. 25–47.

7 C. Beitz, *Political Theory and International Relations*, 2nd edn (Princeton, NJ: Princeton University Press, 1996), pp. 152–3; D. Moellendorf, *Cosmopolitan Justice* (Boulder, CO: Westview Press, 2002), pp. 78–84.

8 T. Pogge, 'A Global Resources Dividend', in D. A. Crocker and T. Linden (eds), *Ethics of Consumption: The Good Life, Justice and Global Stewardship* (Lanham, MD: Rowman & Littlefield, 1998), pp. 501–36.

9 M. Nussbaum, 'Duties of Justice, Duties of Material Aid', *The Journal of Political Philosophy*, 8 (2000), 176–206; Nussbaum, 'Patriotism and Cosmopolitanism', in J. Cohen (ed.), *For Love of Country: Debating the Limits of Patriotism* (Boston, MA: Beacon Press, 1996), pp. 2–17.

10 B. Hooker, *Ideal Code, Real World: A Rule-Consequentialist Theory of Morality* (Oxford: Oxford University Press, 2001), pp. 162–4.

11 P. Singer, 'The Singer Solution to World Poverty', *New York Times Sunday Magazine*, 5 September 1999, pp. 60–3; see also Singer, *One World: The Ethics of Globalization* (New Haven, CT: Yale University Press, 2002), p. 189.

12 G. Hardin, 'Lifeboat Ethics: The Case Against Helping the Poor', *Psychology Today*, September 1974, 38–43.

13 D. Parfit, *Reasons and Persons* (New York: Oxford University Press, 1984), pp. 381–90; 'Symposium on Derek Parfit's *Reasons and Persons*', *Ethics*, 96 (1986),

703–872; T. Cowen, 'What do We Learn from the Repugnant Conclusion?', *Ethics*, 106 (1996), 754–75.

14 See also O. O'Neill, *Faces of Hunger* (London: Allen & Unwin, 1989). In a neo-Kantian frame, O'Neill urges treating the global poor as moral agents themselves.

15 P. Singer, 'Reconsidering the Famine Relief Argument', in P. G. Brown and H. Shue (eds), *Food Policy: The Responsibility of the United States in Life and Death Choices* (New York, Free Press, 1977).

16 See O. O'Neill, *Bounds of Justice* (Cambridge: Cambridge University Press, 2000), pp. 163–7.

17 K. Johnson, 'Politics of International and Domestic Adoption in China', *Law & Society Review*, 36 (2002), 379–96, esp. pp. 388–90.

18 M. H. Cooper, 'Foreign Aid after Sept. 11', *The CQ Researcher Online*, 12 (2002), 361–92.

19 P. Hoy, *Players and Issues in International Aid* (West Hartford, CT: Kumarian Press, 1998), p. 71. For a response to criticisms of such conditionalities, see IMF Chief Economist Kenneth Rogoff, 'The IMF Strikes Back', *Foreign Policy* (2003), 38–46; see also World Bank, *A Case for Aid: Building a Consensus for Development Assistance* (Washington, DC: The World Bank, 2002).

20 See G. Crawford, *Foreign Aid and Political Reform: A Comparative Analysis of Democracy Assistance and Political Conditionality* (New York: Palgrave, 2001).

21 M. Holland, *The European Union and the Third World* (New York: Palgrave, 2002).

22 Millennium Challenge Account, 'Overview', online at http://www.mca.gov.

23 S. Kosack, 'Effective Aid: How Democracy Allows Development Aid to Improve the Quality of Life', *World Development*, 31 (2003), 1–22; World Bank, *Assessing Aid: What Works, What Doesn't and Why* (New York: Oxford University Press, 1998); J. Beynon, 'Policy Implications for Aid Allocations of Recent Research on Aid Effectiveness and Selectivity', in B. M. Arvin (ed.), *New Perspectives on Foreign Aid and Economic Development* (Westport, CT: Praeger, 2002), pp. 199–264.

24 'Ranking the Rich 2004', *Foreign Policy* (2004), 46–56.

25 A. F. Alesina and D. Dollar, 'Who Gives Foreign Aid to Whom and Why?', *NBER Working Paper No. W6612* (Cambridge, MA: National Bureau of Economic Research, June 1998), online at http://ssrn.com/abstract=226334.

26 At times, especially in the 1980s, macroeconomic structural adjustment has been seen as opposed in its effects to poverty-reduction efforts. See J. P. Lewis, *Pro-Poor Aid Conditionality: Policy Essay No. 8* (Washington, DC: Overseas Development Council, 1993), pp. 1–2.

27 For detailed background, see V. Miller, 'The Human Rights Clause in the EU's External Agreements', *House of Commons Library Research Paper 04/33*, 16 April 2004, online at http://www.parliament.uk/commons/lib/research/rp2004/rp04-033.pdf.

28 J. Stiglitz, *Globalization and its Discontents* (New York: W. W. Norton, 2002); see Rogoff, 'The IMF Strikes Back', for a response.

29 World Bank, *A Case for Aid*, pp. 18–19.

30 For details on such input, see C. Adam *et al.*, 'Performance-Based Conditionality: A European Perspective', *World Development*, 32 (2004), 1,059–70.

31 Beitz, 'Social and Cosmopolitan Liberalism', p. 129.

32 See T. Pogge, 'Economic Justice and National Borders', *ReVision*, 22 (1999), 27–43; B. Barry, 'Statism and Nationalism: A Cosmopolitan Critique', in I. Shapiro and L. Brilmayer (eds), *Nomos XLI: Global Justice* (New York: New York University Press, 1999), pp. 12–66, p. 40; Moellendorf, *Cosmopolitan Justice*, esp. pp. 171–6.
33 Cabrera, *Political Theory of Global Justice*, especially ch. 4.
34 John Locke, *Second Treatise of Government*, ch. 2, section 13; see also J. Mayerfeld, 'The Myth of Benign Group Identity: A Critique of Liberal Nationalism', *Polity*, 30 (1998), 555–78.
35 M. Nussbaum, 'Women and Equality: The Capabilities Approach', *International Labour Review*, 138 (1999), 227–53, esp. p. 232.
36 European Commission, 'The European Union and the External Dimension of Human Rights Policy from Rome to Maastricht and Beyond', Communication from the Commission to the European Council and European Parliament, COM (95) 567, final, suppl. 3/95, p. 33. Cited in E. Fierro, *The EU's Approach to Conditionality in Practice* (The Hague: Martinus Nijhoff, 2003), p. 157.
37 C. Brand, 'Berlusconi to Plead for Leniency after Italy Violates EU Deficit Rules', *The Associated Press*, 4 July 2004.
38 N. Nugent, *The Government and Politics of the European Union*, 5th edn (Basingstoke: Palgrave Macmillan, 2002), pp. 504–7.
39 J. McCormick, *The European Union: Politics and Policies* (Boulder, CO: Westview, 1999), p. 68.
40 See A. Geddes, *The Politics of Migration and Immigration in Europe* (London: Sage, 2003).
41 For extensive information on the enlargement process, see the EU Enlargement web site at http://europa.eu.int/comm/enlargement/index.htm.
42 See W. Brown, *The European Union and Africa: The Restructuring of North–South Relations* (London: I. B. Tauris, 2002), pp. 2–4.
43 P. D. Broughton, 'Fox Models his Vision of North America on the EU', *The Daily Telegraph*, 10 August 2001, p. 21.
44 US Department of State, 'US–Mexico Partnership for Prosperity', Press Release, 22 March 2002, online at http://www.state.gov/p/wha/rls/fs/8919.htm.
45 R. Alonso-Zaldivar, 'Bush Would Open US to Guest Workers', *Los Angeles Times*, 8 January 2004, p. A-1.
46 For a 'pro-paternalism' approach to social welfare supervision, see L. Mead (ed.), *The New Paternalism: Supervisory Approaches to Poverty* (Washington, DC: The Brookings Institution Press, 1997); for a critical response, see G. Standing, *Beyond the New Paternalism: Basic Security as Equality* (London: Verso, 2002).
47 J. S. Mill, *On Liberty and Other Writings* (Cambridge: Cambridge University Press, 1989); R. Sartorius (ed.), *Paternalism* (Minneapolis, MN: University of Minnesota Press, 1983); D. VanDeVeer, *Paternalistic Intervention: The Moral Bounds on Benevolence* (Princeton, NJ: Princeton University Press, 1986); J. Feinberg, *The Moral Limits of the Criminal Law* (Oxford: Oxford University Press, 1988).
48 R. Pastor, *Toward a North American Community: Lessons from the Old World for the New* (Washington, DC: Institute for International Economics, 2001); see also R. Pastor and R. F. de Castro (eds), *The Controversial Pivot: The US*

Congress and North America (Washington, DC: Brookings Institution Press, 1998), esp. ch. 8.

49 J. Brecher and T. Costello, *Global Village or Global Pillage: Economic Reconstruction from the Bottom Up* (Boston, MA: South End Press, 1994), pp. 97–102.

50 M. Valente, 'Argentina: Second "No to the FTAA" Campaign Kicks Off', *IPS-Inter Press Service*, 1 July 2004.

51 See J. Mercury and B. Schwartz, 'Creating the Free Trade Area of the Americas: Linking Labour, the Environment, and Human Rights to the FTAA', *Asper Review of International Business and Trade Law*, 1 (2001), 37–65; see also the official FTAA web site and its 'open invitation' for civil society groups to provide input, online at http://www.ftaa-alca.org/alca_e.asp.

52 S. Dunphy, 'Clinton Signs Pact to Lessen Child Labor: Respect Environment, Workers, He Tells WTO', *The Seattle Times*, 2 December 1999, p. A-1.

53 J. Bhagwati, 'Symposium: The Boundaries of the WTO: Afterword: The Question of Linkage', *American Journal of International Law*, 96 (2002), 126–34; K. Jones, *Who's Afraid of the WTO?* (Oxford: Oxford University Press, 2004).

54 International Labour Organization, online at http://www.ilo.org.

55 P. Lamy, 'What Are the Options After Seattle?' Speech to European Parliament, Brussels, 25 January 2000, online at http://europa.eu.int/comm/commissioners/lamy/speeches_articles/spla09_en.htm.

56 See D. Bigman (ed.), *Globalization and the Developing Countries: Emerging Strategies for Rural Development and Poverty Alleviation* (Wallingford, UK: CABI Publishing, 2003).

10

Environmentalism as Globalization from Above and Below: Can World Watchers Truly Represent the Earth?

Timothy W. Luke

Introduction

This brief analysis reconsiders the cultural, ideological and practical dimensions of spatiality at the interface of the world environment and globalization, especially as they are being reimagined through global biocomplexity modelling as the key site for globalist intervention. By fusing environmentalism with globalism, many scientific experts and some major governmental and non-governmental science agencies are attempting to generate the theories and practices needed for managing 'the environment' on a local, regional, national and global level of operation. In their models, the prevailing procedures of ecomanagerialism[1] are being reformatted through new 'world watching' technics in data-driven biocomplexity models.[2] Such turns in basic scientific work deserve careful review, and this chapter begins that investigation of planetary ecomanagerialism as a mode of globalization.

To untangle the snarls of globalization, Ulrich Beck distinguishes between globalism, globality and globalization. First, 'globalization', Beck suggests, 'denotes the processes through which sovereign national actors are criss-crossed and undermined by transnational actors with varying prospects for power, orientations, identities, and networks'.[3] The natural and mathematical sciences behind global biocomplexity models are examples of such influences. Second, 'globality' now constitutes some of the more unique existential conditions of what is regarded by millions as a 'world society'. As the cultural roots of globality have spread over the past few centuries, we clearly have been living for quite some time in a world society of one kind or another: that is, a world where 'the totality of social relationships' to a significant degree 'are not integrated into or determined (or determinable) by national-state politics'.[4] Finally, 'globalism' is what now appears most distinctive about the present. It denotes the embeddedness of an extraordinarily virulent worldwide ideology, which is usually embraced by many among the managerial, professional-technical and intellectual classes, that holds 'the world market eliminates or supplants political action – that is, the ideology of rule by the world market, the ideology of neoliberalism... If it mentions at all the other dimensions of globalization – ecology, culture, politics, civil society – it does so only by placing them under the sway of the world-market system.'[5]

Beck asserts that globalism in this contemporary sense entails a highly cohesive set of specific beliefs and operational practices that basically impels all states, societies and cultures to be managed like a corporate capitalist enterprise. Without a single world state to steer this global society, however, many entrepreneurs and firms view globalism as the best possible formula for creating, and then somehow managing, economic growth. This formula is clear: 'a globally disorganized capitalism... For there is no hegemonic power and no international regime either economic or political.'[6] Many business people and major corporations are developing coherent global strategies around the ideologies of globalism. Even though they often underemphasize environmental concerns along with these plans, the business strategies of many firms are to transform their goods and services into a decisive sign of the world market's globalization, an explicit marker of their clients' globality, and an indicator, if only tacitly, of their consumers' and suppliers' submission to the anarchy of globalist exchange.[7] To manage the chaotic anarchy emerging from today's 'globally disorganized capitalism', it now appears to some scientists that global biocomplexity models can serve as the most useful tools for ecomanagerial agencies to exert a manner of environmental restraint over the loose, but still nonetheless effective, systems of worldwide exchange.

Overview of 'global biocomplexity'

This chapter asks us all to closely re-read the emergent project of 'global biocomplexity' research, which has been drawing significant new investment from the National Science Foundation (NSF) and other major science research funding bodies in the USA since 1999. In many ways, it constitutes one of the latest, and most sophisticated, attempts to embed ecomanagerialist policies and politics[8] more deeply into environmental policy practices by relying upon the form of sophisticated biophysical and socioeconomic models.[9] Most importantly, the nature of terrestrial space itself is being re-imagined not as Nature, ecology, or even environment, but rather with new metaphors about service-generating, capacity-sustaining and load-bearing planetary infrastructures.[10]

In turn, the scientific communities engaged in these modelling exercises and policy debates are mobilizing the ambiguous premises of 'globality' and 'biocomplexity' in this new conceptual couplet in order to propound new powers for geological imagining, geophysical sensing, and biochemical scanning communities around new knowledges embedded in the research problematics of global biocomplexity.[11] While the effective management of the Earth's increasingly entwined industrial and natural ecologies is undoubtedly still far beyond human abilities, this new environmental theory appears to be laying the basis for a new 'de-nationalized', or even fully 'trans-nationalized', politics for terrestrial administration tied to 'the findings' of such modelling projects.[12] This analysis questions the notions of Nature, planetary ecology and scientific expertise that such big techno-science projects require, while articulating a political critique of who is doing what to whom and for what purposes in this work.[13]

On one level, 'big science' simply represents the push-and-pull of existing networks of researchers plugging away at the normal science agendas regarded as legitimate by major research universities, national academic professional associations, scientific discipline study committees, corporate entities, and other government agencies.[14] Yet, on another level, the NSF also competes with many other international and national science agencies to define the depth and direction of new research initiatives which draw scientists and advisers into government delegations as policy-makers.[15] The popular and elite concern for the environment, which increased in the 1990s with the twentieth anniversary of Earth Day, the global environment conference in Rio and the debates over global warming, permitted the NSF's higher managers to single out new environment-related research as its number one 'priority area' for 'crosscutting investment strategies'.[16] Yet this declaration also may represent a campaign to nationalize the most basic foundational science being done on ecological topics. Consequently, in 1999 the NSF resolved to make even more 'significant investments' in a new area of investigation, namely, 'biocomplexity in the environment' research, because it is now clear that:

> The environment is a subject of profound national importance and scientific interest, making it a strategic priority for NSF... A centerpiece of NSF's Environmental Research and Education portfolio is the Biocomplexity in the Environment (BE) competition. Initiated in fiscal year (FY) 1999, this special competition promotes comprehensive, integrated investigations of environmental systems using advanced scientific and engineering methods. Biocomplexity refers to the dynamic web of interrelationships that arise when living things at all levels – from molecular structures to genes to organisms to ecosystems – interact with their environment. Investigations of biocomplexity in the environment are intended to provide a more complete and synthetic understanding of natural processes, human behaviors and decisions in the natural world; and ways to use new technology effectively to observe the environment and sustain the diversity of life on Earth.[17]

While these research goals are laudable, it also is clear that a panoply of ecomanagerial strategies are at play here in which creating greater administrative command over, control of, and communication about 'coupled systems' in the environment – for research and education – becomes a critical concern to 'biocomplexity in the environment', or 'BE-science'. This disposition in the NSF's discursive engagement is made quite clear in five thematics of investigation that it stressed in 2002–3:

1 *Dynamics of Coupled Natural and Human (CNH) Systems* – this emphasizes quantitative interdisciplinary analysis of relevant human and natural systems processes and the complex interactions among human and natural systems at diverse scales, with special emphasis given to studies of natural capital; landscapes and land use; and uncertainty, resilience and vulnerability.
2 *Coupled Biogeochemical Cycles (CBC)* – these focus on the interrelation of biological, geochemical, geological and physical processes at all temporal and spatial scales, with particular emphasis on understanding linkages between chemical and physical cycles and the influence of human and other biotic factors on those cycles.
3 *Genome-Enabled Environmental Science and Engineering (GEN-EN)* – this encourages the use of genetic and information technology approaches to gain novel insights into environmental questions and problems.
4 *Instrumentation Development for Environmental Activities (IDEA)* – this supports the development of instrumentation and software that

relies on and takes advantage of microelectronics, photonics, telemetry, robotics, sensing systems, modelling, data mining and analysis techniques to bring recent laboratory instrumentation advances to bear on the full spectrum of environmental biocomplexity questions.

5 *Materials Use: Science, Engineering, and Society (MUSES)* – this supports projects directed towards reducing adverse human impact on the total interactive system of resource use; designing and synthesizing new materials with environmentally benign impacts on biocomplex systems; and maximizing the efficient use of individual materials throughout their life cycles.[18]

Here, biocomplexity's valorization as a codex for knowledges of the interface of natural and industrial ecologies also is connected to new material science breakthroughs, innovative surveillance instrumentation arrays, and genome-enabled ecotechnics as the tools needed to remediate disruptions in 'coupled natural and human systems'. It is being made quite plain here that the projects of environmentality[19] with all of their state-based managerial agendas is what the NSF wishes to bring into focus 'on frontiers of knowledge, where discovery and innovation are likely to produce significant progress'.[20]

The biocomplexity research project

One might believe that these scholarly pursuits are confined only to the laboratories and conferences of a few scientists; and, to an extent, this is true. Yet these research agendas also permit globalization to serve as a pretext for the re-terrestrialization of earthly ecologies in a 'Second Copernican Revolution'[21] that grants additional authority to science and the state, albeit with not much clarity about which scientists or what states, to set about 'managing the Earth'.[22] Partly on their own, partly with national authority, and partly with transnational support, scientists are leveraging their still limited knowledge about global environments to create power for administering these sites and spaces.[23] Global biocomplexity models supposedly will permit scientists and decision-makers to re-evaluate 'the human–environment relationship, operating across humanity as a whole and at the scale of the Earth as a single system'.[24] Indeed, many scientists in the 1990s were pushing research agendas towards global levels of analysis. Whether expressed in terms of Gaia analysis,[25] climatological complexity,[26] or earth system analysis,[27] the spatiality of the world's environments was being re-imagined in registers of global biocomplexity.[28]

A sample research abstract from the NSF's 'BE-science' panel funded for 2002 illustrates this engagement with modelling the interactions between natural and industrial ecologies. Acevedo *et al.*[29] assert that:

> Few ecosystems are now free of extensive human influence, but the ways that human activity affects such systems and their reciprocal effects on human behavior are poorly understood. The major objective of this research project is to develop integrated models that couple forest ecosystem dynamics to human decision making... Changes in forest cover affect ecological processes and functions, leading to predictable changes in water quantity and quality. Human behaviors will be simulated using multi-agent models, and they will be coupled to the forest models through linkages that describe different forms of disturbance of human activities on forest and hydrologic system functions and by receiving feedbacks about the effects of such actions from the forest and hydrological models...The dynamics of the coupled natural and human systems will be analyzed mathematically to identify complex behavior (such as oscillations and 'chaos') resulting from the interaction of the human and natural systems...Results of this research will provide a better quantitative understanding of the interplay between human actions and forest dynamics. This enhanced understanding will give landowners, other stakeholders, and policy makers reliable information about the impact of their decisions on the future composition, structure, and functionality of local ecosystems. It will thereby facilitate a more informed analysis of the long-term consequences of private choices and public policies on the natural systems in which human systems are embedded and with which they interact.

This three-year long project was funded at US$566,020 (estimated), and it illustrates how policy-makers believe that models of complex coupled systems will enhance their understanding with more reliable information. In turn, the state can then direct 'landowners and other stakeholders' to change 'private choices and public policies'.

Yet the discourse here belies a bigger change: namely, the infrastructuralization of the Earth in registers of 'global biocomplexity'. Vegetation growth is transformed in 'forest ecosystem dynamics', 'human behaviors that affect forest ecosystem structure and functions', and four sites in two countries are employed to guarantee 'the feasibility of modeling forest dynamics as they are reciprocally influenced by human decision making' and 'demonstrate the generality of this approach to understanding coupled human and natural systems'.

Strangely enough, the fictive, presumptive or imaginary values and effects of 'BE-science' models also are blatantly confessed. That is, 'human behaviors will be simulated using multi-agent models', forest structure is modelled in hierarchical arrays 'beginning with the dynamics of tree growth and distribution and working up to the stand and landscape scales', and the coupled interactions are seen as an imaginary engine in which human models and forest models are algorithmically engaged in 'linkages that describe different forms of disturbance of human activities on forest and hydrologic system functions and by receiving feedbacks about the effects of such actions from the forest and hydrological models'. Here environmentality's impulse to bring people and things, humans and non-humans, industries and ecologies into the best dispositions to control the conduct of their conduct (by benchmarking them against generalized models of conduct) is made quite plain.[30]

Spatiality: coupled urban/environmental systems

These technoscientific manoeuvres aim to recast the Earth as terrestrial infrastructure, which allegedly exists as such and therefore requires management in accord with its own machinic regularities that biocomplexity models will adduce. It also acquires its own unique spatiality. On one level, such spatiality often is unfixed in setting its localities, stabilities or properties. Here the manifolds of biocomplex spatiality appear as the mediations of practices in place and in process. That is, as De Certeau might suggest, global biocomplexity models constitute the sort of spaces that exist when:

> one takes into consideration vectors of direction, velocities, and time variables. Thus space is composed of intersections of mobile elements. It is in a sense activated by the ensemble of movements deployed within it. Space occurs as the effect produced by the operations that orient it, situate it, temporalize it, and make it function in a polyvalent unity of conflictual programs or contractual proximates.[31]

While it surfaces in second and third order registers away from its articulation in everyday life, contemporary commodity exchange is little more than the incessant intersecting flight of many mobile elements. And here biocomplexity and sociocomplexity fold together globally. The polyvalent unity of conflictual human and non-human metabolisms do orient, situate, temporalize and functionalize ensembles of moving ideas, peoples, goods and energies.

Thus, on another level, globalized biocomplexity modelling finalizes the omnipolitan realities of Lefebvre's 'urban revolution'[32] in which the instrumentally rational organization of space synchronizes human activities with other humans and non-humans into the 'now-wheres', 'now-whens', 'now-whats', and 'now-whos' of constructed spatiality. In these locales, stable interconnected properties, practices and populations instantiate 'place', or 'an instantaneous configuration of positions'[33] that begins to imply stability. For Lefebvre these embedded cycles of emplacement are the fields of 'the urban', infiltrating globally into what once was social and natural, countrified and citified, peasant and proletarian with differential, disjunctive and discontinuous biocomplexities.

In many attempts to gauge such spatiality, a blindness induced by sutures in time or twists in history occlude what is at hand. Lefebvre maintains 'the urban (urban space, urban landscape) remains unseen',[34] because human cognition and perception are trained to be incapable of sighting it. Snagged by the detritus of industry, modernity simply slips into postmodernity; yet there is much more at work beyond the 'blinding (assumptions we accept dogmatically) and the blinded (the misunderstood)' that now are 'complementary aspects of our blindness'.[35] Global biocomplexity models perhaps are efforts to overcome such blindness by grinding new spatial optics to detect disruptive snarls in the worldwide webs of natural and social exchanges,[36] but these lenses also have distortions.

To postulate that global biocomplexity exists, can be defined, assigned reliable metrics, and then managed within zones of sustainable continuation, the NSF and other research funding agencies implicitly concede that 'the urban revolution' has fully taken hold – deruralizing, deindustrializing, and perhaps even dehumanizing the production of human settlements as civilizations – on a global scale. Instead ensembles of systems are seen as coexisting in chaotic, turbulent, complex strings of self-organizing stability, knitting together what once were natural and social elements into the prefigurations of planet-wide community that Lefebvre labelled 'the urban' in 1970. What seemed only like 'a horizon, an illuminating virtuality'[37] a generation ago is now fully recognizable.

These emergent models of global biocomplexity recognize this concretization. While virtual, the urban is abstract, but still a focus of action. Consequently, the planetarian project arises alongside the urban revolution's reconstitutions of all environments and their inhabitants:

> Theoretical knowledge can and must reveal the terrain, the foundation on which it resides: an ongoing social practice, an urban practice in the process of formation. It is an aspect of the critical phase that this practice is currently veiled and disjointed, that it possesses only fragments of a reality and a science that are still in the future. It is our job to demonstrate that such an approach has an outcome, that there are solutions to the current problematic.[38]

Nearly a generation later, then, the NSF's global biocomplexity initiative essentially acknowledges this planetary society now exists along with the 'global city' that constitutes it.[39]

Biocomplexity: re-territorializing power

The NSF's identification of 'biocomplexity in the environment' as an engagement for scientists, which is worth spending the taxpayers' money, transforms it into a legitimate pursuit for individual researchers' studies; yet it is unclear that this topic, concern or object of research exists as such. As Lefebvre asserts:

> Can the concept of an object (of a science) withstand close examination? Apparently more precise and more rigorous than the concept of a 'domain' or 'field', it nonetheless brings with it significant complications. For the object presents itself, or is presented, as *real* prior to any examination. It is said that there is no science without an object, no object without a science... The concept of a scientific object, although convenient and easy, is deliberately simplistic and may conceal another intention: a strategy of fragmentation designed to promote a unitary and synthetic, and therefore authoritarian, model. An object is isolating even if conceived as a system that is dissimulated beneath the apparently 'objective' nature of the scientific object. The sought-for-system constitutes its object by constituting itself. The constituted object then legitimates the system... In other words, the 'real' sociological object is an image and an ideology.[40]

The NSF's endorsement of 'biocomplexity in the environment' exemplifies all of these contradictory conceptual tendencies at once. Its object is unstable, elusive and ideological. Something exists at the interface of Nature and Society, but global biocomplexity becomes 'a real object' in these particular terms only by operationalizing the NSF's preferred precepts of research. In turn, the sought-for-system of 'BE' constitutes itself and its analytical objects all together, and thereby legitimates the system of 'BE-science' and 'BE-policy'.

Here, the re-territorialization of terrestrial processes shifts shape in the NSF's 'BE-science' to conform to the agendas of professional technical analysis as well as governmental activity. Terrestrial spatiality is where the sought-for system of global biocomplexity is posited to unfold. Globality, ecology and complexity, then, congeal into apparently real sociological objects, but they are also discursive constructs, analytical images and managerial ideologies.[41] By postulating the analytical constructs of global biocomplexity, the environment becomes another twist in scientists' and technologists' 'articulation of "time-space", or, if you prefer, the inscription of "time in space", becomes an object of knowledge'.[42]

Once again, however, the positivistic pretence behind power and knowledge here is quite problematic. This research stance draws ideology into the inscriptions of 'time in space', because:

> space is only a medium, environment and means, and instrument and intermediary...The relation between time and space that confers absolute priority to space is in fact a social relationship inherent in a society in which a certain form of rationality governing duration predominates. This reduces, and can even destroy, temporality. Ideology and science are merged.[43]

One again sees the NSF bringing technocratic knowledge and state power through the 'time in space' concept of coupled natural and social systems, which instantiate global biocomplexity. At that juncture, new eco-power and eco-knowledge allegedly can be produced by earth science modellers to advance governmentality as environmentality.[44]

This will to power in 'BE-science' environmentality is naïvely or brazenly illustrated by Schellnhuber and Held[45] in their account of the 'Challenges of a Changing Earth' conference in Amsterdam during July 2001. As they claim, over 1,800 scientists from 100 countries saw this convocation as:

> something like an Earth Summit for Global Change science as it (i) brought together all pertinent parts and disciplines from a worldwide environmental research community, (ii) reviewed and summarized the state of the art in all fields that contribute to the growing understanding of the planetary machinery, and (iii) developed a programmatic vision – a scientific 'Agenda 21' – research for global sustainability.

Even though such efforts are commendable, the evocation of Earth as 'planetary machinery', which must be appraised and administered as a whole, is quite problematic.

Their difficulties begin when tendencies are mistaken as full-blown capabilities and initial possibilities are becoming taken for attained capacities. Schellnhuber and Held, for example, discuss in the past tense 'several developments' that allegedly make Earth System Science, Global Biocomplexity or Biocomplexity in the Environment truly disciplinary artefacts with real technical refinement by repeating the essence of the Amsterdam meeting's consensus. That is, global biocomplexity analysis now rises upon the following:

1 The view of the Earth from a spaceship, a blue-green sphere floating in blackness, triggers emotional *feelings* of a home teeming with life set in a homeless void, as well as more analytical *perceptions* of a materially limited and self-contained entity.
2 Global observation systems allow the application of *concepts* that were only previously applicable at subsystem level, or regional or local scales, to the Earth as a whole.
3 Global databases allow global scale phenomena to be addressed with consistently acquired *data* that have the potential for harmonization and comparison at a global scale.
4 Dramatic advances in the power to infer characteristics of Earth system processes in the past allow contemporary observations to be viewed in a coherent *time continuum*.
5 Enhanced computing power makes possible not only essential data assimilation, but increasingly sophisticated *models* improve understanding or functional interactions and system sensitivities.[46]

Meanwhile, other scientists today cannot accurately predict earthquakes, forecast hurricane intensity or direction, anticipate ozone hole variations, or account for many climatological changes. Yet, on the other hand, this group of Earth System modellers is convinced they can actually manage the planet right now as a single rapidly evolving biotic/abiotic system.

Their certainty about how humanity now knows what to do, and how to do what to do when, where and why has a finalist teleology that, in turn, implies a new ontopolitical transition, which is regarded as a 'Second Copernican Revolution' by many in the global biocomplexity community on both epistemological and sociopolitical grounds:

> The first Copernican Revolution put the Earth in its correct astrophysical context, but it also shattered the medieval perception of our home planet as the hub of God's creation. As a consequence, the elites of feudal hierarchy, who arrogated themselves central positions in this creation, lost their singularity in the eyes of the ordinary people, and the stage was set for the rise of the civil individual. The second Copernican revolution now discovers our planet as one whole and unique entity by watching it from outerspace, by probing its digital caricatures, in the virtual reality of cyberspace, or by reproducing parts of it in miniature. As a consequence, a deep consciousness of global interconnectedness is about to arise that reintegrates the individual into some planetary hierarchy – the *real* hierarchy of biogeochemical cycles, atmospheric circulation patterns, syndromes of land use change, international economic oscillations, and worldwide technological waves. Thus, in a sense, the second revolution reverts and completes the first one.[47]

Hearing scientists claim that they know all peoples and societies on the Earth must submit to this sort of reintegration into *real* hierarchies, which only Earth System Science can apprehend and administer, is highly disturbing. Even more upsetting, however, is their absurd, naïve or self-serving analysis of the political questions posed by their finalist scientific research programmes. That is, they ask:

> if everything goes right, some 8 to 10 billion beings will run this planet carefully and interactively and sustainably in the not too distant future. But what if something goes terribly wrong? Is the earth so fragile that it can be ruined by careless handling? And, if so, what must we do, at the very least, to avoid this?[48]

With these pronouncements, the questions are ultimately all begged: their recommendation is clear – 'let us try to sketch a few tentative answers'.[49] The 'us', who answer the 'we', who ask 'what to do?' is the same tiny vanguard: namely, those Earth System Scientists convinced that eight to ten billion human beings cannot run the planet sustainably, because of their past record of careless handling. So what 'we' all must do to avoid this terribly wrong outcome is to acknowledge that advent of 'a Global Subject'[50] or 'human superorganism',[51] which faces 'the supreme task' that Earth System Science[52] now presents: 'the selection and implementation of a tolerable environmental future from the infinity of optional co-evolutions of ecosphere and anthroposphere'.[53] Global biocomplexity models suggest 'the Global Subject' is a 'whole pool of robust adaptive strategies (reminiscent of "fuzzy control")'; and this could be seen as discouraging reality, but Schellnhuber and Held answer the big 'What Shall We Do?' questions with an open invitation 'not to hesitate to realize the fascinating options involved for the further development of our common scientific enterprise'.[54]

Such work on global biocomplexity unfortunately seems to forget that model construction is never free from criticism. In fact, the best use of models comes from comparing their tentative results to what is agreed provisionally to be real. Mistaking the model for the mechanisms is to confuse the map with the terrain. As Lefebvre argues, models are always provisional, and no method guarantees 'absolute "scientificity"', because:

> Even mathematics and linguistics are unable to guarantee a perfectly and definitively rigorous methodology. Although there are models, none of them can be realized completely satisfactorily, none of them can be generalized, or transferred, or exported, or imported outside the sector within which they were constructed without exercising considerable precaution The methodology of models is said to continue and refine the methodology of concepts. There are specific concepts, characteristic of each partial science, but none of them can completely determine an object by tracing its contours, by grasping it. The effective realization of an object involves considerable risk; even if the analyst constructs objects, these are provisional and reductive. Consequently, there are many models that do not constitute a coherent and completed whole.[55]

Still, the presumption of the NSF that the object of 'biocomplexity in the environment', as its 'BE' investment initiatives define it, actually exists then becomes dangerous. There is a finalism in the 'sought-for-system' emerging from 'BE-science' as the 'searched-for-system-now-found'.

While traditional forms of religious or transcendental finalism have been discredited by rigorous philosophical criticism, this new variety of cybernetic finalism being unveiled in cybernetic, stochastic or probabilistic modelling goes unchallenged. Yet 'BE-science', and the statist goals of environmentality behind it, must be ardently challenged. Despite what the NSF would have its clients and consumers believe about terrestrial spatiality and its intrinsic ecological processes, reifying planetary dynamics in biocomplexity models as systems of space-time compression is leading to a false finalism to steer the world's political economy.[56]

These aspirations and applications for environmental science should be resisted, since:

> in terms of historical becoming, and given the inevitability of change, there is no definite, prefabricated goal, one that is therefore already achieved by a god or in his name, by an Idea or absolute Spirit. There is no objective that can be posited as an object (already real). Conversely, there is no preexisting impossibility associated with a planned goal, for an objective that is rationally claimed to be the meaning of action and becoming. No synthesis can be accomplished in advance.[57]

Obviously, even Lefebvre admits this cycle of complexification is real, and the urban revolution's unceasing colonization of Nature is investing natural and industrial systems with even greater complexity. Nonetheless, flawed finalistic models of such complexity cannot reveal any definite goals or final objectives with completely secure meaning for either action or reflection.

Conclusions

The imaginary of biocomplexity must be questioned severely at this juncture. Viewed as Life's place in the Cosmos, and considered as sites where the forces of technoscientific production are in constant contention with resistances of everyday life, the Earth – or the spatiality of terrestrial ecologies in this life-sustaining planet – continues to unfold through 'world watching' with all of its known and unknown qualities.[58] As De Certeau concedes, place remains little more than a palimpsest:

> Scientific analysis knows only its most recent text; and even then the latter is for science no more that the result of its epistemological decisions, its criteria and its goals. Why should it then be surprising that operations conceived in relation to this reconstitution have a 'fictive' character and owe their (provisional?) success less to their perspicacity than to their power of breaking down the complexion of these interrelations between disparate forces and times?[59]

The project of global biocomplexity therefore clearly marks the latest efforts to expand 'the empire of the evident in functionalist technocracy',[60] as this overview has sought to demonstrate with regard to Earth System

Science's reimagination of planetary places, processes, and practices at the interface of industrial and biophysical ecologies.

In fact, ideas such as 'a Second Copernican Revolution', 'a Global subject', or 'the Human Superorganism' surfacing in the world's environment do little more than empower global biocomplexity modellers to express the rationalist technics at the heart of planetary management. The spatiality of the Earth is granted attributes which no longer support:

> the inferences that create opacity and ambiguity in planning projects or reductions to two dimensions. It has its own mode of operation, that of *legibility* and *distinguishing* between functions, on the page where it can *write* them side by side, one after the other, in such a way as to be able to transfer this image onto the ground or onto the facade of cities or in machines.[61]

Biocomplexity models tangle with chaotic, turbulent or complex processes via the enlargements, focalizations and reliefs of instrumentalist operations of market exchange. The planetarian projects rising from this, and several other 'big science' undertakings share a common aim: allowing all the biochemical, geophysical and sociopolitical processes of the Earth's many intertwined ecologies now 'to be a readable artifact, an object open from end to end to the survey of an immobile eye'.[62]

More critical analyses, such as the one being undertaken here, must question the artefactualization of an entire planet through scientific analysis. There is far too much pretence implied by presuming the Earth's ecologies can be made essentially legible. In turn, even more arrogance manifests itself in scientists backing a regulatory regime based upon this shaky science. The everyday realities of globalization plainly have been pushing a planetarian project forward since the late 1960s or early 1970s. That these everyday realities bring an impulse to recast regularities in ecological and economic interaction as stable terrestrial functions with real, or apparent, mechanisms to be controlled as 'natural' forces and resources gets forgotten in the everyday practices of planetarian strategies. Nonetheless, spatiality here both imposes transnational technology's capacities and exposes national science's limits. Planetarian engineers intent upon the infrastructuralization of the environment obviously do not, or even cannot, 'perceive the fictive character instituted in an order by its relationship to everyday reality. But they must *not* acknowledge this relationship. It would be a sort of *lèse majesté* to talk ironically about this subject in offices, and the guilty person would be cashiered.'[63]

Notes

1 T. W. Luke, 'Environmentality as Green Governmentality', in E. Darrier (ed.), *Discourses of the Environment* (Oxford: Basil Blackwell, 1999).
2 T. W. Luke, 'Identity, Meaning and Globalization: Space-Time Compression and the Political Economy of Everyday Life', in S. Lash, P. Heelas and P. Morris (eds), *Detraditionalization: Critical Reflections on Authority and Identity* (Oxford: Basil Blackwell, 1996), pp. 109–33; T. W. Luke, 'Worldwatching at the Limits to Growth', *Capitalism Nature Socialism*, 5 (1994), pp. 43–64.
3 U. Beck, *What is Globalization*? (Malden, MA: Polity Press, 2000), p. 11.
4 Ibid., p. 10.
5 Ibid., p. 9.
6 Ibid., p. 13.
7 Luke, 'Identity, Meaning and Globalization'.
8 Luke, 'Environmentality as Green Governmentality'.
9 United Nations Environmental Program (UNEP), *Global Environmental Outlook* (London: Earthscan, 2000).
10 National Science Foundation, *Biocomplexity in the Environment (BE): Integrated Research and Education in Environmental Systems: Program Solicitation NSF 03-597* (Washington, DC: National Science Foundation, 2003), online at http://www.nsf.gov/pubs/2003/nsf03597/nsf03597.htm#cnh; National Science Foundation, *Complex Environmental Systems: Synthesis for Earth, Life, and Society in the 21st Century: A 10-Year Outlook for the National Science Foundation* (Washington, DC: National Science Foundation, 2003), online at http://www.nsf.gov/ere; National Science Foundation, *Environmental Research and Education: Funding Opportunities: Biocomplexity in the Environment* (Washington, DC: National Science Foundation, 2003), online at http://www.nsf.gov/geo/ere/ere-web/fund-biocomplex.cfm; UNEP, *Global Environmental Outlook*; WCRP, *World Climate Research Program* (2001), online at http://www.wmo.ch/web/wcrp/about.htm.
11 C. Bright *et al.*, *State of the World: 2003* (Washington, DC: Worldwatch Institute, 2003); UNEP, *Global Environmental Outlook*.
12 IHDP, *International Human Dimensions Programme on Global Environmental Change: Annual Report 2000* (Bonn: IHDP Secretariat, 2001), online at http://www.uni-bonn.de/ihdp; IPCC, *Climate Change 2001: The Scientific Basis; Contribution of Working Group I to the Third Assessment Report of the IPCC* (Cambridge: Cambridge University Press, 2001); IPCC, *Climate Change 2001: Impacts, Adaptation and Vulnerability; Contribution of Working Group II to the IPCC Third Assessment Report* (Cambridge: Cambridge University Press, 2001); WCRP, *World Climate Research Program*.
13 Luke, 'Identity, Meaning and Globalization'.
14 D. Dickson, *The New Politics of Science* (New York: Pantheon, 1984), pp. 11–15.
15 S. Jasanoff, *The Fifth Branch: Science Advisers as Policymakers* (Cambridge, MA: Harvard University Press, 1990).
16 NSF, *Cross Cutting Investment Strategies: NSF Priority Areas* (2003), online at http://www.nsf.gov/od/lpa/news/publicat/nsf03009/cross/priority.htm.
17 Ibid.
18 Ibid.
19 Luke, 'Environmentality as Green Governmentality'.
20 NSF, *Cross Cutting Investment Strategies: NSF Priority Areas*.

21 J. C. Briden and T. E. Downing, *Managing the Earth: The Lineacre Lectures 2001* (Oxford: Oxford University Press, 2002), p. 2
22 Ibid.
23 FCCC, *United Nations Framework on Climate Change* (Bonn: FCCC Secretariat, 1995); FCCC, *United Nations Framework on Climate* (Bonn: FCCC Secretariat, 1992); IHDP, *International Human Dimensions Programme on Global Environmental Change: Annual Report 2000*; IPCC, *Climate Change 2001: The Scientific Basis*; IPCC, *Climate Change 2001: Impacts, Adaptation and Vulnerability*; UNEP, *Global Environmental Outlook*; WCRP, *World Climate Research Program*; WBGU, *WissenschafftLicher Beirat Der Bundesregierung Globale Unweltveränderungen, 'Szenario zur Ableitung Globaler CO_2-Reduktionsziele und Umsetzsstrategium'* (Bremerhaven: WBGU, 1995); UNDP, *Human Development Report 1996* (Oxford: Oxford University Press, 1996).
24 H.-J. Schellnhuber and H. Held, 'How Fragile is the Earth System?', in J. C. Briden and T. E. Downing (eds), *Managing the Earth*, p. 7.
25 J. E. Lovelock, *The Ages of Gaia: A Biography of our Living Earth* (Oxford: Oxford University Press, 1995).
26 V. Petoukhov *et al.*, 'Cuimber-2: A Climate System Model of Intermediate Complexity: Part I: Model Description and Performance for Present Climate', *Climate Dynamics*, 16 (2000), 1–17.
27 H.-J. Schellnhuber, '"Earth System" Analysis and the Second Coperican Revolution', *Nature*, 402 (1999) suppl. C19–C23; H.-J. Schellnhuber, 'Discourse: Earth System Analysis – the Concept', in H.-J. Schellnhuber and V. Wenzel (eds), *Earth System Analysis* (Berlin: Springer, 1998).
28 J. N. Thompson *et al.*, 'Frontiers of Ecology', *Bioscience*, 51 (2001), 15–24; J. N. Thompson *et al.*, *Frontier of Ecology: Results of a Workshop held at NSF on December 6–8, 1999; Final Report: December 22* (1999), online at http://ibrcs.aibs.org/reports/pdf/Frontiers.pdf.
29 M. F. Acevedo *et al.*, 'NSF Award no. 0216722: Integrating Models of Natural and Human Dynamics in Forest Landscapes Across Scales and Cultures', *National Science Foundation BE/CNH Biocomplexity* (Washington, DC: National Science Foundation, 2002), online at http://www.fastlane.nsf.gov/serv/eet/showaward?award + 0216722.
30 Luke, 'Environmentality as Green Governmentality'.
31 M. De Certeau, *The Practice of Everyday Life* (Berkeley, CA: University of California Press, 1988), p. 117.
32 H. Lefebvre, *The Urban Revolution* (Minneapolis, MN: University of Minnesota Press, 2003), pp. 1–22.
33 De Certeau, *The Practice of Everyday Life*, p. 117.
34 Lefebvre, *The Urban Revolution*, p. 29.
35 Ibid., p. 32.
36 F. Dodds and T. Middleton, *Earth Summit 2002: A New Deal* (London: Earthscan, 2000).
37 Lefebvre, *The Urban Revolution*, p. 17.
38 Ibid.
39 T. W. Luke, *Ecocritique: Contesting the Politics of Nature, Economy and Culture* (Minneapolis, MN: University of Minnesota Press, 1997).
40 Lefebvre, *The Urban Revolution*, pp. 56–7.
41 Luke, 'Environmentality as Green Governmentality'.

42 Lefebvre, *The Urban Revolution*, p. 73.
43 Ibid., pp. 73–4.
44 Luke, 'Environmentality as Green Governmentality'
45 Schellnhuber and Held, 'How Fragile is the Earth System?', p. 5.
46 Ibid., pp. 6–7.
47 Ibid., p. 7.
48 Ibid.
49 Ibid.
50 Schellnhuber, 'Discourse: Earth System Analysis – the Concept'.
51 A. Jolly, 'The Fifth Step', *New Scientist*, 164 (1999), 78–9.
52 H. Nowotny, P. Scott and M. Gibbons, *Re-Thinking Science: Knowledge and the Public in an Age of Uncertainty* (Cambridge: Polity Press, 2001).
53 Schellnhuber and Held, 'How Fragile is the Earth System?', pp. 15–16.
54 Ibid., p. 29.
55 Lefebvre, *The Urban Revolution*, p. 66.
56 Luke, 'Identity, Meaning and Globalization'.
57 Lefebvre, *The Urban Revolution*, p. 67.
58 T. W. Luke, 'Worldwatching at the Limits to Growth', *Capitalism Nature Socialism*, 5 (1994), 43–64.
59 De Certeau, *The Practice of Everyday Life*, p. 202.
60 Ibid., p. 203.
61 Ibid., p. 199.
62 Ibid.
63 Ibid., p. 200.

11
Globalization, Terrorism and Democracy: 9/11 and its Aftermath

Douglas Kellner

Globalization has been one of the most hotly contested phenomena of the past two decades.[1] It has been a primary attractor of books, articles and heated debate, just as postmodernism was the most fashionable and debated topic of the 1980s. A wide and diverse range of social theorists have argued that today's world is organized by accelerating globalization, which is strengthening the dominance of a world capitalist economic system, supplanting the primacy of the nation-state by transnational corporations and organizations, and eroding local cultures and traditions through a global culture. Contemporary theorists from a wide range of political and theoretical positions are converging on the position that globalization is a distinguishing trend of the present moment, but there are hot debates concerning its nature, effects and future.[2]

For its defenders, globalization marks the triumph of capitalism and its market economy,[3] while its critics portray globalization as negative.[4] Some theorists see the emergence of a new transnational ruling elite and the universalization of consumerism,[5] while others stress global fragmentation and 'the clash of civilizations'.[6] Driving 'post' discourses into novel realms of theory and politics, Hardt and Negri present the emergence of 'Empire' as producing evolving forms of sovereignty, economy, culture and political struggle that unleash an unforeseeable and unpredictable flow of novelties, surprises and upheavals.[7]

Discourses of globalization initially were polarized into pro or con celebrations or attacks. For critics, it provides a cover concept for global capitalism and imperialism, and is accordingly condemned as an ideological cover for the imposition of the logic of capital and the market on ever more regions of the world and spheres of life. For defenders, it is the continuation of modernization and a force of progress, increased wealth, freedom, democracy and happiness. Its champions present globalization as beneficial, generating fresh economic opportunities, political democratization, cultural diversity and the opening to an exciting new world. Its detractors see globalization as harmful, bringing about increased domination and control by the wealthier overdeveloped nations over the poor underdeveloped countries, thus increasing the hegemony of the 'haves' over the 'have nots'. In addition, supplementing the negative view, globalization critics assert that globalization produces an undermining of democracy, a cultural homogenization, and increased destruction of natural species and the environment.[8] Further, some imagine the globalization project – whether viewed positively or negatively – as inevitable and beyond human control and intervention, whereas others view globalization as generating new conflicts and new spaces for struggle, distinguishing between globalization from above and globalization from below.[9]

I wish to sketch aspects of a critical theory of globalization that will discuss the fundamental transformations in the world economy, politics and culture in a dialectical framework that distinguishes between progressive and emancipatory features and oppressive and negative attributes. This requires articulations of the contradictions and ambiguities of globalization and the ways that globalization is both imposed from above and yet can be contested and reconfigured from below in ways that promote democracy and social justice. I argue that the key to understanding globalization critically is theorizing it at once as a product of technological revolution and the global restructuring of capitalism in which economic, technological, political and cultural features are intertwined. From this perspective, one should avoid both technological and economic determinism and all one-sided optics of globalization in favour of a view that theorizes globalization as a highly complex, contradictory and thus ambiguous set of institutions and social relations, as well as involving flows of goods, services, ideas, technologies, cultural forms and people.[10] To illustrate my approach, I argue that the 9/11 terrorist attacks and the subsequent wars in Afghanistan and Iraq, as part of the ensuing Terror War, put on display contradictions and ambiguities embedded in globalization that demand critical and dialectical perspectives to clarify and illuminate these events and globalization itself.[11]

9/11 and globalization

The 9/11 terrorist attacks and Bush administration's subsequent military response have dramatized once again the centrality of globalization in contemporary experience and the need for adequate conceptualizations and responses to it. The 9/11 terrorist acts against the USA dramatically disclose the downside of globalization, and the ways that global flows of technology, goods, information, ideologies and people can have destructive as well as productive effects. The disclosure of powerful anti-Western terrorist networks shows that globalization divides the world just as it unifies, that it produces enemies as it incorporates participants. The events reveal explosive contradictions and conflicts at the heart of globalization and that the technologies of information, communication and transportation which facilitate globalization can also be used to undermine and attack it, and generate instruments of destruction as well as production.

The experience of 9/11 points to the objective ambiguity of globalization, showing that positive and negative sides are interconnected, and that the institutions of open society unlock the possibilities of destruction and violence, as well as democracy, free trade and cultural and social exchange. Once again, the interconnection and interdependency of the networked world was dramatically demonstrated as terrorists from the Middle East brought local grievances from their region to attack key symbols of American power and the very infrastructure of New York. Some saw terrorism as an expression of 'the dark side of globalization', while I would conceive it as part of the objective ambiguity of globalization that simultaneously creates friends and enemies, wealth and poverty, and growing divisions between the 'haves' and 'have nots'. Yet the downturn in the global economy, intensification of local and global political conflicts, the repression of human rights and civil liberties and the general increase in fear and anxiety have certainly undermined the naïve optimism of globophiles who perceived globalization as a purely positive instrument of progress and well-being.[12]

The use by terrorists of powerful technologies as weapons of destruction also disclosed current asymmetries of power and emergent forms of terrorism and war, as the new millennium exploded into dangerous conflicts and military interventions. As technologies of mass destruction become more available and dispersed, perilous instabilities have emerged that have elicited policing measures to stem the flow of movements of people and goods across borders and internally. In particular, the USA Patriot Act has led to repressive measures that are replacing the spaces of the open and free information society with new forms of surveillance, policing and restrictions of civil liberties, thus significantly undermining US democracy.[13]

The spectacular 9/11 events have led to new reflections on globalization and the contemporary era. Jean Baudrillard, for instance, had long complained that the contemporary era was one of weak events, that no major historical occurrences had happened, and that therefore life and thought were becoming increasingly boring. Yet the 9/11 terror attacks on New York and Washington and subsequent military responses by the Bush administration in Afghanistan and Iraq were obviously strong events that elicited wide-ranging responses. Baudrillard had often written on terrorism, was beginning to reflect on globalization, and produced one of the more controversial books on the 9/11 events, *The Spirit of Terrorism and Requiem for the Twin Towers*.[14] For Baudrillard, the 9/11 attacks represent a new kind of terrorism, exhibiting a 'form of action which plays the game, and lays hold of the rules of the game, solely with the aim of disrupting it . . . they have taken over all the weapons of the dominant power'. That is, the terrorists used aircrafts, computer networks and the media associated with Western societies to produce a spectacle of terror to frighten US citizens, disrupt the stock market and New York and Washington, and recruit followers of Islamic Jihad.

Baudrillard conceded that 9/11 constituted 'the absolute event, the mother of all events, the pure event uniting within itself all the events that have never taken place'. Baudrillard perceives that the terrorists hope that the system will overreact in response to the multiple challenges of terrorism: 'It is the terrorist model to bring about an excess of reality, and have the system collapse beneath that excess.' The Bush administration, of course, responded with an excess of unilateral militarism in Afghanistan and Iraq, and has made a war against terrorism the fundament of its domestic and foreign policy, and infamously declared that 'you are with us or against us', in effect saying that anyone who did not support Bush's war on terrorism was aiding and abetting terrorism.

Baudrillard himself was accused of justifying terrorism when he stated in an article in the French newspaper *Le Monde*:

> Because with its unbearable power, it has fomented this violence pervading the world, along with the terrorist imagination that inhabits all of us, without our knowing. That we dreamed of this event, that everyone without exception dreamed of it, because no one can fail to dream of the destruction of any power become so hegemonic – that is unacceptable for the Western moral conscience. And yet it's a fact, which can be measured by the pathetic violence of all the discourses that want to cover it up. To put it in the most extreme terms, they did it, but we wanted it.[15]

Baudrillard defended himself claiming:

> I do not praise murderous attacks – that would be idiotic. Terrorism is not a contemporary form of revolution against oppression and capitalism. No ideology, no struggle for an objective, not even Islamic fundamentalism, can explain it ... I have glorified nothing, accused nobody, justified nothing. One should not confuse the messenger with his message. I have endeavored to analyze the process through which the unbounded expansion of globalization creates the conditions for its own destruction.[16]

Baudrillard has also produced some interesting reflections on globalization. In 'The Violence of the Global', he distinguishes between the global and the universal, linking globalization with technology, the market, tourism and information, and equating the universal with 'human rights, liberty, culture, and democracy'.[17] While 'globalization appears to be irreversible ... universalization is likely to be on its way out'. Elsewhere, Baudrillard writes:

> the idea of freedom, a new and recent idea, is already fading from the minds and mores, and liberal globalization is coming about in precisely the opposite form – a police-state globalization, a total control, a terror based on 'law-and-order' measures. Deregulation ends up in a maximum of constraints and restrictions, akin to those of a fundamentalist society.[18]

Most theorists, including myself, see globalization as a matrix of market economy, democracy, technology, migration and tourism, and the worldwide circulation of ideas and culture.[19] Baudrillard, who has become increasingly apolitical over the years and anti-Leftist, curiously, takes the position of those in the anti-corporate globalization movement who condemn globalization as the opposite of democracy and human rights. For Baudrillard, globalization is completely a process of homogenization and standardization that crushes 'the singular' and heterogeneity. This position, however, fails to note the process of hybridization linked with globalization and that the anti-corporate globalization movement is fighting for social justice, democratization and increased rights, factors that Baudrillard links with a dying universalization. In fact, the struggle for rights and justice is an important part of the ever-expanding anti-corporate globalization movement and Baudrillard's cavalier dismissal of rights, democratization and justice as part of an obsolete universalization being erased by globalization is theoretically and politically problematical.

Ultimately, however, the abhorrent terror acts by the bin Laden network and the violent military response by the Bush administration may be an anomalous paroxysm whereby a highly regressive premodern Islamic fundamentalism has clashed with an old-fashioned patriarchal and unilateralist Wild West militarism. It could be that such forms of terrorism, militarism and state repression will be superseded by more rational forms of politics that globalize and criminalize terrorism, and that do not sacrifice the benefits of the open society and economy in the name of security. Yet the events of 9/11 may open a new era of Terror War that will lead to the kind of apocalyptic futurist world depicted by cyberpunk fiction.[20]

In any case, the events of 9/11 have promoted a fury of reflection, theoretical debates, and political conflicts and upheaval that put the complex dynamics of globalization at the centre of contemporary theory and politics. To those sceptical of the centrality of globalization to contemporary experience, it is now clear that we are living in a global world that is highly interconnected and vulnerable to passions and crises that can cross borders and can affect anyone or any region at any time. The events of 11 September 2001 and their aftermath also provide a test case to evaluate various theories of globalization in the contemporary era. In addition, they highlight some of the contradictions of globalization and the need to develop a highly complex and dialectical model to capture its conflicts, ambiguities, and contradictory effects.

Consequently, I argue that in order to properly theorize globalization one needs to conceptualize several sets of contradictions generated by globalization's combination of technological revolution and restructuring of capital, which in turn generate tensions between capitalism and democracy, and 'haves' and 'have nots'. Within the world economy, globalization involves the proliferation of the logic of capital, but also the spread of democracy in information, finance, investing and the diffusion of technology.[21] Globalization is thus a contradictory amalgam of capitalism and democracy, in which the logic of capital and the market system enter ever more arenas of global life, even as democracy spreads and more political regions and spaces of everyday life are being contested by democratic demands and forces. But the overall process is contradictory. Sometimes globalizing forces promote democracy and sometimes they inhibit it, so that either equating capitalism and democracy, or simply opposing them, are problematical.

The processes of globalization are highly turbulent and have generated new conflicts throughout the world. Benjamin Barber describes the strife between McWorld and Jihad, contrasting the homogenizing, commercialized, Americanized tendencies of the global economy and culture with anti-modernizing Jihadist movements that affirm traditional cultures and are resistant to aspects of neoliberal globalization.[22] Thomas Friedman makes a more benign distinction between what he calls the 'Lexus' and the 'Olive Tree'.[23] The former is a symbol of modernization, of affluence and luxury, and of Westernized consumption, contrasted with the olive tree which is a symbol of roots, tradition, place and stable community. Barber, however, is too negative towards McWorld and Jihad, failing to adequately describe the democratic and progressive forces within both. Although Barber recognizes a dialectic of McWorld and Jihad, he opposes both to democracy, failing to perceive how they generate their own democratic forces and tendencies, as well as opposing and undermining democratization. Within Western democracies, for instance, there is not just top-down homogenization and corporate domination, but also globalization-from-below and oppositional social movements that desire alternatives to capitalist globalization. Thus it is not only traditionalist, non-Western forces of Jihad that oppose McWorld: likewise, Jihad has its democratizing forces as well as the reactionary Islamic fundamentalists who are now the most demonized elements of the contemporary era, as I discuss below. Jihad, like McWorld, has its contradictions and its potential for democratization, as well as elements of domination and destruction.[24]

Friedman, by contrast, is too uncritical of globalization, caught up in his own Lexus high-consumption lifestyle and failing to perceive the depth of the oppressive features of globalization and breadth and extent of resistance and opposition to it. In particular, he fails to articulate the contradictions between capitalism and democracy, and the ways that globalization and its economic logic undermine democracy as well as encourage it. Likewise, he does not grasp the virulence of the premodern and Jihadist tendencies that he blithely identifies with the olive tree, and the reasons why globalization and the West are so strongly resisted in many parts of the world. Hence it is important to present globalization as a strange amalgam of both homogenizing forces of sameness and uniformity, *and* heterogeneity, difference and hybridity, as well as a contradictory mixture of democratizing and anti-democratizing tendencies. On one hand, globalization unfolds a process of standardization in which a globalized mass culture circulates the globe creating sameness and homogeneity everywhere; but globalized culture also makes possible unique appropriations and developments all over the world, thus proliferating hybrids, difference and heterogeneity.[25] Every local context involves its own appropriation and reworking of global products and signifiers, thus proliferating difference, otherness, diversity and variety.[26] Grasping the fact that globalization embodies these contradictory tendencies at once, that it can be both a force of homogenization and heterogeneity, is crucial to articulating the contradictions of globalization and avoiding one-sided and reductive conceptions.

My intention is to present globalization as conflictual, contradictory and open to resistance and democratic intervention and transformation and not just as a monolithic juggernaut of progress or domination as in many other discourses. This goal is advanced by distinguishing between 'globalization from below' and 'globalization from above' of corporate capitalism and the capitalist state, a distinction that should help us to get a better sense of how globalization does or does not promote democratization. 'Globalization from below' refers to the ways in which marginalized individuals and social movements and critical pedagogues resist globalization and/or use its institutions and instruments to further democratization and social justice.

Yet one needs to avoid binary normative articulations, since globalization from below can have highly conservative and destructive effects, as well as positive ones, while globalization from above can help produce global solutions to problems such as terrorism or the environment. Moreover, on one hand, as Michael Peters argues, globalization itself is a kind of war and much militarism has been expansive and globalizing in many historical situations.[27] Yet, on the other hand, anti-war and peace movements are also increasingly global, and hence all forms of globalization are marked by tensions and contradictions.

Thus, while on one level globalization significantly increases the supremacy of big corporations and big government, it can also give power to groups and individuals that were previously left out of the democratic dialogue and terrain of political struggle. Such potentially positive effects of globalization include increased access to education for individuals excluded from sharing culture and knowledge, the possibility of oppositional individuals and groups participating in global culture and politics through gaining access to global communication and media networks, and the opportunity to circulate local struggles and oppositional ideas through these media. The role of information technologies in social movements, political struggle and everyday life forces social movements and critical theorists to reconsider their political strategies and goals and democratic theory to appraise how new technologies do and do not promote democratization.[28]

In their book *Empire*, Hardt and Negri present contradictions within globalization in terms of an imperializing logic of 'Empire' and an assortment of struggles by the multitude, creating a contradictory and tense situation.[29] As in my conception, Hardt and Negri present globalization as a complex process which involves a multidimensional mixture of expansions of the global economy and capitalist market system, information technologies and media, expanded judicial and legal modes of governance, and emergent modes of power, sovereignty and resistance.[30] Combining poststructuralism with 'autonomous Marxism', Hardt and Negri stress political openings and possibilities of struggle within Empire in an optimistic and buoyant text that envisages progressive democratization and self-valorization in the turbulent process of the restructuring of capital.

Many theorists, by contrast, have argued that one of the trends of globalization is depoliticization of publics, the decline of the nation-state, and the end of traditional politics.[31] While I would agree that globalization is promoted by tremendously powerful economic forces and that it often undermines democratic movements and decision-making, one should also note that there are openings and possibilities for both a globalization from below that inflects globalization for positive and progressive ends, and that globalization can thus help promote as well as destabilize democracy.[32] Globalization involves both a disorganization and reorganization of capitalism, a tremendous restructuring process, which creates openings for progressive social change and intervention as well as highly destructive transformative effects. On the positive ledger, in a more fluid and open economic and political system, oppositional forces can gain concessions, win victories and effect progressive changes. During the 1970s, new social movements, new NGOs and new forms of struggle and solidarity emerged that have been expanding to the present day.[33]

However, it was not only the anti-corporate globalization of the 1990s that emerged as a form of globalization from below, as al-Qaeda and various global terror networks also intensified their attacks and helped generate an era of Terror War. This made it difficult simply to affirm globalization from below while denigrating globalization from above, as clearly terrorism was an emergent and dangerous form of globalization from below that was a threat to peace, security and democracy. Moreover, in the face of Bush administration unilateralism and militarism, multilateral approaches to the problems of terrorism called for global responses and alliances to a wide range of global problems,[34] thus demanding a progressive and cosmopolitan globalization to deal with contemporary challenges.

Moreover, the present conjuncture is marked by a conflict between growing centralization and organization of power and wealth in the hands of the few contrasted with opposing processes exhibiting a fragmentation of power that is more plural, multiple and open to contestation. Both tendencies are observable and it is up to individuals and groups to find openings for progressive political intervention, social transformation and the democratization of education that pursue positive values such as democracy, human rights, literacy, equality, ecological preservation and restoration, and social justice, while fighting poverty, ignorance, terror and injustice. Thus, rather than just denouncing globalization, or engaging in celebration and legitimation, a critical theory of globalization reproaches those aspects that are oppressive, while seizing upon opportunities to fight domination and exploitation and to promote democratization, justice, and a forward looking reconstruction of the polity, society and culture.

Against capitalist globalization from above, there has been a significant eruption of forces and subcultures of resistance that have attempted to preserve specific forms of culture and society against globalization and homogenization, and to create alternative forces of society and culture, thus exhibiting resistance and globalization from below. Most dramatically, peasant and guerrilla movements in Latin America, labour unions, students, and environmentalists throughout the world, and a variety of other groups and movements have resisted capitalist globalization and attacks on previous rights and benefits.[35] Several dozen people's organizations from around the world have protested against World Trade Organization policies and a backlash against globalization is visible everywhere. Politicians who once championed trade agreements such as the General Agreement on Tariffs and Trade (GATT) and NAFTA are now often quiet about these arrangements. As early as 1996 at the annual Davos World Economic Forum, its founder and managing director published a warning entitled: 'Start Taking the Backlash Against Globalization Seriously'. Reports surfaced that major representatives of the capitalist system expressed fear that capitalism was getting too mean and predatory, that it needs a kinder and gentler state to ensure order and harmony, and that the welfare state may make a comeback.[36] One should take such reports with the proverbial grain of salt, but they express fissures and openings in the system for critical discourse and intervention.

Indeed, by 1999, the theme of the annual Davos conference was making globalization work for poor countries and minimizing the differences between the 'haves' and 'have nots'. The growing divisions between rich and poor were worrying some globalizers, as were the wave of crises in Asian, Latin American, and other 'developing countries'. In James Flanigan's report in the *Los Angeles Times*, the 'main theme' is to 'spread the wealth. In a world frightened by glaring imbalances and the weakness of economies from Indonesia to Russia, the talk is no longer of a new world economy getting stronger but of ways to "keep the engine going".'[37] In particular, the globalizers were attempting to keep economies growing in the more developed countries and capital flowing to developing nations. US Vice-President Al Gore called on all countries to spur economic growth, and he proposed a new US-led initiative to eliminate the debt burdens of developing countries. The South African President, Nelson Mandela, asked: 'Is globalization only for the powerful? Does it offer nothing to the men, women and children who are ravaged by the violence of poverty?'

As the new millennium opened, there was no clear answer to Mandela's question. In the 2000s, there have been ritual proclamations of the need to make globalization work for the developing nations at all major meetings of global institutions such as the WTO or G-8 convenings. For instance, at the September 2003 WTO meeting at Cancun, organizers claimed that its goal was to fashion a new trade agreement that would reduce poverty and boost development in poorer nations. But critics pointed out that in the past years the richer nations of the USA, Japan and Europe continued to enforce trade tariffs and provide subsidies for national producers of goods such as agriculture, while forcing poorer nations to open their markets to 'free trade', thus bankrupting agricultural sectors in these countries that could not compete. Significantly, the September 2003 WTO trade talks in Cancun collapsed as leaders of the developing world concurred with protesters and blocked expansion of a 'free trade zone' that would mainly benefit the USA and overdeveloped countries. Likewise, in Miami in November 2003 the 'Free Trade Summit' collapsed without an agreement as the police violently suppressed protesters.[38]

Moreover, major economists such as Joseph Stiglitz,[39] as well as anti-corporate globalization protesters and critics, argued that the developing countries were not adequately developing under current corporate globalization policies and that divisions between the rich and poor nations were growing. Under these conditions, critics of globalization were calling for radically new policies that would help the developing countries, regulate the rich and overdeveloped countries, and provide more power to working people and local groups.

Concluding comments

And so, to paraphrase Foucault, wherever there is globalization from above, globalization as the imposition of capitalist logic, there can be resistance and struggle. The possibilities of globalization from below result from transnational alliances between groups fighting for better wages and working conditions, social and political justice, environmental protection, and more democracy and freedom worldwide. In addition, a renewed emphasis on local and grass-roots movements has put dominant economic forces on the defensive in their own backyard. Often, the broadcasting media or the Internet have called attention to oppressive and destructive corporate policies on the local level, putting national and even transnational pressure upon major corporations for reform. Moreover, proliferating media and the Internet make possible a greater circulation of struggles and the possibilities of new alliances and solidarities that can connect resistant forces who oppose capitalist and corporate-state elite forms of globalization-from-above.[40]

Globalization should thus be seen as a contested terrain with opposing forces attempting to use its institutions, technologies, media and forms for their own purposes. A critical theory of globalization should be normative, specifying positive values and potentials of globalization such as human rights, rights for labour, women, children and oppressed groups; ecological protection and enhancement of the environment; and the promotion of democracy and social justice. Yet it should also critique negative aspects to globalization which strengthen elite economic and political forces over and against the underlying population, and specify in detail bad aspects of globalization such as destructive IMF policies, unfair policies within the WTO, and environmental, human rights and labour abuse throughout the world.

Consequently, a dialectic of globalization seeks both positive potential while criticizing negative and destructive aspects. Other beneficial openings include the opportunity for greater democratization, increased education and health care, and new opportunities within the global economy that open entry to members of races, regions and classes previously excluded from mainstream economics, politics and culture within the modern corporate order. In the light of the neoliberal projects to dismantle the Welfare State, colonize the public sphere and control globalization, it is up to citizens, activists and educators to create alternative public spheres, politics and pedagogies. In these spaces, which could include progressive classrooms, students and citizens could learn to use information and multimedia technologies to discuss what kinds of society people today want and to oppose the society against which people resist and struggle. This involves, minimally, demands for more education, health care, welfare and benefits from the state, and a struggle to create a more democratic and egalitarian society. But one cannot expect that generous corporations and a beneficent state are going to make available to citizens the bounties and benefits of the globalized information economy; rather, it is up to individuals and groups to promote democratization and progressive social change.

Thus, in opposition to the globalization of corporate and state capitalism, I would advocate an oppositional democratic, pedagogical and cosmopolitan globalization, which supports individuals and groups using information and multimedia technologies to create a more multicultural, egalitarian, democratic and ecological globalization. Of course, the new technologies might exacerbate existing inequalities in the current class, gender, race and regional configurations of power and give dominant corporate forces powerful tools to advance their interests. In this situation, it is up to people of good will to devise strategies to use emergent technologies to promote democratization and social justice on a planetary scale because, as the proliferating technologies become ever more central to everyday life, developing an oppositional technopolitics in alternative public spheres and pedagogical sites will become increasingly important. Changes in the economy, politics and social life demand a constant rethinking of politics and social change in the light of globalization and the technological revolution, requiring new thinking as a response to ever-changing historical conditions.

Notes

1 In this study, I draw upon previous studies of globalization in A. Cvetkovich and D. Kellner, *Articulating the Global and the Local: Globalization and Cultural Studies* (Boulder, CO: Westview, 1997); D. Kellner, 'Globalization and the Postmodern Turn', in R. Axtmann (ed.), *Globalization and Europe* (London: Cassells, 1998), pp. 23–42; D. Kellner, 'Theorizing Globalization', *Sociological Theory*, 20 (2002), pp. 285–305; S. Best and D. Kellner, *The Postmodern Adventure* (London and New York: Routledge and Guilford press, 2001); and D. Kellner, *From 9/11 to Terror War: Dangers of the Bush Legacy* (Lanham, MD: Rowman & Littlefield, 2003).

2 Attempts to chart the globalization of capital, decline of the nation-state, and rise of a new global culture include the essays in M. Featherstone (ed.), *Global Culture: Nationalism, Globalization and Modernity* (London: Sage, 1990); A. Giddens, *Consequences of Modernity* (Cambridge: Polity, 1990); M. Featherstone, S. Lash

and R. Robertson (eds), *Global Modernities* (London: Sage, 1995); B. Axford, *The Global System* (Cambridge: Polity, 1995); D. Held, *Democracy and the Global Order* (Cambridge: Polity, 1995); P. Hirst and G. Thompson, *Globalization in Question* (Cambridge: Polity, 1996); D. Held, A. McGrew, D. Goldblatt and J. Perraton, *Global Transformations* (Cambridge: Polity, 1999); M. Hardt and T. Negri, *Empire* (Cambridge, MA: Harvard University Press, 2000); M. Steger, *Globalism: The New Market Ideology* (Lanham, MD: Rowman & Littlefield, 2002); J. E. Stiglitz, *Globalization and its Discontents* (New York: Norton, 2002); and G. Ritzer, *The Globalization of Nothing* (Thousand Oaks, CA, and London: Pine Forge Press and Sage, 2004).

3 F. Fukuyama, *The End of History* (New York: Free Press, 1992); T. Friedman, *The Lexus and the Olive Tree* (New York: Farrar, Straus & Giroux, 1999).

4 J. Mander and E. Goldsmith, *The Case Against the Global Economy* (San Francisco, CA: Sierra Club Books, 1996); Z. Eisenstein, *Global Obscenities: Patriarchy, Capitalism, and the Lure of Cyberfantasy* (New York: New York University Press, 1998); K. Robins and F. Webster, *Times of the Technoculture* (London and New York: Routledge, 1999).

5 L. Sklair, *The Transnational Capitalist Class* (Oxford: Basil Blackwell, 2001).

6 S. Huntington, *The Clash of Civilizations and the Remaking of World Order* (New York: Touchstone Books, 1996).

7 Hardt and Negri, *Empire*. Advocates of a postmodern break in history argue that developments in transnational capitalism are producing a new global historical configuration of post-Fordism as an emergent cultural logic of capitalism. See D. Harvey, *The Condition of Postmodernity* (Oxford: Basil Blackwell, 1989); E. W. Soja, *Postmodern Geographies: The Reassertion of Space in Critical Social Theory* (New York: Verso, 1989); and F. Jameson, *Postmodernism, or the Cultural Logic of Late Capitalism* (Durham, NC: Duke University Press, 1991). Others define the emergent global economy and culture as a 'network society' grounded in new communications and information technology: see M. Castells, *The Information Age: The Rise of the Network Society* (Oxford: Basil Blackwell, 1996); M. Castells, *The Information Age: The Power of Identity* (Oxford: Basil Blackwell, 1997); M. Castells, *The Information Age: End of Millennium* (Oxford: Basil Blackwell, 1998).

8 What now appears at the first stage of academic and popular discourses of globalization in the 1990s tended to be dichotomized into celebratory globophilia and dismissive globophobia. There was also a tendency in some theorists to exaggerate the novelties of globalization and others to dismiss these claims by arguing that globalization has been going on for centuries and there is not that much that is new and different. For an excellent delineation and critique of academic discourses on globalization, see Steger, *Globalism*.

9 J. Brecher, T. Costello and B. Smith, *Globalization from Below* (Boston, MA: South End Press, 2000).

10 A. Appadurai, *Modernity at Large* (Minneapolis, MN: University of Minnesota Press, 1996).

11 By 'Terror War', I refer to the Bush administration's 'war against terrorism' and its doctrine of pre-emptive and unilateral strike against any state or organization presumed to harbour or support terrorism, or to eliminate 'weapons of mass destruction' that could be used against the USA. The Right

wing of the Bush administration seeks to promote a war on Terror as the defining struggle of the era, coded as an apocalyptic battle between good and evil. See Kellner, *From 9/11 to Terror War*, and D. Kellner, 'Postmodern Military and Permanent War', in C. Boggs (ed.), *Masters of War: Militarism and Blowback in the Era of the American Empire* (New York and London: Routledge, 2003), pp. 229–44.

12 See, for example, C. Johnson, *The Sorrows of Empire: Militarism, Secrecy, and the End of the Republic* (New York: Metropolitan Books, 2004).

13 See Kellner, *From 9/11 to Terror War*.

14 J. Baudrillard, *The Spirit of Terrorism and Requiem for the Twin Towers* (London: Verso, 2002).

15 J. Baudrillard, citied in Mark Goldblatt, 'French Toast: America wanted Sept. 11' (2001), online at http://www.nationalreview.com/comment/comment-goldblatt121301.shtml.

16 J. Baudrillard, 'This is the Fourth World War', an interview with *Der Spiegel* (2002), online at http://www.ubishops.ca/baudrillardstudies/spiegel.htm.

17 J. Baudrillard, 'La violence du Mondial', in *Power Inferno* (Paris: Galilee, 2002), pp. 63–83. Available online at http://www.ctheory.net/text_file.asp?pick=385.

18 Baudrillard, *The Spirit of Terrorism and Requiem for the Twin Towers*, p. 32.

19 Kellner, 'Theorizing Globalization'.

20 Kellner, *From 9/11 to Terror War*.

21 See Friedman, *The Lexus and the Olive Tree*, and Hardt and Negri, *Empire*.

22 B. R. Barber, *Jihad vs. McWorld* (New York: Ballatine Books, 1995).

23 Friedman, *The Lexus and the Olive Tree*.

24 B. R. Barber's recent *Fear's Empire: War, Terrorism, and Democracy* (New York: Norton, 2004) sharply criticizes the Bush administration policy of 'pre-emptive strikes' and 'preventive wars' as unilateralist militarism, destructive of international law, treaties, alliances, and the multilateral approach necessary to deal with global problems such as terrorism, a critique that I would agree with; see D. Kellner, *Media Spectacle* (London and New York: Routledge, 2003). I also am in accord with Barber's position that both bin Laden's terrorism and Bush's militarism promote a politics of fear that is not helpful to building a strong democracy. Hence, while I find Barber's general categorical explication of globalization problematically dualistic and his categories of McWorld and Jihad too homogenizing and totalizing, I am in general agreement with his criticism of Bush administration policy.

25 For example, as G. Ritzer argues, McDonald's imposes not only a similar cuisine all over the world, but circulates processes of what he calls 'McDonaldization' that involve a production/consumption model of efficiency, technological rationality, calculability, predictability, and control. See *The McDonaldization of Society: An Investigation into the Changing Character of Contemporary Social Life* (Thousand Oaks, CA: Pine Forge Press, 1996). Yet, as J. L. Watson *et al.* argue in *Gelen Arches East: McDonald's in East Asia* (Stanford, CA: Stanford University Press, 1997), McDonald's has various cultural meanings in diverse local contexts, as well as different products, organization and effects. But the latter goes too far towards stressing heterogeneity, downplaying the cultural power of McDonald's as a force of a homogenizing globalization and Western corporate logic and system; see D. Kellner 'Globalization From Below? Toward a Radical Democratic Technopolitics', *Angelaki*, 4 (1999), 101–13, and *Media Spectacle*.

26 A. Luke and C. Luke, 'A Situated Perspective on Cultural Globalization', in N. Burbules and C. Torres (eds), *Globalization and Education* (London and New York: Routledge, 2000), pp. 275–98.
27 M. A. Peters, 'War as Globalization: The "Education" of the Iraqi People', in M. A. Peters (ed.), *Education, Globalization and the State in the Age of Terror* (Boulder, CO: Paradigm Press, 2004).
28 D. Kellner, 'Intellectuals and New Technologies', *Media, Culture and Society*, 17 (1995), 201–17; D. Kellner, 'Intellectuals, the New Public Spheres, and Technopolitics', *New Political Science*, 41–2 (1997), 169–88; Kellner, 'Globalization From Below? Toward a Radical Democratic Technopolitics'; Best and Kellner, *The Postmodern Adventure*.
29 Hardt and Negri, *Empire*.
30 While I find *Empire* an impressive and productive text, I am not sure, however, what is gained by using the word 'Empire' rather than the concepts of global capital and political economy. While Hardt and Negri combine categories of Marxism and critical social theory with poststructuralist discourse derived from Foucault and Deleuze and Guattari, they frequently favour the latter, often mystifying and obscuring the object of analysis. I am also not as confident as Hardt and Negri that the 'multitude' replaces traditional concepts of the working class and other modern political subjects, movements and actors, and find the emphasis on nomads, 'New Barbarians' and the poor as replacement categories problematical. Neither am I clear on exactly what forms their poststructuralist politics would take. The same problem is evident, I believe, in an earlier decade's provocative and post-Marxist text by E. Laclau and C. Mouffe, *Hegemony and Socialist Strategy: Towards a Radical Democratic Politics* (London: Verso, 1985); the authors valorize new social movements, radical democracy and a postsocialist politics without providing many concrete examples or proposals for struggle in the present conjuncture.
31 C. Boggs, *The End of Politics* (New York: Guilford Press, 2000).
32 I am thus trying to mediate in this chapter between those who claim that globalization simply undermines democracy and those who claim that globalization promotes democratization like Friedman. I should also note that in distinguishing between globalization from above and globalization from below, I do not want to say that one is good and the other is bad in relation to democracy. As Friedman shows, capitalist corporations and global forces might very well promote democratization in many arenas of the world, and globalization from below might promote special interests or reactionary goals, so I am criticizing theorizing globalization in binary terms as primarily 'good' or 'bad'.
33 Hardt and Negri, *Empire*; R. Burbach, *Globalization and Postmodern Politics: From Zapatistas to High-Tech Robber Barons* (London: Pluto Press, 2001); Best and Kellner, *The Postmodern Adventure*; and J. Foran (ed.), *The Future of Revolutions: Rethinking Radical Change in the Age of Globalization* (London: Zed Books, 2003).
34 See Kellner, *From 9/11 to Terror War*, and Barber, *Fear's Empire*.
35 On resistance to globalization by labour, see K. Moody, *An Injury to One* (London: Verso, 1988), and 'Toward an International Social-Movement Unionism', *New Left Review*, 225 (1997), 52–72; on resistance by environmentalists and other social movements, see the studies in Mander and Goldsmith,

The Case Against the Global Economy, while I provide examples below from several domains.

36 See the article in *New York Times*, 7 February 7 1996, A15. Friedman (*The Lexus and the Olive Tree*, p. 267) notes that George Soros was the star of Davos in 1995, when the triumph of global capital was being celebrated, but that the next year Russian Communist Party leader Gennadi A. Zyuganov was a major media focus when unrestrained globalization was being questioned, although Friedman does not point out that this was a result of a growing recognition that divisions between 'haves' and 'have nots' were becoming too scandalous and that predatory capitalism was becoming too brutal and ferocious.

37 J. Flanigan, *Los Angeles Times*, 19 February 1999.

38 On the Cancun meetings, see C. Kraul, 'WTO Meeting Finds Protests Inside and Out', *Los Angeles Times*, 11 September 11 2003, A3; P. Hewitt, 'Making Trade Fairer', *The Guardian*, 12 September 2003; and N. Klein, 'Activists Must Follow the Money', *The Guardian*, 12 September 2003. On the collapse of the so-called 'Free-Trade Summit', see C. J. Williams and H.-T. Dahlberg, 'Free-Trade Summit Ends Without Pact', *Los Angeles Times*, 21 November 2003. On the growing division between rich and poor, see B. M. Friedman, 'Globalization: Stiglitz's Case', *The New York Review of Books*, 15 August 2002, and G. Monbiot, 'The Worst of Times', *The Guardian*, 12 September 2003.

39 Stiglitz, *Globalization and its Discontents*.

40 N. Dyer-Witheford, *Cyber-Marx: Cycles and Circuits of Struggle in High-Tech Capitalism* (Urbana, IL: University of Illinois Press, 1999).

Part III

Rethinking Globalization, Resistance and Transformative Politics

12

'Alter-Globalization' and Social Movements: Towards Understanding Transnational Politicization

Martin Weber

Over the past decade or so, we have witnessed the ascendancy of new forms of transnational solidarization, politicization and developments of social consciousness, as well as the by now well established channels of engagement involving NGOs, national governments and international organizations. From the 'Battle in Seattle' through the 'Global Carnival' to the global and regional Social Forum movements, it has become clear that a different type of political challenge is in formation from the kind anticipated in much of the globalization literature, which stipulated reform and a gradual democratization of existing institutions based on the increasing involvement of an emergent 'global civil society'. While the counterhegemonic thrust of the 'alter-globalization' constellation may not be articulated in the form of a 'coherent project', it deploys features of an alternative 'universalizing discourse' compared with the dominant one lodged in the expansion and entrenchment of modernity characterized by capitalist-liberal states.

Below, I argue that the analytical lenses deployed in the globalization literature for dealing with non-state actors' – such as 'alter-globalists' – role in changing world order fail to adequately grasp the qualitative difference of the politics of 'alter globalization', and that such failures are themselves not politically innocent. Though I do not wish to overstate (empirically) the political importance of the alter-globalization movement – I think it is far from settled whether it will sustain momentum and its distinctiveness – I think its potential significance needs to be properly understood even at what is now still an early stage in its formation. In so far as it is apposite to summarize the diverse activities, action-contexts and objectives as being meaningful parts of a larger 'alter-globalist' counterhegemonic project, it is clearly a movement with emancipatory aims and transnational scope. These features cannot be adequately understood within the analytical idioms offered in the globalization literature of 'global' or 'international' civil society, or through recent attempts to refine such analysis with the use of the concept of public spheres. I reconstruct these positions through the works of key proponents, maintaining that their respective emancipatory interests are – quite appropriately – lodged in the role of 'public reason'. Contrary to their inclusive conceptualizations of 'publicness', I argue that it is the notion of the *public* as 'the good public' itself that is subject to the politicization-drives advanced in the alter-globalist mode, and that the latter ought to be read as significantly constituted as a 'counter-public'. Thus, from the perspective of the alter-globalists, many of the offers of participation in 'public reasoning' (typically extended as 'consultative status') are disingenuous attempts at incorporating dissent into a pseudo-public sphere, in which the *public* commitment to openness conceals tightly circumscribed conceptions of what counts and what does not count as reasonable contributions or proposals. The constriction of the possibility to communicate the adverse experiences of 'globalizing modernity' lies behind both the creative repertoire of alter-globalists' engagement, and the insistence on utopianism as a politically instructive, legitimate and practical conversation, which enables the pose of the authentic voice of counterhegemony.

Social movements as agents of change: problems in the analysis of global politics

To focus on social movements as agents of change is to draw attention away from the more formalized avenues of political engagement (NGOs and consultative networks), which have been well explored in the wider circle of studies on globalization.[1] Keck and Sikkink explored the transnationalization of networks of advocacy, based on increasing collaboration among mainly NGOs, who have increased their effectiveness by circumventing the constrictions of sovereign boundedness.[2] Such organizational successes have, however, begun to draw criticisms, both from the perspective of democratic theory (who do such organizational agents 'represent', and is such representation legitimate?), as well as from the angle of ideology critique (to what degree are they successes, or should they be rather seen as part of a strategy of cooptation by 'hegemonic' forces?). To get somewhat closer to these concerns, the focus on 'movements' is instructive, not least because NGOs (or other, more formal non-state actors) rely to a significant degree on their – perceived or real – connectedness to social mobilization, even if the latter's articulation is often in an idiom aside from discourses geared towards policy-relevance (for instance, rejectionist stances, or revolutionary rhetoric).

Movements, however diffuse their appearance in the global public may be, articulate social struggle, concern and discontent, galvanizing around injustices, over practices of domination and exploitation, or the struggle for alternative ways of life and the conditions preventing these. In widening or creating the space for articulating such aims, they engage in challenging the status quo and its institutional setting. It is for these reasons that the globalization literature has engaged notions of informal agency in global politics from the perspective of seeking out social forces promoting emancipatory change in global politics. By far the most effort went into the exploration of 'civil society' as a generalized site from which such change emanated. Conceptualized either in terms of global or international civil society, this strand of interpretations has followed in the footsteps of Robert Cox, who early on argued that the forces of civil society were the most potent and plausible agents for political transformation.[3] I want to first turn to global civil society conceptions, before discussing the international civil society analysis offered by Colas.[4] My aim is to seek out their respective limitations for political analysis. I then turn to the more recent revival of interest in 'public spheres',[5] which seems more conducive to understanding universalizing discourses as part of efforts to democratically overcome pernicious forms of social and political fragmentation and hierarchization, but, as I argue, carries the risk of obscuring the significance of oppositional politicization practices, which are an important part of social movement struggles. The reconstruction of the posture of emancipatory action in the alter-globalization movement, I argue then, is captured better by focusing on it as an example of 'counter-public' contest.

Global civil society

Most studies utilizing the concept of global civil society in the context of transnational politics proceed by conceding the contradictory tendencies immanent to its constitution. Hence, civil society is identified in accordance with the Hegelian proviso of society distinct from the organizational complex of the state, the realm of 'private interests'.[6] This results in the identification of civil society as a 'domain' from which impulses register which 'affect' societal constellations as a whole, and effect changes within functionally circumscribed systems. In 'critical IR', this domain-reading of civil society (as if it were 'space') is then routinely supplemented with agent-centred accounts focusing on who acts out what kinds of political project. The structural constellation that forms the accepted conceptual framework for analysing the contestation or affirmation of world order formation consists usually in the separating out of the three spheres (state/economy/civil society), complemented by their dynamic trajectories (internationalization/global integration/global extension). The political story in turn thus becomes one told in terms of the actions and struggles within the 'third column', which results in adaptive changes or transformative knock-on effects in the realms of the other two (depending on the significance accorded to political action in 'civil society').

The conceptualization of global civil society as a 'domain' or a space leads to sociological orientations with which the various tensions within it are recorded, and a book like Keane's is an example of what rich and thick descriptions are possible on that basis.[7] But the domain reading imposes the cost of a lack in differentiation of the kinds of political projects, their scope, and the depth of their challenge as they are advanced within the 'domain'. In the last instance, the normative criteria introduced in such accounts are not particularly helpful for identifying progressive political projects, because they are not developed out of accounts of the *experience* which give rise to the contest out of which the normative demands themselves are generated and derive their cogency. This can be seen in Keane's uneasy treatment of the universalizing ethical ideal of global civil society, which, on his interpretation, is animated by the celebration of 'social diversity' by asking after the 'universal conditions' which enable it.[8] This ethical ideal is sustained by a positive orientation to life, which views alterity as dialectically mediated with notions of 'self', and hence de-emphasizes conflictual social relations.[9] Though such an ethical vision is appealing, it overglosses the constitutive features of civil society as comprising hierarchical relations, and relations of power and domination, which themselves are in need of 'normative constraint'. That the latter may be sought in the struggles within the domain of civil society provides no guidance on beginning to seek out differences between emancipatory and reactionary social forces, or orientation on possible formations of political projects.

Not global, but international civil society?

The situation is not much helped when one turns to more substantive restatements of 'international civil society'. These reintroduce a 'constraining agency' through which the apprehension of normative ideals becomes possible, namely the state and its legislative response to social and political pressure. An internationalist take on the scope for emancipatory change and progressive politicization is presented in Colas, who suggests that the political significance of civil society remains dependent on the sovereign nation-state.[10] The inter-position of state sovereignty in the web of global social relations provides in this analysis the focal point of the political demands emanating from civil society, and hence the primary site of struggle. Such an analysis inadvertently reifies the 'state' in terms of sovereignty, autonomy and membership (citizenry), and invites the familiar charge, laid at the door of many 'Marxisms', of oversimplification. As Offe and Ronge argued, the conception of the state as a 'neutral' site of political authority, open to seizure in the interest of classes, misconceives the constitutive dimension of social relations reproducing the capitalist state.[11] What is intended, therefore, as a means of making transparent sociopolitical power relations in a way conducive to the idea that collective struggle can bring about significant change, amounts in the end to a relativization of emancipatory action within the process of the reproduction of the capitalist state form, both nationally and internationally. Despite these criticisms, the notion of emancipatory agency in 'international' civil society is not wholly implausible, either analytically or descriptively. This is because the analysis holds firm for conceptions of civil society explicitly conceived in terms of actors seeking to participate. In this vein, the constitutive actors' interest can be apprehended in accordance with Gramsci's conception of the 'war of movement', even if this is not to be equated with the actual comprehensive seizure of the means of violence and control over society as a whole. Movement, rather, implies the orientation towards the appropriation of the state through the centring of class interest advanced out of struggle.

The merit of this analysis is undoubtedly to recast the genealogy of the 'international' in terms of social relations and specifically class relations. In so far as the state is the 'site' of the struggle of class interests, the preoccupation of realist/liberal IR theory with state autonomy and anarchy is comprehensively blocked.

However, this would not leave us with a plausibly refined framework for the political analysis of current social movement politics expressed in the transnational sense (for example, 'alter-globalization'). This can be seen with reference to the 'participation' focus already alluded to above, for it now appears that the emancipatory political content of the struggle of social movements seeking to effect structural transformation would need to rely on the *internationalist scope* of their organizational vision. The latter serves at the same time as a yardstick for assessing the (politically) progressive nature of respective movements: only movements which thus constitute themselves internationally while enacting correspondingly their influence on national governments can count as 'progressive', according to this logic.

The internationalization of social movements appears as a historically and politically necessary reaction as the transnationalization of elite interests proceeds. Seeking *participation* in this way throws collective social agents such as NGOs back towards engagement at national levels as they find that 'the form, content and eventual outcomes of such gatherings (International Organization Summits) are so heavily circumscribed by the interests of states' that it seems that 'global civil society is what states make of it'.[12]

The position advanced by Colas on social movement politics is thus not statist – in the sense that the state is not imputed 'autonomous corporate agency' – but state-centric, in the sense that the state is the instrument through which collective will can be 'universalized'. This account is analytically blinkered from grasping politicization discourses directed at radically contesting the institutional set-up of sovereign state authority, and its extension through global governance, which we can discern in the postures of 'alter-globalization' movement actors.

When political projects look dangerous: the return of pluralism via the 'public sphere'

We have seen that 'global civil society', despite attempts to develop it as a concept for political agency with a normative edge, counts for little if anything when we are faced with the question of what may constitute emancipatory social struggle within the domain and what may not. Likewise, I have gestured at the problems which arise from the refocusing of civil society in internationalist terms, where the dilemma is from the outset whether states, international systems and their institutions represent merely neutral 'sites' for political struggles, or part of a 'global politics' which as such may be the target of contestation.

In both cases complexity abounds to a degree which can make the search for emancipatory sociopolitical agency and its contents look futile in the face of the sheer plurality of interests, motivations and orientations. In this vein, *pluralism* makes a comeback. Corresponding to the basic orientation towards participation in Colas' internationalist analysis is a pluralist/pragmatist understanding of the scope of representative politics, which has begun to explore the potential of analysis oriented towards *public spheres* more systematically. On this view too, organized political representation – party politics and political party membership mobilization – loses in significance *vis-à-vis* the contest of interests among movements, groups, organizations and lobbies, representing a shift away from 'ideological' contests and towards the 'managerial' state.[13] This implies a general normalization of political reality – animated significantly by the perception of the demise of classical class conflict,[14] and the ensuing multiplication of social-political 'interests' – reflected in the shift in political science towards 'Pluralism'.[15] Pluralism, in Coxean terms, represents the classical 'problem-solving' approach, in that it takes the social/political reality as given – including the fact of social complexity – and, in its basic constitutive features, stable, in order to map, explain and project bargaining processes and outcomes, as well as electoral behaviour in accordance with its 'interface' with the pregiven foundational order. This research programme, as well as the 'public transcript' it sustains – the image of politics as facilitating compromise between mutually exclusive or reciprocally damaging claims of 'interest groups' – is consistent with the ideological rendition of the increasing range of life-choices which have become available under late capitalist development, and hence a material/utilitarian conception of 'freedom' as 'freedom of choice'.

The anticipated mode of 'state–society' relations in this context becomes one of lobbying, of 'organization', in which organizational models reflect each other as associations geared to communicating to the political centre, so as to elicit policy responses: the payoff for sustained engagement. The conflict model underpinning this conception of a bargaining politics allows for a relatively small range of antagonistic forms of struggle, and is biased from the outset towards the 'incorporation' of collective claims via compromise 'solutions'.

The public sphere

In the context of the advance of pluralism in IR, a shift away from the language of 'civil society' as the site of movement struggle can be apprehended. Motivated perhaps by an attempt to distance pluralist inquiry from neo-Gramscian IR, which probes the resistance potentials from within civil society from the perspective of the contradictions of capitalist modernity, the move towards the more 'liberal' concept of the public sphere was advanced. Though the debate over 'public spheres' in political theory and social theory was itself significantly influenced by both Marxist and liberal theories,[16] the concept was appropriated in IR in the context of the study of regimes and international institutions and, more recently, attempts to merge pragmatist inspired political theory and institutionalism in IR, directed by the goal to conceive of forms of democratic legitimacy not 'overburdened' by the demands of substantive democratic self-rule.

This pragmatist challenge to the perceived formalism in global constitutional projects pitches a different understanding of the rule of legitimate law against the one implicit in the cosmopolitan institutionalist model proposed for democracy by Held *et al.* The conceptual anchor for this challenge to the constitutive conception of legitimate cosmopolitan democratic governance is a specific understanding of the role of the public sphere in the institution of democratic constraint upon sovereign government. In this context, a conception of the democratization of global governance is advanced, whose emancipatory content is purged of the influences of neo-Marxist thought (in the widest sense), and oriented more clearly towards classical Liberalism. I take the work of Molly Cochran as a point of reference, because this tendency towards liberal pluralism and away from the themes of Marxist-inspired crisis theories is quite pronounced in her work, and can be used to problematize the pluralist conception of public spheres which operates to circumscribe emancipatory agency.[17]

Cochran develops her conception of a 'bottom-up' approach to cosmopolitan democracy through a critique of what she identifies as general disregard for the role of social movements, NGOs, and what she summarizes (for better or worse) as the 'institutional sites' of International Public Spheres (IPSs) in the work of David Held.[18] Her critique revolves significantly around the notion of institutionalization, which she identifies as the core concern of Held's promotion of cosmopolitan democracy. She correctly traces the normative backdrop of this conception to Held's development of the tension-field of autonomy/nautonomy, and asks whether the norms of public participation elaborated on this basis are not part of an overtaxing of democratic citizens' willingness and capacity to participate (raising sociological limits to democratization generally, but in particular with reference to the cosmopolitan scope of the project).[19]

The focus she takes on the question of cosmopolitan democratic transformation is then developed in distinction to Bohman's 'centrism',[20] which involves the idea that the bottom-up pressures for global democratization are met by the appropriate development of sufficiently universal legal instruments, and in equal distinction to Dryzek's focus on discursive political will-formation in public spheres to which he attributes, via expanding networks, transformative capacity.[21]

Her primary charge is that both Dryzek and Bohman let themselves be restricted by a Habermasian conception of the public sphere, which is not sufficiently flexible to account for the multifarious functions fulfilled by actors representing 'public spheres' in the formation of cosmopolitan transformation.[22] The restrictions they share with Habermas's account are argued to lie with an unduly rigidified conception of the public as a sphere of 'private individuals', which prevents 'international public spheres' from being seen as 'institutions invested with public authority'.[23]

Instead of the 'Habermasian' public sphere, Cochran proposes the adoption of Dewey's conception of public spheres, which he developed along a consequentialist approach in the context of his exploration of participation in government. Cochran reconstructs Dewey's approach to participation as distinguished by the absence of the clear role distinction found in Bohman, Dryzek and Habermas, between political will-formation and the dispensation of public authority (or civil society and the governmental state). Public spheres thus conceived share with states the pragmatist definition of their purpose: 'a shared interest in controlling indirect consequences that affect those associated'.[24] It is upon this outlook that publics 'have traits of a state'. Each public can thus be seen as a 'tool, which serves the specialized function of helping individuals, through co-operative social inquiry, to work towards more effective control of the indeterminate situations in which they share common interests'.[25]

This notion of public spheres, more geared towards the dispensation of public authority, is more easily adaptable to the international context as their constitutive substance is no longer conceptualized in the heavy language of normative theory and emancipatory universalizing discourse, but rather conceived of as a shared concern with the unintended consequences of globalizing modernity. This allows for international public spheres to be analysed in terms of problem-driven communities of interest: 'A functional understanding of a public constituted by the shared affects of indirect consequences, as compared to a Habermasian epistemological one, will have a better chance of affecting expectations of responsible action between persons in world politics.'[26]

Cochran develops the reasoning for a defence of this pluralized notion of International Public Spheres. It is here that we can begin with a critical appraisal of the limits of her argument. We can contrast her conception of problem-constituted IPSs with the conception of the public sphere which Habermas developed earlier, in his attempt to apprehend the emancipatory aspects of the unfolding bourgeois public sphere. Key to his treatment of the normative aspect of public sphere is Kant's conception, introduced in 'What is Enlightenment?', of 'the public use of reason' or 'the reasoning public', understood in terms of the free exchange of ideas and criticisms.[27] The bourgeois public sphere as a sphere of the free exchange of ideas and critique served, according to Habermas's historical analysis, emancipatory interests with which an emboldened 'public' could confront the entrenched power structures of state institutions. However, Habermas also shows that the bourgeois public sphere with its production of critical media (newspapers), and use of public spaces (cafés) had socially exclusionary features, and that it was the contradiction between the normative demand to inclusiveness and openness on the one hand, and the fact of bourgeois elitism on the other, which ultimately destabilized the emancipatory force of the bourgeois public.[28] The emancipatory force of public spheres is a precarious good, not guaranteed by simple reference to something 'made public' or involving public opinion. In keeping with the Frankfurt School line of critical analysis, the ideal of free critical argumentation is maintained as the normative backdrop for the development of a self-reflective reason with which social and political pathologies can be confronted.[29] By reorienting the notion of public spheres towards the notion of problem-solving, Cochran urges, in effect, a foreshortening of the critical reflective process in favour of conceptions of problems which have to be already shared by the actors involved in 'functional public spheres'.

While on her reading engagement, participation and accession may be modes sought by many social movements, NGOs or 'IPSs', the pluralism of her stance compels the interpretation of all repertoires of collective political agency as oriented by the desire to 'join' procedural settings which ultimately may themselves be targets of the politicization-efforts of informal political agency. This is clearly the case with regard to the 'alter-globalization' movement, whose oppositional stance *vis-à-vis* pressures to institutionalize has persisted, although not by remaining within the framework of a fetishized politics of resistance. One of the much overlooked features of the movement is the relatively high degree and high quality of information exchange, learning, teaching and dispensation of knowledge and experiences across boundaries (see, for instance, the impact of ATTAC in this regard).

Cochran's approach leads back to 'problem-solving' theory, but although Habermas's notion of the critical function of public reason helps to steer clear of reducing emancipatory social and political agency in such a manner, it does not yet provide us with enough conceptual vocabulary to engage the problem we are now facing: if the role of 'public reasoning' can degenerate, how are we to differentiate between forces sustaining 'pseudo-public spheres', and those set out – in whatever form or idiom – to counter the 'deformations of reason' which reproduce experiences of suffering and denigration?[30] We are looking, in other words, to differentiate our account of emancipatory agency further.

Refocusing political analysis: the counter-public sphere

Negt and Kluge argued early on that Habermas's conception of the public sphere was too underspecified.[31] Their critique is, however, not addressed by a simple 'pluralization' (that is, the stipulation of many, coordinated, competing or co-operating public spheres) as is the case in Cochran's proposal.

In keeping with Marxist insights, Negt and Kluge maintain a hierarchical understanding of societies, the conflictual and crisis-ridden nature of social relations expressed in the relations of (re)production.[32] Their conceptual juxtaposition of the bourgeois public sphere and the proletarian public sphere raises terminological problems in that these denominators invoke the image of rigid class society in terms of folk-readings of nineteenth-century capitalist society. However, they use these 'anachronisms' deliberately to denote spheres of experience, rather than bounded socialization-contexts. In Negt and Kluge's work, experience is mobilized to account for the refraction of 'the public sphere' along lines of domination and subordination, and the contradictions which unfold in light of the 'inclusiveness' of the public sphere as the domain of public reason (its normative and democratizing function in the approaches sketched above) on the one hand, and its function as the domain of the reproduction of the 'Dominant Social Paradigm' on the other. Here, the parallels with Gramscian accounts of hegemony/counterhegemony are obvious.

The counter-public sphere: origins and instances

If the pluralist take on the internal political scenes in Western liberal democracies took its cue from the relative 'stability' of contemporary social relations,[33] its focus on social conflicts framed by interest-divergence and choice limitations was revealed, in turn, by changes in social reality which burst its conceptual shell. If 'pluralism', both as a research programme nested in the normative assumptions outlined above and as an operative social consensus with political efficacy, was oriented towards the dynamics of conflict against the background of a secured conception of relations among state, society, civil society and individuals, it was ill prepared for conceptualizing a challenge directed at the very 'system' upon which it sought to resolve the problems of analysing formations of claims, counterclaims and the pursuit of privileges. That, however, was the challenge presented, in the late 1960s and early 1970s by New Social Movements (NSMs) with more explicitly postmaterial and contra-establishment demands, combined with a political refusal to engage on the terms laid down on behalf of established political interest formations. The student movements in Europe in particular raised the possibility of a comprehensive disruption of the very 'modern' political order taken as constitutive by pluralism. The emergence of 'counter-public spheres',[34] the strategic-practical refusal of forms of dialogue which depended, from the perspectives of the protesters and activists, on major concessions to particular ways of doing politics, has led to the interpretation of this form of engagement in terms of what we could term meta-political practices. The reasons for this conceptualization have to do with the comprehensive impact these challenges made, not least, for instance, with reference to contesting the state's 'monopoly on violence'. Although subsequently often belittled as 'life-style politics', the emergence of NSMs from this context represented the most formidable challenge to liberal nation-states 'from within' in the postwar era.[35]

Significantly the political contest initiated by the NSMs cannot be circumscribed without major problems in terms of particular 'state–civil society' relations. Instead, the very form of state–civil society relations (as described, analysed and reproduced continuously in pluralist research) was itself the target of a political challenge. Hence, the transformed Left, no longer as of primary significance rooted in terms of 'capital–labour' relations, develops a distinct vocabulary and action repertoire with which to raise the contradictions of modern capitalist social life to actionable political protest, and the generation of properly transformation-oriented solidarity.

As is obvious and well established, the brief 'spring' of meta-political practice oriented to the comprehensive disruption of the dominant order (the student protests of 1968) ended in its various nation-state settings in 'defeat', incurred variously through an exhaustion of 'revolutionary' energy, lack of credible alternative political programmes, cooptation, coercion and repression, and fragmentation. Yet the question of success or failure is secondary to the more important problem of the conditions, sustenance and likelihood of radical political challenges to the modern state formation, and it is here that the peculiar political challenge of social movements such as those comprising 'alter-globalists' show themselves to be aligned with the latently present threat of the contradictions of modern nation-states to become apparent and subject to politicization. Meta-political practices are most pronouncedly what differentiate an approach to collective agency that includes a working notion of the counter-public sphere from approaches which focus on access and participation from an institutionalist perspective. The latter routinely miss the 'power' dimension of public spheres, but also foreclose an analytical interest in the substantive content and expressive repertoire of social struggles where these include disenchantment with consolidated forms of opportunities for participation which are experienced as, at the very least, systematically biased. The focus on counter-publics brings to the attention of political analysis practices of collective agency *directed at politicizing the dominant mode of political engagement itself.*

What 'brings on' this political form of counter-public engagement is the recognition that experiences of domination, hierarchy and denigration cannot be authentically represented in the 'public sphere' as such. Hence the path to the kind of pragmatic participation in a public sphere for problem-solving is blocked, because the criterion for 'access' is premised upon a perspective-shift, which cannot be taken for granted as unproblematic. The role of 'experience' for the formation of counter-publics is circumscribed in terms of three elements:

> The experience of re/production under capitalist, that is, alienated, conditions; the systematic blockage of that experience as a horizon in its own right, that is, the separation of the experiencing subjects from the networks of public expression and representation; and, as a response to that blockage, resistances and imaginative strategies grounded in the experience of alienated production – protest energies, psychic balancing acts, a penchant for personalization, individual and collective fantasy, and creative re-appropriations.[36]

Negt and Kluge investigate under the impressions left by the failures of the student movement, and the arrival of the re fractured identity-political formations grouped together under the NSM label, the dialectical nature of public spheres. In keeping with the general themes of critical theory, they, too, view public spheres as the key social sites for emancipation, a feat they achieve primarily through the mobilization of symbolic resources out of public discourse, which *can* lead to the politicization or re-politicization of the 'societalization process'. In contrast to Habermas, however, for whom the main interest lies in the formation of historically dominant public spheres and their relationship within civil society to the ordering powers of the political and the economic systems, Negt and Kluge focus on the heterogeneous composition of publics themselves. They discern a dialectical interplay between the 'organized' and 'organizing' dominant public sphere, which they identify with the bourgeoisie, and the subaltern, disarticulated public spheres which they summarize under the label of the proletarian. It is essential to reconstruct just what the dialectical understanding is of the interplay of the two domains, and their respective relationships with organized power.

Negt and Kluge proceed in three steps. Initially, they clarify their concept of experience, which they derive from Hegel's dialectical conception of consciousness. The second step of their conceptual groundwork is the reconstruction of the bourgeois understanding of the public sphere. This they do with the specific interest in the 'production' of the conditions of proletarian experience (that is, with a view to the self-insuring tendencies in the reproduction of the bourgeois public sphere). It is only then that the formation of counter-publics in the context of the proletarian horizon of experience can be grasped both analytically and in substantive analysis.

The same logic is invoked by Negt and Kluge in their reconstruction of the dialectical conception of experience from the perspective of the 'worker', for whom the range of self-knowledge remains 'privatist', elated only by the remote possibility of the worker as the macro-subject of history – a condition comprehensively removed from the sphere of action, but tentative in the 'production' of alternative realities (fantasy). Like Ulysses' oarsmen in Horkheimer and Adorno's *Dialectic of Enlightenment*, Negt and Kluge's worker 'is prevented from understanding what is taking place through him, because the media whereby experience is constituted all participate in the mystificatory process of commodity fetishism'.[37]

The second step, the reconstruction of the 'bourgeois public sphere', is done with regard to the 'organization' of bourgeois hegemony, which is analysed as 'industrial-capitalist' publicity. From the perspective of the dominant form of 'publicity' reinforced by the business interest of mass-media and the attempt of powerful actors to control, or at least shape and delimit the possibilities of public debate, counter-public movements must be neutralized (not necessarily 'suppressed'). Neutralization can take many different forms, but the identification of, for instance, 'alter-globalizers' with incurable romantic Luddites, anti-modern forces or adolescent hooligans in 'public' discourse is a fine example. The critical thrust of 'counter-publics' *vis-à-vis* the dominant publicity is thus directed at the veneer of inclusiveness of the latter, which masks the screening capacity with which 'potentially dangerous' dissent is managed.

The third step makes plausible the possibility of the formation of counter-publics in which 'silenced' experience seeks articulation initially for itself, and in distinction to the symbolic modes of 'dominant publicity'. For Negt and Kluge, the ground for the formation of counter-public spheres is the proletarian public sphere, which they qualify in terms of a concept of production, which is widely cast.

How far we can follow Negt and Kluge's substantive conclusions when transposing their conceptual inventory to the study of 'alter-globalization' and formations of transnational counter-publics is a question which has to be deferred. However, their analysis directs us towards the diversity of creative challenges which query the dominant logics of globalization: from the 'copyleft' movement, and alternative 'subaltern' news media, to street protest and other symbolic events, such as the Social Forum gatherings. From 'global civil society' as the least differentiated conceptual frame of movement agency, we have now arrived at a differentiated conception of the public sphere that may begin to emerge, in its 'counter-public' form, transnationally. As such, it remains part of 'global civil society', but a part about which we can tell a much clearer political story despite the fact that 'alter-globalization' is only very loosely integrated organizationally.

Restoring the notion of 'counter-publics' in order to flag the way in which publicity itself is a contested realm enriches social and political theory with normative outlooks, without dispensing with a strong notion of emancipatory agency. It does, however, also complicate the account of the latter. A key problem for the question of the political force of 'counter-public' formations is their interaction with the *social fact* of complexity, the stubborn notion that social and political change is risky because it endangers highly integrated complex social systems, which cannot plausibly be politically appropriated.[38] Such a conceptualization of social reality renders struggles for alternative orders inappropriate, and political agency on their behalf hazardous, or irresponsible. However, it is itself the target of the kind of public critical reason for which 'alter-globalists' are seeking a voice. The discourse on the naturalization of social complexity, as evident in functionalist approaches (systems theoretic as well as pragmatist ones) is a *political* discourse, and the counter-public challenge duly re-politicizes it.

Notes

1 On the importance of distinguishing movements from organizations, see D. Dela Porta and M. Diani, *Social Movements* (Oxford: Basil Blackwell, 1999).
2 M. Keck and K. Sikkink, *Activists Beyond Borders: Advocacy Networks in Global Politics* (Ithaca, NY: Cornell University Press, 1998), p. 13.
3 R. Cox, *Approaches to World Order* (Cambridge: Cambridge University Press, 1996).
4 A. Colas, *International Civil Society* (Cambridge: Polity, 2001).
5 See J. Bohman, 'Citizenship and the Norms of Publicity', *Political Theory*, 27 (1999), 176–202; M. Cochran, 'A Democratic Critique of Cosmopolitan Democracy: Pragmatism from the Bottom-Up', *European Journal of International Relations*, 8 (2002), 517–48.
6 J. Keane, *Global Civil Society?* (Cambridge: Cambridge University Press, 2003).
7 Ibid.
8 Ibid., p. 201.
9 Ibid., p. 204.
10 Colas, *International Civil Society*; see also R. Axtmann, 'What's Wrong with Cosmopolitan Democracy?', in N. Dower and J. Williams (eds), *Global Citizenship: A Reader* (Edinburgh: Edinburgh University Press, 2002).
11 C. Offe and V. Ronge, 'Theses on the Theory of the State', in R. Goodin and P. Pettit (eds), *Contemporary Political Philosophy* (Oxford: Basil Blackwell, 1997).
12 Colas, *International Civil Society*, p. 153.
13 C. Offe, *Contradictions of the Welfare State* (Cambridge, MA: MIT Press, 1984), pp. 35–64. It is important to note that such shifts are, at one level, effected by certain sets of action coming to closer and more prominent attention than previously: the managerial tasks of states thus slip in and out of popular perception and the realm of politicization in accordance with the visibility of the states' presence in the direction of domestic affairs. That this basic pattern changes, however, when the 'relative autonomy' of states is rendered more remote in networks of global governance with constitutional features, is one of the operating hypotheses behind this account.
14 M. Horkheimer and T. Adorno, *Dialectic of Enlightenment* (New York: Continuum, 1995).
15 See C. B. MacPherson on the 'Dahl–Schumpeter axis' in *Democratic Theory: Essays in Retrieval* (Oxford: Oxford University Press,1973), pp. 78–9.
16 C. Calhoun, *Habermas and the Public Sphere* (Cambridge, MA: MIT Press, 1994).
17 Cochran, 'A Democratic Critique of Cosmopolitan Democracy'.
18 D. Held, *Democracy and the Global Order: From the Modern State to Cosmopolitan Governance* (Cambridge: Polity, 1995).
19 Cochran, 'A Democratic Critique of Cosmopolitan Democracy', p. 520.
20 Bohman, 'Citizenship and the Norms of Publicity'.
21 J. Dryzek, 'Transnational Democracy', *Journal of Political Philosophy*, 7 (1999), 30–51.
22 See J. Habermas, *Strukturwandel der Oeffentlichkeit* (Frankfurt: Suhrkamp, 1974); and 'Further Reflections on the Public Sphere', in Calhoun, *Habermas and the Public Sphere*.
23 Cochran, 'A Democratic Critique of Cosmopolitan Democracy', p. 531.
24 Ibid.
25 Ibid.

26 Ibid., p. 536.

27 See I. Kant, 'Beantwortung der Frage: Was ist Aufklaerung?', *Werke, Vol. 9* (Darmstadt: Wissenschaftliche Buchgesellschaft, 1983), p. 55.

28 Calhoun, *Habermas and the Public* Sphere, pp. 20–1.

29 A. Honneth, 'A Social Pathology of Reason: On the Intellectual Legacy of Critical Theory', in F. Rush (ed.), *The Cambridge Companion to Critical Theory* (Cambridge: Cambridge University Press, 2004), pp. 356–7.

30 Ibid., p. 346.

31 O. Negt and A. Kluge, *Public Sphere and Experience* (Minneapolis, MN: University of Minnesota Press, 1993).

32 Ibid., p. 14.

33 See Held, *Democracy and the Global Order.*

34 Negt and Kluge, *Public Sphere and Experience.*

35 K. Eder, 'The "New Social Movements": Moral Crusades, Political Pressure Groups, or Social Movements?', *Social Research*, 52 (1985), 868–90.

36 Negt and Kluge, *Public Sphere and Experience*, p. xxxii. I can only gesture towards the problem of 'scale', which is obviously connected to the notion of collective social experiences, and would require appropriate treatment for the intended political analysis of transnational counter-publics. Under what conditions 'localized' experiences of suffering or denigration can lead to generalized solidarities is not straightforward, but the fact that 'alter-globalists' can confront globally extended governance agencies which are (despite diverse impacts) the same from all angles of the globe may render early forms plausible.

37 Negt and Kluge, *Public Sphere and Experience*, p. 6.

38 N. Luhmann, *Die Gesellschaft der Gesellschaft* (Frankfurt: Suhrkamp, 1997).

13

'Horizontals', 'Verticals' and the Conflicting Logics of Transformative Politics

Andrew Robinson and Simon Tormey

Anyone who follows the politics of the Movement for Global Justice (MGJ) will be under no illusions as to the difficulty of the task that confronts it in terms of developing a politics that is effective as well as noisy. Within the movement (or, better, movement of movements) there are many different *kinds* of grouping as well as many different *visions* of global justice.[1] In terms of the kinds of movement, there are obviously huge numbers of political parties. There are Marxist parties, green parties and more reformist or social democratic parties engaged with the process as well. There are activist groupings and networks such as People's Global Action, *Ya Basta!* and the Wombles. There are NGOs such as Greenpeace and Oxfam. There are religious groupings. There are single issue activist groupings such as those campaigning for the abolition of debt or the installation of clean water supplies. There are representatives from governments and trade unions. There are all manner of hybrid or 'in-between' groups such as ATTAC, which is itself an umbrella for a variety of radicalisms and activisms.

In terms of *visions* it almost goes without saying that the span of ideological and postideological conceptions of the world, of ethical positions, or fundamentalisms is equally impressive. There are liberal interventionists who wish for a 'compassionate' or responsible globalization with reformed institutions and more inclusive political practices. There are a myriad of social democratic visions involving varying accounts of global governance. There are all sorts of radical visions, some with roots in the far-flung past such as Marxism and others of less certain pedigree such as the primitivists, the Immediatists and many other 'isms' besides. There are those such as the Zapatistas who repudiate the idea that any one conception of the world can encompass the complexity of life and who thus call 'only' for a world in which all worlds are possible – except the neoliberal world they are struggling so desperately to keep at bay. This is without question one of the most plural, diverse and heterogeneous political assemblages that can ever have been 'gathered' literally or metaphorically under one banner. Yet it is one that to date has managed to maintain a kind of unity – if only in negation. While specific groupings such as the World Social Forum and People's Global Action have their own criteria of inclusion and exclusion, the incompletion of the representative function of any of these organizations, indeed their tendency towards non-representative modes of coming-together which do not foreclose the possibility of other encounters beyond their scope, prevent such criteria from forming into rigid boundaries. This openness has maintained the energy and openness of the movement in the context of its everyday expressions and the various major mobilizations – the logic of the ant-swarm, as Arquilla and Ronfeldt describe it.[2]

On the other hand it is clear that there is a kind of impatience for the development of a concrete or effective oppositional force that would be able to confront global capitalism. This is a concern which is sharpening for various reasons, one of them being the increasing problems involved in organizing major mobilizations in a context of escalating repression and where major events are often moved to locations (Qatar, Savannah, Kananaskis, Evian) which are inaccessible to protesters. This raises a 'where now?' problem for those involved in the movement, and the party model proposes itself as an easy solution. For instance, Naomi Klein complained recently that the MGJ is stuck in a form of 'serial protesting'.[3] Alex Callinicos of the Socialist Workers Party says it suffers from 'movementism', meaning that it is failing to develop into the full party form that can mobilize masses effectively behind the global justice message.[4] The examples can be multiplied across the many individuals who have issued manifestos and programmes, to the groups and groupuscules who urge that we unite around the particular conception of the world that they hold to be valid. Here lie the origins of what 'verticalism' means as a political logic and as a model of effective politics. It is a politics premised on the necessity for the development of a programme, for the building of a party to win supporters for the programme and to capture power so as to put the programme into operation. Let us look at these elements in closer detail.

The programme outlines what it is broadly speaking that a movement or group stands for, what its vision is that it is trying to realize. The vision can be more or less ideologically based. It can be based on a rigorous, methodologically sophisticated account of the nature of the world and the world to be created. This is the case for Marxist parties and for those with ready-made doctrines and philosophies that are awaiting implementation. When they are highly worked out they resemble something more fundamentalist, a doctrine that brooks no argument or reinterpretation (or very little). At the other extreme are groups with shared values or morals who seek to influence public policy in the direction of those values. Social democratic parties, for example, are rarely characterized by a particular vision so much as a desire to increase equality of opportunity and mitigate the damaging effects of the trade cycle. Some groups contain both kinds of 'believer'. A *programme* usually translates into a manifesto in which otherwise abstract, philosophical or ethical positions are mapped in terms of a readily digestible formula which will guide the party or group once in power. The object of the manifesto is to attract new members and also voters where the group is pursuing an electoral strategy. The manifesto or programme functions as an ideological centre or core, a kind of trunk out of which the various subdivisions of the movement are assumed to grow, and to which in the last instance they all return.

Beyond that the objective is to *capture power* in order to implement the vision or to reshape the environment in accordance with the shared values of the group. This idea is based on an image of power as a macrosocial resource which one can possess, rather than as a microsocial relation which, as Foucault puts it, 'circulates' in social networks. There is thus a 'centre' of power which can be occupied and which, once occupied, provides the power-holder with the basis for moulding society in a particular image. (It is also, of course, implicitly assumed that such a 'centre' *should* exist, since otherwise the problem would be one of its elimination, not its seizure.) Once in power the object is the maintenance of power to ensure that the programme is realized and that rival visions are held at bay. This is not only the case for Leninists, but for political parties of all kinds. This is what political parties are *for*. The rationale of radical green parties is the same as conservative parties: what unites them is a shared conception of political effectivity that stems from the possession of a particular conception of the world. Whether that 'world' is radically green or radically neoliberal is irrelevant from the point of view of the criterion of 'effectiveness'. Effectiveness means capturing (macro-) power, and capturing power means mobilizing a majority of people behind the party whether through the device of election, providing access to Parliament as the centre of power, or through the device of a revolutionary seizure directed at the supposed centres of power, however defined (the stock exchange, the central bank, the media headquarters, the Winter Palace).

At the same time parties can be more or less democratic in the manner by which they seek to realize their ideals. In this particular respect there *is* a considerable difference between, say, the greens and many conservative parties. No doubt an 'anti-capitalist party' or movement would correspond more closely to the model of the greens. It would have numerous spokespersons, occasions for discussion of the programme, and a heavily federated structure with the full paraphernalia of democratically accountable political institutions. But it should be noted that this structure would still involve a centre and a trunk, however democratic the means by which it is established. It would involve some kind of party discipline whereby the minority, rather than forming their own 'bloc' or 'affinity group', would accept the victory of the majority and alienate themselves from their own agenda. It would involve a singular programme, refusal of which would mean exclusion from the movement and the 'world' it is to create. It would also, necessarily, be a movement of the Spectacle, in the Situationist sense. Its focus would be outside everyday life, on the 'centre' of power, and would direct the energies of the movement outside the micropolitics of everyday relations, into struggles to win or seize this centre.

So in terms of the effectiveness or otherwise of political action we can see clearly the teleological character of vertical political organizations. As the political sociologist Robert Michels was to note at the start of the last century, it is this teleological character, the fact that there is a clear end point or vision to be reached, that pushes parties and movements in an 'oligarchical' direction.[5] It is easier to effect a 'coalescence' where there are fewer people involved, just as it is 'easier' to come to a decision the fewer people are involved in making it; to pursue power if the lines of power and accountability are 'clear' with a single leader able to project the message of the party without contradiction or mixed messages occluding the minds of potential supporters or voters; to maintain power where decision-making is confined to a small number of officials. In this sense the quest for 'effectiveness' makes desirable, and under certain conditions, necessitates the elaboration of vertical political structures. These are such well-established patterns of political behaviour that we barely need to look for empirical case studies to back the argument that verticalism is intrinsically exclusionary: the more ideas, people or, variables are excluded the more effective vertical politics becomes. Real-world examples abound, from the de-radicalization of the German Greens and their evolution towards complicity in NATO imperialism and EU enlargement, to the recent reversion of the Brazilian Workers' Party to authoritarian centralism and the expulsion of activists critical of President Lula's increasingly pro-neoliberal line.

The representative claim

What becomes evident in summarizing the logic of verticalist politics is the centrality of *representation* to the formation of political effectiveness. This begins with the formulation of the programme or manifesto which is to 'represent' the best interests of ordinary people, or of the majority. This is to articulate their needs and wants and to articulate them in ways that ordinary people find difficult if not impossible to do themselves (and thus to create a division between representers and represented which reproduces alienation and the society of the spectacle). Tony Blair once claimed that New Labour was 'the official ideology of the British people', thus articulating in stark terms what is at stake: the more people one can claim to represent, the more legitimate the claim on power. Representing the universal – or, in the context of national politics, the nation – is the ultimate goal of verticalist conceptions of politics. That such a claim is without empirical foundation does not matter. The key is the hegemonic action of asserting that a given programme stands for what 'everyone' wants. But this is, of course, a recipe for social exclusion, as the representative relationship is often defined tautologically; someone who does not support the programme or the party is interpellated by it as therefore outside the 'nation', the 'people', the 'class', the majority. What if not 'everyone' recognizes themselves or their needs in the manifesto or programme?

Such a question poses the classic dilemma of political leadership. The job of the leader is to lead, not to follow. It is to remain consistent to the truth of the vision or doctrine and this means educating people to understand their own beliefs and interests. It was Gramsci's great insight in his account of hegemony to assert that these operations are not Leninist, but characteristics of the 'war of position' that characterizes politics under modern conditions, for which read vertical politics. 'Vanguardism' and 'substitutionism' are not in this sense mechanisms that pertain only to radical political forces, but to any party or movement that is seeking power. It is more generally a function of what might be termed 'the representative claim'. This leads to the paradoxical but by no means false conclusion that Blairism, conservatism and social democracy are variants of the same logic of substitution which generated the Stalinist purges. It is the state (or representatives of the state) who act and are sovereign, not the people. It is for this reason that representation has been recognized as a mechanism of control and exclusion – for elite rule – since antiquity. The point of representation is not to empower people but to divest them of power so that it may be used for 'rational', 'beneficial' or 'enlightened' ends.

Another paradox of representation is that the power of the representative can only be the inverted or reconfigured or articulated power of the represented – a view expressed in Deleuze and Guattari's discussion of the reactive entrapment of desire in 'microfascisms', and by autonomist Marxism in the image of capital as the alienated expression of workers' own labour(-power). By constructing a Leviathan, one is exerting one's own power and one's libidinal energies and capacities for action, but one is doing so in a way which negates them, which denies that they are one's own or that they are properties of micropolitics of social groups and of desires, and which instead insists that they are 'really' the agency of the non-existent big Other – the Leviathan, the state, the party, the bosses. Of course in practice this feeds into the strength of actually-existing others, which is to say, of those who seek mastery. Against the self-positing mastery of free subjectivity, there rises up a vampiric mastery which can exist only through the constant self-flagellation of the 'represented', the alienated, the enslaved.

Organizational hierarchy is a disaster for movements of resistance for a number of reasons. First, it concentrates power in the hands of an elite who are able to use the movement to their own advantage, should a division emerge between themselves and the mass. Capitalism is well-structured to allow the cooption of such elites through their incorporation into structures such as parliamentary politics and the media 'celebrity' circuit. This has happened even to the German Green Party, who went out of their way to avoid such results through methods such as rotating leadership positions. In the last election, their main posters featured the face of Joschka Fischer, as if this coopted ex-militant is the party personified.

Second, organizations are open to infiltration, precisely because of their centralization. If the centre of an organization can be compromised or undermined, the entire organization can be weakened throughout its structure. A good example is the Black Panther Party, which collapsed in large part because the FBI was able to assassinate, discredit or otherwise eliminate its core leadership. Despite the fact that the Panthers were a grass-roots organization with a social basis in the ghettos, they were open to such tactics because of their adoption of an arborescent structure. Similar points could be made about the Bolshevik Party in Russia, not only in relation to its frequently compromised prerevolutionary situation (such as an occasion when a police agent was able to acquire entire membership lists from the Party Secretariat), but also in relation to the alleged 'betrayal' by Stalin. Whether one puts this down to a project inherent in Leninism or to a takeover by a Bonapartist faction after the revolution, it is clear that it was possible only because of the militaristic, centralized structure of the party itself.

Third, arborescent organization tends to draw activities away from the grass-roots base and into a combination of regular, formalized meetings, lobbying within the political system and set-piece actions arranged by the central leadership. Piven and Cloward clearly demonstrate this argument in relation to a number of social movements, showing how trade unions, civil rights protesters and unemployed groups, among others, were misled by the fallacy of hierarchic organization into tactics which weakened their ability to capitalize on their necessarily located and territorial potentials.[6] If the Bolsheviks seem like a counterexample, it should be recalled that the bulk of the party hierarchy opposed Lenin's *April Theses*, that Lenin himself failed to foresee or take advantage of the June insurrection and that the party leadership consistently overestimated the party's popularity in the countryside.[7] Instead of the desires of the oppressed feeding into social forms which tend towards their emancipation, these desires are channelled into a new master-signifier which then redirects the energies of activism as it sees fit. Thus, the energies subsumed in the movement, instead of being released and freed in emancipatory activity, become trapped in their own *image*, as an element in the Spectacle.

Furthermore, organizations tend towards crude and clumsy tactics. Disavowing fragmentation, they make it difficult for those with different tactical preferences or different social positions to work together. Despite the frequently cited image of people functioning harmoniously as cogs in a whole, organizations are usually torn apart with infighting and unable to extend their support-base. If disagreements occur, there are only two possibilities: the subsumption of the disagreement under a repressively-constructed illusion of consensus, or the fracturing of the organization itself. It is no coincidence that the most effective anti-capitalist events are often those where diverse tendencies are able to form separate spaces, without being expected to subordinate themselves to overarching structures. In addition, it should be realized that the pressures driving an organization in cases of disagreement will be those either of an elite or a majority. In the former case, one has a simple return to direct hierarchy, and in the latter, the appeal of the spectacle and the uneven development of oppositional ideas will guarantee that it is the most conservative strands which normally triumph. Deleuze and Guattari are right that pressures for emancipation are necessarily minoritarian, because majorities are compared to what Margaret Thornton terms 'Benchmark Man', an image of social normality.

Perhaps most importantly, the traditional organizational model fails to alter the relationship between the spectacle and everyday life, or between desire and social production. Actual activities are still channelled into forms governed by their own image, rather than the image altering in proportion to the actual and immediate. Similarly, desires are sublimated into the production of a new master-signifier which one seeks to advance in alterity, rather than operating in ways which problematize the primacy of social production and which tend to reverse the dominant ordering by making social production a function of the production of flows of desire. Since activists do not overcome their character-armouring, the 'cops in their heads', they are not able to construct social relations able to similarly restructure the world.

Fortunately, there is an alternative to the many repetitions of this flawed logic of organization, an alternative which takes us beyond the repetition of the organizational Oedipus complex of the master-signifier as name of the father, and which opens instead on to difference. A logic of horizontal *and anti-representational* political action (already present in traditions such as Situationism, primitivism, immediatism, insurrectionism and autonomism) stems from the critique of representation both as a mechanism for the articulation of needs and preferences and as a basis for thinking about how other worlds might be thought about and created. This has different aspects but rotates around the idea of the alienating nature of essentialism and 'fixity' whether conceptual, philosophical or organizational (for instance, the critique of roles in the work of Vaneigem, of domestication in primitivism, of the Spectacle in Debord, of spooks in Stirner, of alienation into capital in autonomism, and so on). This in turn implies the need to provide a critique of the key elements of representation upon which a vertical politics relies.

Switch 'the programme' off

Traditionally, political theory has equated to the search for some essential definition of humanity's needs, interests or essence. Having found such a notion a programme can then be constructed that promises to restore or enshrine the particular notion to the self or class or nation. As we noted above a manifesto is the translation of the programme into readily digestible terms for electoral purposes or for purposes of mobilizing individuals in some other way to support the cause. To take the example of the early Marx, the idea of communism is a direct response to the alienation Marx saw in capitalist relations, or wage labour. The species-essential character of labour is subordinated to the task of making a profit. Communism meant the restoration of labour and thus of 'life's prime want' through the socialization of the means of production. The 'essentializing' of labour is thus an essential step towards privileging communism as a normative ideal and at the same time combating rival conceptions of how the world should look, whether radical or conservative.

Stirner's critique of Marx inaugurated 'horizontalism' in that he identified such a manoeuvre not as the liberation of 'man' from the spooks that otherwise ensure our repression, but the erection of another spook ('Communism') that would in turn provide the basis for a new form of servitude.[8] Stirner's approach was instead to wage war on spooks, to encourage release from the perceived necessity of spooks. He insisted that individuals re-evaluate the terms and conditions of their attachment to projects and principles on an 'egoistic' basis. This is to say he wanted us to 'own' ourselves instead of being in thrall to something that lay outside ourselves in 'fixity'. His politics was thus similarly 'egoistic', rejecting revolution as an abstraction in favour of rebellion: the on-going and permanent war against the alienation of self from the 'representatives' of our own immediate desires. Stirner's rebellion set the template for a war against programmes, against the fixity of revolutionary ideology more generally. Stirner's critique of conceptual representation as a basis for thinking about the programme became a template for later attempts to free emancipatory struggle from the tyranny of ideology. In the wake of 1968 a succession of theorists and movements stressed the necessity for 'thinking for oneself' instead of becoming enslaved to a perspective or worldview lorded over by a theocratic caste of individuals whose task it was to maintain 'the line'. The Situationists and Immediatists (to name two groups) are both insistent on the necessity to reject 'ideology' in favour of forms of action between those who see 'through' the spectacle. The essay 'The Revolutionary Pleasure of Thinking for Yourself', for instance, posits a radical egoism as the very basis for a concern for others and for openness to difference, as ways of resisting the packaged-commodity model which above all demeans the self and destroys individual freedom.[9] But the Stirnerian critique poses the question of what next? How does the gesture of rejecting the need for a programme translate into collective action?

To pose such a question is to ask whether or not it is possible to act except on the basis of a unifying ideology of the kind represented by orthodox Marxism and neoliberalism, an ideology, that is, which is able to give an account of social and historical development and thus of the nature of the better world to come. How can a movement cohere or be effective without an ideology to guide its actions? It is perhaps instructive here to return to Stirner, for his point was not that individuals should act alone or necessarily in their own interests; rather, they should act 'egoistically' – that is, on the basis that they do not surrender their own capacity or facility to review the terms and conditions of acting. The point about rebellion is that it is a continual process, not a one-off 'act' of transcendence; but it is a process that admits of collusion and alliances. It is therefore a praxis of micropower, a micropolitics of resistance in everyday life, which rejects the myriad of spooks which construct the hyperreality of the Spectacle. Thus the union of egoists which Stirner termed the form of interaction made possible by the emergence of humanity from the world of spooks and phantoms is a contingent and negotiable coalition. Individuals could therefore act together on whatever basis they saw fit, as opposed to having to sign up for a vision of the world or a conception of a better place.

Immediatism, as for instance in the work of Hakim Bey, enlarges this notion by stressing the way in which action can be motivated in a multiplicity of different ways and to different intensity and effect, better expressed in ontological terms as chaos and complexity rather than as order. Thus the terms and conditions of collective action should reflect the different desires and affects that motivate people even confronted by the same injustices or by the hope of constructing something similar. Difference of affect, of emotion, of perception elicits differences in terms of the way in which we perceive the need or otherwise to act. The issue then is less to aim at programmatic orthodoxy than how to provide linkages for the various ways in which people do and will rebel, resist and revolt. Indeed, for the Immediatists, the Situationists, Deleuze, Reich and Foucault, the liberation of desire itself from its entrapment in the shackles of the status quo, from its repressive reduction to packaged commodities (including the repressive tolerance of 'opinions' as possessions of the self, the reduction of sexuality to heterosexual fixity and the repression of madness beneath neurotic conformity) becomes a central issue of political liberation.

This in turn points to the desirability for the generation of spaces in which people can interact to mutual benefit – as opposed to, say, the annual congress mechanism of 'democratic centralism' designed to create a line to which everyone will adhere. It is clear, for example, that one of the reasons why many activists, particularly 'horizontals', have invested so heavily in the social forum process is that they see the forums as providing such spaces: spaces of discussion, of comparison, of shared pedagogies, of affinity and affiliation. What they are not geared up for is the generation of a party line, orthodoxy or programme. Of course there are frustrations here too. The social forums can have the appearance of political ineffectuality, of being a kind of Glastonbury experience where we leave behind the worries and cares of everyday life in search of a short-lived 'high'.[10] But this in turn ramps up the expectations, whetting the appetite for more and greater highs, more creativity, more interactions of a non-instrumental kind. As McLeish has suggested, with the addition of databases in which participants could log their own passions, interests, activisms and connections, the forums have the potential to become this kind of 'immediatist' hive in which activists can find common cause with others, multiplying and remultiplying the activist base – and all without a programme, or the perceived need to generate one.[11] The social forums facilitate what might be termed an activist rhizomatics: a way in which networks can coalesce, develop, multiply and re-multiply. A network does not have a programme, and neither does it need one. What it needs are zones of encounter, shared learning, solidarity, affiliation, and the coalescence provided by networks of support, affinity groups and the ability to mobilize together without the need for a trunk to convert the rhizomes into branches.

It's (not) party time

As we have noted above, the party is the vehicle for 'modernist' radical politics. There are of course many variations of the party, but also some constants. The party is the arbiter of the line to be pursued by members and activists in their dealings among themselves and with others they seek to mobilize. It is the point of reference for matters of conflict between members. It is responsible for discipline within the ranks. It has an inside and an outside, so that one either is or is not a member. It provides the fulcrum or space within which strategy and tactics are formulated. It provides the political leadership without which the ensemble will fail to be 'effective'. It provides leaders for the next administration or for the transition to some point where the party itself will become unnecessary. The party is a government in waiting. As such it mirrors the apparatus of the state itself. It is hierarchical, based on a division of labour and a teleological notion of effectivity – the rationale of the party is capturing power. It thus becomes in itself a Leviathan, an alienation of power which reproduces amongst its mass membership the same subordination which exists in the wider society.

It follows from the above that for those who wish to develop 'horizontal' relationships the party cannot be the vehicle for thinking about the MGJ. If not the party, what else? Again we find a certain tradition of theorizing outside the party which can be useful for contemplating alternative models and conceptualizations. We have already mentioned Stirner and the union of egoists which revolves around notions that are more familiar as the 'revolution in everyday life' – a succession of resistances and rebellions tied together through bonds of empathy and affinity – or not. One can think in this context of the very concrete resistances discussed in the work of authors such as James Scott, who recounts how such activities arise in the context of peasant societies, Rick Fantasia, who demonstrates the need for similar everyday constellations as a generative matrix operating behind unionized and non-unionized worker resistances, and Hecht and Simone's discussion of the 'art of African micropolitics', the diverse, hybrid social forms which enable survival and resistance in even the harshest contexts.[12] The work of Sartre is also a key reference point, not least for Deleuze and Guattari, the two thinkers who in turn gave the most sustained thought to the nature of combination and recombination after 1968.

To Sartre, collective entities divided into those that were intentional and those that were accidental.[13] As he famously describes it a line of people queuing for bread is at one level a collective entity, but it is one he characterized as 'seriality', the appearance of a group in the same space but without shared goals or objectives. Intentional groups such as revolutionary organizations themselves divided into two: the group-in-fusion (GIF) and the pledged group. The difference between the two kinds of grouping is the degree to which agents remain autonomous and thus able to influence the nature and direction of the group itself. The pledged group is bound by an oath of loyalty or allegiance that transfers autonomy of the subject to the autonomy of the leader or leadership (the 'pledge' which gives this form its name). It is a group premised on the necessity for discipline and subordination to the party line, a necessity enforced through what Sartre terms 'fraternity-terror', a terroristic mutual panopticism operating among activists themselves, a surveillance of all against all. It punishes transgressors and regards the carrying out of orders as the highest task for most members. The GIF is a much more protean and complex ensemble, predicated as it is on ability and proclivity of members to interact with each other in an active and free-flowing manner. It makes no demands on individuals, but is instead premised on the active desire of individuals to want to be involved. There are no penalties for transgression or for querying and questioning aims and objectives. Indeed such discussions are what characterizes the GIF and without them it is likely to lapse into a pledge group.

Deleuze and Guattari were heavily influenced by Sartre, particularly Guattari whose early work concerned the nature of interactions between individuals and groups.[14] Whilst staying close to the model outlined by Sartre they stress the centrality of active desire to the construction of GIF, re-christened as 'subject groups' or 'nomadic assemblages'. The group is constructed on a minoritarian, univocal basis as opposed to the majoritarian, representative basis evinced by pledged groups (including most revolutionary groups) and mainstream political parties. These would for Guattari be 'dependent groups', secondary to the functioning of existing society and 'bogged down in the phantasies of the dominant group', and therefore fundamentally alienating and non-revolutionary.[15] Thus, Guattari calls for 'the deployment of new conceptual references, the production of new forms of organisation not even hinted at in the regular assortment currently on offer on the Marxist–Leninist market'.[16] We have noted that representation is based on 'speaking for' – speaking for 'us', 'everyone', the oppressed, the majority, the working class, the black community. It is constructed from the point of view of a static molar subject which Deleuze and Guattari term a 'denumerable' set.[17] This is a set or group that conforms to the logic of molar identities, identities which are constructed *for* people, rather than *by* people. A classic denumerable set in political rhetoric is 'the majority', as in 'the majority is in favour of cracking down on delinquents'. Who is the majority? A fictive 'set' – the more than 50 per cent. It is the ostensibly objective nature of the denumerable set that permits those speaking for it to claim legitimacy for their actions, which is in turn the 'move' made by vertical groups and bodies to cement the hierarchy, need for order and discipline: 'The party speaks for the working class'; 'the people of the developing world want more development'; 'the black community wants to integrate into society'; 'everyone knows that . . .'. And yet the resistance of rhizomatic movements exceeds and overflows this representationality. 'The power of the minorities is not measured by their capacity to enter and make themselves felt within the majority order, nor even to reverse the necessarily tautological criterion of the majority, but to bring to bear the force of the nondenumerable sets, against the axiomatic of denumerable sets.'[18]

A nomadic assemblage is one premised on the idea that there are only minorities ('ours is becoming an age of minorities') and thus that there is no denumerable set which can or should be spoken for. Given the non-denumerable nature of the group, there can be no speaking-for.

There is 'univocity', which is to say the recognition of difference as constitutive of each singularity within the group itself. Such an assemblage is a molecular as opposed to molar entity. Each singularity retains its own autonomy, its own voice, its own presence within the larger aggregate of which it is a part. This is not to say that the group cannot act as an agent, or that it has no 'agentic' properties: far from it. As Deleuze and Guattari make clear in *A Thousand Plateaus*, when they discuss singularity they do not mean individuals, they mean *any* assemblage that is capable of becoming singular.[19] This means individuals but it also means groups and larger aggregates still. The point is not to dissolve agency, but to make it more substantial and effective by drawing on the active 'becoming-revolutionary' of the singularities that compose it. The singularity does not submit to the authority of the group, it creates and underwrites its very existence as part of its molecular structure.

The singularity does not pledge an oath of allegiance, promise to obey or carry out commands. It is not a matter of duties or obligations – of submitting to something that one wills for oneself ('my party right or wrong'). It is a matter of becoming-revolutionary, of allying oneself to everything and everyone that represents a challenge to the axiomatics of representation, of fixed identities, of molar subjects, of hierarchy, oppression, denumerability, alienation. It is a becoming-nomadic: a continual and perpetual dissolution of bonds, ties and 'duties' that keep one from 'moving', a permanent 'line of flight' which breaks out of the cages of capitalism and statism and the traps laid by the various parties to reterritorialize the emancipated flows. 'Horizontality' is from this point of view not a question of joining a party, but of dissolving the axiomatic of parties in the quest for combinations that fully express the availability of autonomy and authentic modes of univocal engagement with and alongside others. The proliferation of rhizomes is also an effective way of multiplying points of challenge so as to reduce the effectiveness of measures of repression. As any gardener who has tried to eliminate dandelions knows, a rhizome system is very difficult to reach because, when a rhizome is destroyed, others will form and re-link, re-forming the networks which have been damaged. An arborescent organization, in contrast, can be cut down far more easily.

The state we're (not) in

It is typical of vertical approaches that the assumption is that change is produced for 'the people' by an agent which is not itself 'the people'. It is the state or states acting in combination which 'act' as opposed to individuals, groups, movements and collectivities acting in combination.

Here lies the source of Bakunin's critique of Marxism, and more generally of the anarchist and libertarian suspicion of the transitional strategies favoured by communists after Marx.[20] Bakunin's critique is one based on the logic of the state itself as opposed to the inclinations of those who run or control it. For Bakunin, as indeed for realist and neorealist commentators on global politics, the world of states is a Hobbesian 'state of nature'. There is no superior force to the state, and yet the state finds itself in competition with other states for territory, resources, people. This in turn necessitates a strategy of alliance between states in turn excluding those other states that do not share the values or priorities of the alliance. Here is a repetition of the logic of power that characterizes the history of the state and the wars fought by them. As Bakunin makes clear, only a break with such a logic can secure the transformation of social relations and so it is only by making a break with the state – sooner rather than later – that those concerned with the pursuit of alternative visions of social and global justice can begin the task of reconstituting the political. It is in this context that Bakunin can refer to a freedom which, instead of stopping at the boundaries of others, instead enriches itself in a continual expansion along with others' freedom. As Deleuze and Guattari put it, the position of the excluded precludes their reformulation as a state. 'It is hard to see what an Amazon-State would be, a women's State, or a State of erratic workers, a State of the "refusal" of work.'[21] For Bakunin, Marxism excludes such others by trying to form a state which must necessarily become the state of the *organized* workers, the labour aristocracy, if not of the party bureaucrats and intellectuals, thereby excluding the precarious workers, the unrecalcitrant peasants and the lumpenproletarian 'rabble'. There can be no state of the 'rabble', so a politics of the 'rabble' must necessarily be anti-statist and non-statist.

Horizontalist strategies do not merely avoid the state as a means or instrument, they are anti-statist: that is, they self-consciously eschew the capturing of power in favour of alternative strategies that maintain the integrity and autonomy of all constituent singularities. Stirner's 'Union of Egoists' is not of course a state – the term 'union' from *Eigenheit* conveys the horizontal nature of the bonds to be created by autonomous egos. What Stirner was concerned to demonstrate (and which continues in the work of later anarchists and libertarians) is the necessarily 'continuous' nature of the transformation of social relations. In this sense there are no 'stages' or transitions on the way to something. There is no split temporally, conceptually and politically between Today and Tomorrow. It is on such a basis that it would be more accurate to describe horizontalist strategies not as a process of 'capture' and subsequent transformation but as continual unfolding, extension and enlargement of present networks, affiliations and resistances. This in turn entails the undermining, emptying out, draining and curtailing of the power of states, indeed of all molar representational entities.

Here we are reminded of the figure of the rhizome in Deleuze and Guattari's *A Thousand Plateaus*.[22] The rhizome represents non-linear continuity and fuzzy aggregates that are interlinked or interwoven, but on the basis of horizontal or transversal connection as opposed to the stasis of arborescent structures with their segmentarities and hierarchies. By contrast the world of nomadic combination is a world of smooth space, which is to say of *ungoverned* space. It is a space of combination and recombination on a minoritarian, non-denumerable basis, again stressing the redundancy of the state as a basis for thinking horizontal relations. In such a space possibility and contingency are held open by virtue of the immanence of the relations into which we as singularities enter. There is no fiction of an imagined community, no ties that bind, no imagined social contract tying our fates together in some one-off act of communal obligation. There is nothing above or beyond the terms of combination and recombination itself. A horizontal world is, as Marcos puts it, a world of 'many worlds'; but what makes many worlds possible is the delight and celebration of our autonomy from those who speak for others. It is a world beyond representatives, fixed and known identities, obligations and duties that others erect for us and call 'transcendental'. It is a world beyond the dialectics of historical progression, beyond utilitarianism and the 'hard choices' of revolutionaries caught between the promise and the reality. Is it a utopian world?

Horizontalism and the politics of im/possibility

But surely 'horizontalism' is a dream – a utopian dream. Are horizontals not in the same category as all those dreamers and utopians who imagined the beyond or outside of power? The answer is very clearly 'yes and no'. On the one hand what is imagined in invoking smooth space, the rhizome, is so far removed from the reality of day-to-day politics, of life under advanced capitalist conditions, of interactions between those who have little faith in the possibilities and creativeness of human desire that it is *clearly* utopian. It is an 'impossible' politics. But with Žižek we might say that this is precisely why it is important to stand by 'horizontalism'. It is the very 'impossibility' of genuinely transformative politics that assures us that it is actually worth pursuing. Unlike Žižek, however, the point is not to evoke horizontal politics as an Act or Event – both of which are inevitably 'betrayed' on his reading.[23] It is not to 'go through' utopia in order to reinscribe social reality anew with its antagonisms and alienations, lacks and emptinesses. It is to insist that as a politics horizontalism is an ethics, just as a horizontal ethics is at the same time a politics. Becoming-minor, becoming-revolutionary is a stance *towards* the world, a stance *in* the world. It is the embodiment of a practice the generalization of which is a transformative politics. As we mentioned above, the point is to stress the absolute continuity between desiring production, the singular and the social, and thus the necessity to break down the sense of disjuncture that characterizes verticalist notions of transformation, with their stages, transitions between A and B, dialectical movements and feats of organizational acrobatics. Becoming-minor is also becoming-immanent, a recognition of the flat or 'smooth' nature of the transformative process itself, the absence of transcendent macro-powers and master-signifiers and the refusal of the illusion of a trunk. Tolstoy remarked in reply to the revolutionary utilitarianism he saw around him in the Russia of the late nineteenth century that 'everybody thinks of changing humanity, and nobody thinks of changing himself'.[24] In reply to this inkling of the doctrine of 'the revolution in everyday life', we would assert that the detachment of the one from the many, of the individual and society, of the molecular and the molar is creating a break between the singular and plural, when it is clear to us that there is no such break – or rather there should not be one. It is a mark of our own alienation that we accept the dichotomy between ethics and politics as implied in Tolstoy's remarks. Ethics is politics, politics is ethics. Rebellion, rejection, revolt against the representatives are political and ethical gestures – they are the gestures of those who have decided to speak for themselves and not let others speak for them. As such they represent the germ of a flat, immanent, smooth politics of networks, not parties.

The MGJ has entered a new phase. It has moved beyond the temporary and contingent convergences that marked the period up to and including Seattle and the large-scale protests that followed in its wake. It has moved into the phase where the aims, objectives and principles upon which the movement will develop are being debated and decided upon. So far the signs are mixed. Clearly verticalism is a default setting for many within the MGJ just as it is for many outside unused to the idea that there is life beyond parties, elections, voting, central committees, manifestos, plenaries, speaking for, speaking on behalf of, remaining silent. Already the social forum process seems perennially beset with catering for the needs of those who have narrow or limited interests, but who have the money and resources to override the hopes of many activists and smaller groupings. For this reason it is likely that the phenomenon of the parallel social forum will gather force with autonomists, libertarians and anarchists as well as elements excluded by lack of resources, untouchability or invisibility holding sessions outside the official setting. The various personality cults that 'necessitate' set-piece plenaries, roundtables and media interviews in turn reinforce the 'spectacular' nature of the forums and in turn the MGJ itself. Yet in and around are signs of 'another world', from the resistances and revolts of everyday life that puncture the surface of what Castoriadis aptly termed the 'air-conditioned comfort' of the North to the growing unwillingness of those in the South, in Brazil, Argentina, South Korea or the Chiapas to obey the masters. To all those who say 'Ya Basta!' not only to the old masters, but also to the new – the would-be masters of the revolutionary party – we need to reaffirm that another world is possible: a world of many worlds.

Notes

1 S. Tormey, *Anti-Capitalism: A Beginner's Guide* (Oxford: Oneworld, 2004), chs 3 and 4.

2 J. Arquilla and D. Ronfeldt, 'Swarming and the Future of Conflict' (2000), online at http://www.rand.org/publications/DB/DB311/.

3 N. Klein, *Fences and Windows* (London: Flamingo, 2002).

4 A. Callinicos, 'Regroupment, Realignment and the Revolutionary Left' (2002), online at http://www.swp.org.uk/INTER/regroupen.pdf.

5 R. Michels, *Political Parties: A Sociological Study of the Oligarchical Tendencies of Modern Democracy* (New York: Transaction, 1998).

6 F. F. Piven and R. A. Cloward, *Poor People's Movements: Why They Succeed, How They Fail* (New York: Random House, 1988).

7 M. Liebman, *Leninism under Lenin* (London: Merlin, 1975), pp. 162–80.

8 M. Stirner, *The Ego and its Own* (London: Rebel Press, 1993).

9 Anon, 'The Revolutionary Pleasure of Thinking for Yourself' (1975), online at http://deoxy.org/rst.htm.

10 S. Tormey, 'The 2003 European Social Forum: Where Next for the Anti-Capitalist Movement?', *Capital & Class*, 84 (2004), 151–60.

11 P. McLeish, 'The Promise of the European Social Forum', *The Commoner*, 8 (2004) online at www.commoner.org.uk/01–12 groundzero.

12 R. Fantasia, *Cultures of Solidarity: Consciousness, Action and Contemporary American Workers* (Stanford, CA: University of California Press, 1988); J. C. Scott, *Domination and the Arts of Resistance* (New Haven, CT: Yale University Press, 1992); D. Hecht and A. M. Simone, *Invisible Governance: The Art of African Micro-Politics* (New York: Autonomedia, 1994).

13 J.-P. Sartre, *The Critique of Dialectical Reason, Volume 1* (London: Verso, 1976).

14 G. Genosko, *Felix Guattari: An Aberrant Introduction* (London: Continuum, 2002).

15 F. Guattari, *Molecular Revolution: Psychiatry and Politics* (Harmondsworth: Penguin, 1984), p. 191.
16 Ibid., p. 199.
17 G. Deleuze and F. Guattari, *A Thousand Plateaus: Capitalism and Schizophrenia* (London: Athlone Press, 1984), p. 470.
18 Ibid., p. 471.
19 Ibid.
20 M. Bakunin, 'Marxism, Freedom and the State' (1867–72). Available at: http:Harmondsworth//www.marxists.org/reference/archive/bakunin/works/mf-state/.
21 Deleuze and Guattari, *A Thousand Plateaus: Capitalism and Schizophrenia*, p. 472.
22 Ibid., pp. 3–25.
23 S. Žižek, *The Sublime Object of Ideology* (London: Verso, 1989), pp. 211–12.
24 L. Tolstoy, *Government is Violence: Essays on Anarchism and Pacifism* (London: Phoenix Press, 1990), p. 19.

14

American Globalism 'Madison Avenue-Style': A Critique of US Public Diplomacy after 9/11

Manfred B. Steger

Introduction

More than three years after al-Qaeda's devastating attacks on the most recognized symbols of American power, it is easy to forget the worldwide outpouring of sympathy that followed on the heels of the strikes. Granted, some individuals may have revelled in the callous notion that the USA had finally received its just deserts, but most ordinary people around the globe appeared to be genuinely upset by the massive loss of life in New York City and Washington, DC. Even the most inveterate critics of American foreign policy paused in amazement as the headline of a major French newspaper proclaimed that 'We are all Americans now', and thousands of Iranian youths staged touching solidarity vigils in central Tehran.[1] Unable to rally the Muslim world behind its violent vision, al-Qaeda actually presented the USA with a golden opportunity to enhance its global leadership by pulling together a transnational coalition of equal partners committed to seeking out and punishing those criminals responsible for the atrocities of 9/11.

Failing to take advantage of this auspicious moment, the Bush administration rushed instead into a global War on Terror, thereby not only elevating the political status of a private network to that of a war-making entity, but also casting an exceedingly wide semantic net around the notion of 'terrorists'. Unwilling to involve itself in genuine multilateral efforts to combat global terrorism, the US government acted as though it had all the right answers, demanding from its 'allies' nothing less than unquestioning loyalty. Claiming that his country's responsibility to history was to 'rid the world of evil', President George W. Bush famously put the world on notice that whoever was not with America was against it.[2] Bush's persistent Manichean portrayal of his country as the force of good battling the barbaric hordes of evil – combined with his administration's obvious disdain for the United Nations – fuelled public perceptions around the world that America was an arrogant bully indifferent to what the rest of humanity thought. Within months of the attacks, the thrilling prospect of a caring America leading a collective struggle for a better world had turned into the dark reality of a vengeful hyperpower unleashing its awesome military arsenal without much international consultation.

A series of global opinion polls tracked the rising tide of anti-Americanism, particularly in the Muslim world. For example, a 2002 Pew Charitable Trust Poll found that 69 per cent of Egyptians, 75 per cent of Jordanians, 59 per cent of Lebanese, 69 per cent of Pakistanis, and 55 per cent of Turks had unfavourable views of the USA.[3] Surprised by the sharp increase of negative perceptions, the US government remained nonetheless wedded to its militant unilateralism, doggedly pursuing its imperial vision for a 'new American century'.[4] Wrapped in its flag and donning the rhetorical cloak of waging a 'just war on terror', the USA escalated its military operations in the Middle East while at the same time seeking to convince sceptical audiences around the world that its real aim was to bring noble 'American values' such as 'freedom' and 'democracy' to the region's oppressed people.

This double-pronged strategy was rooted in the influential view that the War on Terror involved both military and ideological confrontations with radical Islamism. As many US foreign policy experts emphasized, winning the 'battle for the hearts and minds' in the Muslim world required a major public relations effort.[5] Touted as 'twenty-first century public diplomacy', the State Department launched a massive propaganda campaign to fix America's global image problem. Substituting neoliberal advertising techniques for a genuine cross-cultural dialogue committed to addressing serious problems such as the global redistribution of wealth and technology, the Bush administration vigorously pushed its imperial version of 'American globalism'.[6] However, within less than a year, there were clear signs that anti-American sentiments around the world were intensifying rather than subsiding. A few months later, the campaign for a new and improved 'Brand USA' came to a screeching halt.

This chapter opens with a brief historical overview of US public diplomacy and its cultural embeddedness in American globalism. Discussing the various elements of the post-9/11 public diplomacy campaign, it then offers a critique of the ill-fated attempt to spread American values 'Madison Avenue-style'. Ending on a constructive note, the chapter suggests that solving America's image problems abroad requires far more than infusing public diplomacy with slick marketing techniques.

US public diplomacy before 9/11

Coined in the mid-1960s by Dean Edmund Guillon at Tufts University, 'public diplomacy' refers to government-sponsored programmes and initiatives designed to inform and shape public opinion in other countries with the ultimate goal of promoting US national interests.[7] While complementing and supporting traditional diplomacy, public diplomacy does not engage other governments primarily through formal channels but seeks to influence diverse non-governmental segments of foreign societies. Moreover, as Peter van Ham notes, it focuses on *values* as opposed to traditional diplomacy's concern with *issues*.[8] Created specifically for media consumption and carried out by a variety of public and private agents, public diplomacy has been an amorphous enterprise operating primarily on the level of rhetoric. As former US ambassador Richard Holbrooke put it, 'Call it public diplomacy, or public affairs, or psychological warfare, or – if you really want to be blunt – propaganda.'[9]

Given Americans' long-standing suspicions of government propaganda, US public diplomacy never enjoyed the high status it was afforded in other countries. Early efforts by Benjamin Franklin and Thomas Jefferson to cultivate a 'decent respect for the opinions of mankind' represented a rather instrumental strategy by a young republic eager to establish itself as a fully-fledged member of the international community. Indeed, it was not until America's entry into the First World War that public diplomacy turned into a substantive enterprise. The Wilson administration created the Committee on Public Information which, at its peak, employed 150,000 people. The objective was not only to strengthen the 'war will' among an ethnically diverse home population, but also to convince foreign publics that a reliable and invincible America would defeat the German war machine and 'make the world safe for democracy'.[10]

After the Second World War, public diplomacy added a new dimension with US Senator J. William Fulbright's immensely successful scholarly and cultural exchange programmes designed to 'tell the American story' in academic settings. In 1953, the Eisenhower administration inaugurated the era of modern public diplomacy by creating the gigantic US Information Agency (USIA). Still wary of government-sponsored propaganda, Congress prohibited the domestic distribution of its periodicals, newspapers, magazines, articles, broadcasts and films.[11] Operating on a billion-dollar budget and employing more than 12,000 people at its peak in the mid-1960s, USIA oversaw such well-known broadcast programmes as Voice of America, Radio Free Europe/Radio Liberty, Radio Free Asia, and Worldnet TV, which reached millions of people in dozens of countries. Born of the dynamics of the Cold War, USIA developed a surprisingly decentralized and semi-autonomous organizational structure, led by public affairs officers with a keen eye for existing cultural diversity in the world. The heads of the Agency's posts in each country were given some leeway to design their own programmes and to decide how much or how little of Washington-produced media material they wanted to include in their initiatives.[12]

At the same time, however, US public diplomacy during the Cold War period operated in a foreign policy climate characterized by America's globalist impulse to treat the whole world as a proper sphere for its political influence. Intensely nationalistic at its core, American globalism was born in the flames of Pearl Harbor and represents an ideology dedicated to the spread of 'American values' – freedom, democracy, rule of law, and so on – ostensibly for the benefit of humankind.[13] Indeed, at the core of American globalism one finds the unshakeable conviction that the universality and superiority of American national values justifies and even necessitates the *global* projection of US power.

American globalism, in turn, cannot be understood apart from a broader cultural matrix that developed around the idea of American exceptionalism. Siobhan McEvoy-Levy identifies two major strands of this doctrine. One calls for the wholesale remodelling of the world according to American ideals, while the other promotes American superiority within the limits of the established international order.[14] But even the proponents of the second, more moderate variant of American exceptionalism, regard liberty, democracy, individualism, diversity and free markets as values that are fundamentally 'American' in character. Their assumed universal applicability implies that anyone opposed to those values can only be 'irrational' or 'evil'. In fact, the vehement rejection of American globalism during, say, the Vietnam years or the 1980 Iran hostage crisis tended to generate in many Americans sentiments of anger and humiliation as they struggled to understand why anybody would want to reject their country's precious gift to the world. Anger was usually followed by one of two extreme reactions: temporary retreat (fuelling, in turn, the flames of isolationism), or aggression, manifested in renewed attempts to impose American values and social arrangements on dissenting nations.

During the 1980s, President Reagan's preference for the second approach resulted in the creation of an Office of Public Diplomacy dedicated to 'managing' foreign media. Moreover, it was to encourage popular support at home and abroad for America's arms race with the Soviet Union and its aggressive military interventions in Central America.[15] Assuming the presidency after the collapse of the 'Evil Empire' and President George H. W. Bush's successful prosecution of the 1991 Gulf War, President Clinton developed his approach to public diplomacy in the shadow of Francis Fukuyama's influential idea that American liberalism had defeated all of its ideological competitors, thus leaving the world no alternative to Anglo-American liberal democracy and free markets. As Peter van Ham notes, the main conclusion following from this conceptual framework was that the newly liberated Eastern European nations would spontaneously opt for the market-oriented 'American model'.[16] This neoliberal reliance on the 'free market' as the 'natural' agent for the global spread of American values meant that the state had to get out of the way and leave public diplomacy to a phalanx of corporate forces that made the case for a new world order based on 'turbo-capitalism'. Arguing that the 'new economy' of the information society required fully deregulated and globally integrated markets, American globalists in the Clinton era primarily opted for 'soft power' to secure US hegemony: that is, the use of cultural and ideological appeals to shape favourable outcomes without commanding allegiance.[17]

The embrace of market fundamentalism during the 1990s turned American globalism into a fiercely deterministic doctrine centred on the ideological claim that globalization – understood as the liberalization of markets and the worldwide spread of American values – was inevitable and irreversible.[18] This faith in economic Providence translated not only in a significant drop in US military spending, but also in a decrease of government funds earmarked for public diplomacy. Between 1989 and 1999, USIA's annual budget shrank by $150 million, or 10 per cent. The resources for its mission in Indonesia, the world's largest Muslim nation, were cut in half.[19] By the end of the decade, USIA had ceased to exist as an independent agency as it was decided to 'integrate' it into the State Department as the Office of International Information Programs and the Bureau of Educational and Cultural Affairs under the jurisdiction of a new Undersecretary of State for Diplomacy and Public Affairs.[20] As William Kiehl notes, the once formidable public affairs agency was 'reduced to a shadow on the periphery of foreign policy'.[21]

US public diplomacy after 9/11

The events of 9/11 marked the reversal of the Clintonian laissez-faire approach to public diplomacy, as it became clear that the magnitude of the terrorist challenge required the development of effective war propaganda by the US government. Neoconservative hawks in the Pentagon vied with neoliberal doves in the State Department for control over US public diplomacy. Defense Secretary Rumsfeld's cohorts eventually self-destructed when their ill-conceived attempt to set up an Office for Strategic Influence (OSI) was derided in the national media as the creation of an 'Office for Disinformation' designed to spread false 'news stories' to the foreign press. Secretary of State Colin Powell emerged as the clear winner in this contest, but his sole control over the public diplomacy agenda ended in January 2003 when President Bush established the White House Office of Global Communications, an agency charged with 'improving America's image abroad by better conveying U.S. policies'.[22] In the aftermath of 9/11, however, the main responsibility for dealing with the rising tide of anti-Americanism rested with Charlotte Beers, the newly appointed Undersecretary of State for Public Diplomacy and Public Affairs.

Powell's choice of Beers reflected the emerging partnership between government reinvigorated by the new security agenda and the corporate sector struggling to keep alive its globalist project of expanding markets and trade in a time of global terror. Prior to her appointment, Beers had served as Chief Executive Officer of J. Walter Thompson and Ogilvy & Mather (two of the world's top ten advertising corporations), handling the multimillion dollar advertising accounts of such powerful clients as IBM. Thus, she brought to her new government job a thorough understanding of cutting-edge commercial marketing and public relations techniques developed specifically to meet the new challenges of the global information society. Hence, it is hardly surprising that she approached the task of improving America's image in the world in terms of 'branding': that is, the attempt to establish a positive relationship between the commercial 'product' – American values – and its 'users' or 'buyers' abroad.[23]

Convinced that four decades in the advertising industry had been the perfect preparation for her new position, Beers saw herself as the salesperson-in-chief hawking America's 'intangible assets – things like our belief system and our values' to her 'target audience' in the Muslim world. Indeed, for Beers, public diplomacy and commercial advertising were linked by the same market logic: 'You'll find that in any great brand, the leverageable asset is the emotional underpinning of the brand – or what people believe, what they think, what they feel when they use it. I am much more comfortable with that dimension of the assignment, because I have dealt with it before.'[24] Agreeing wholeheartedly with Beers's Madison Avenue approach to public diplomacy, Secretary Powell countered public criticisms of appointing a politically inexperienced advertising executive to such an important post by saying, 'There is nothing wrong with getting somebody who knows how to sell something.' 'After all', he added, 'we are selling a product. We need someone who can rebrand foreign policy, rebrand diplomacy. And besides, Charlotte Beers got me to buy Uncle Ben's rice.'[25]

As a priority, Undersecretary Beers had a meeting with the Ad Council – an umbrella organization of the advertisement industry specializing in so-called 'public service announcements' – to develop a series of television commercials that would capture the 'essence' of 'American freedom and democracy'. The most striking of these commercials shows a typical American suburban street with the caption '9/11 has changed the USA forever', followed by a depiction of the same street with flags flying from every house while a confident voice praises the patriotism exhibited by US citizens. Carried by national networks, such messages violated the traditional prohibition against the domestic dissemination of government propaganda. As Peter van Ham observes, Beers countered this charge by arguing that the ads were part of 'a broader exercise to reposition and recharge the "American brand"'.[26]

Upon launching her public relations blitz in early 2002, Undersecretary Beers identified three main strategic goals of her campaign for a new and improved Brand USA: (1) countering anti-American sentiments by effectively conveying genuine American values and beliefs to the rest of the world, especially the Middle East, and by applying the most up-to-date communication techniques and methods; (2) demonstrating the global opportunities that result from democratization, good governance, and open markets; and (3) supporting an appropriate education of the younger generation in crisis regions. At the same time, however, she consistently emphasized that her task was not to participate in policy-making, but to inform 'many publics of the content of U.S. policy – accurately, clearly and swiftly'.[27] To those ends, the Undersecretary agreed to a number of new initiatives.

Perhaps her most substantive project was the creation of the Middle East radio network 'Sawa' (Arabic for 'together') and a 24-hour Middle East television network. The latter was meant to compete with al-Jazeera and other regional Arab broadcast networks. Specifically targeting listeners aged 30 or under, Radio Sawa's programming was music-driven with periodic newscasts that presented the US government's view. In addition, Beers oversaw the creation of a brochure on 9/11 titled 'The Network of Terrorism'. More than a million copies were distributed in the Muslim world. She also collaborated with California-based Globe TV to fund an exchange of Arab and US journalists, including Shereen el Wakeel, the anchorwoman of the popular Egyptian television show 'Good Morning Egypt'. Moreover, her office embarked on the systematic search for thousands of foreign professionals, students and artists who had participated in past decades in US government-sponsored exchange programmes, hoping to pressure them into serving in their respective countries as 'mini-ambassadors' for the USA. Finally, she advocated English teaching to foreigners in their own schools as 'an effective way of exposing them to American values and preparing them for productive lives in a modern world'.[28]

When Beers resigned unexpectedly in March 2003 – ostensibly for health reasons – commentators were united in their negative assessment of her campaign. After all, world opinion polls actually pointed to *intensifying* anti-American sentiments. The war in Iraq and the difficult occupation of the country by coalition forces only made matters worse. Even in the UK, America's closest and most sympathetic partner, positive attitudes towards the USA dropped from 75 per cent in July 2002 to 58 per cent in March 2004.[29] Congress was so dismayed at the results of Beers's efforts that it appointed a special commission to recommend new and better public diplomacy strategies for the Muslim world. Criticisms of Beers's performance included accusations that she failed to take into consideration the fundamental cultural differences between Americans and Arabs; charges that she was not trying to measure scientifically what impact her public relations efforts were having on her target audience; and allegations that she did not spend enough time in the Middle East. Indeed, a few days before her resignation, the frustrated Undersecretary conceded that 'the gap between who we [Americans] are and how we wish to be seen and how we are in fact seen, is frighteningly wide'.[30]

In addition to having fallen far short of its professed goal, Beers's campaign was also counterproductive and dangerous. Let me offer four reasons for this assessment. First, the central metaphor of Beer's message – 'American values' – is historically incorrect, culturally insensitive, and politically foolish. Given that broad ideals such as freedom, democracy and diversity can be found in almost all cultures at various times, the exclusivist claim of any single country to these values runs the risk of generating intense sentiments of resentment and inferiority in non-Americans. For example, the widespread American conviction that 'democracy' was 'invented' in Greece 2,500 years ago and culminated in the American republic overlooks a number of important qualifications: (1) ancient Greece was culturally much closer to the Mediterranean societies of West Asia and North Africa than to those of Northern Europe; (2) Greek democracy was never 'democratic' in the modern sense; (3) the evolution of democracy did not lead smoothly from point A (Greece) to point Z (USA), but is characterized by long interruptions, dramatic reversals, and vital contributions from many cultures; (4) existing forms of democracy are far too varied and complex to be reduced to one ideal type; (5) American democracy consistently fails to live up to its advertised standards (as demonstrated, for example, by the Presidential elections in 2000).

Indeed, the constant representation of freedom and democracy as 'American' values reveals the unabated strength of exceptionalist thinking in US politics – the cultural impulse behind the rise of American globalism and its mission to remake the entire world in its image. In fact, the semiotic prominence of 'American values' in Beers's communicative strategy reveals its cultural embeddedness in powerful diffusionist and orientalist models that portray 'modernization' or 'globalization' as a civilizing process originating in the 'West'. Imagined as the permanent navel of the world, the 'West' is inscribed with a superior cultural essence that must be diffused to the inferior, 'backward' periphery. The West represents the active masculine principle, whereas the East appears as a passive feminine vessel waiting to be filled with accidental knowledge. James Blaut has referred to this hegemonic conceptual regime as 'the colonizer's model of the world' – a worldview constructed by Europeans and their American descendents to explain, justify and assist their colonial expansion. It is not grounded in facts of history and geography, but in imperialist and colonialist ideology.[31]

An instructive example of the contemporary pervasiveness of such pejorative and historically flawed strains of 'diffusionism' pervading American globalism can be found in the writings of influential foreign policy experts such as Michael Mandelbaum, who boldly asserts that 'the ideas that conquered the world' (peace, democracy, and free markets) were 'invented' in Great Britain and France in the seventeenth and eighteenth century. Claiming that 'it was natural for Britain and France to lead the world into the modern age', Mandelbaum never acknowledges that these countries owe much of their 'meteoric rise' to the previous scientific and cultural contributions made by non-European civilizations.[32]

Cultural insensitivity and the failure to recognize the achievement of others is crystallized in the notion of 'American values'. It explains, at least in part, why Beers's campaign faced such a steep uphill battle in the Muslim world. After all, it operated on a symbolic level that was easily recognizable by the inhabitants of that region as yet another form of Euro-American imperialism. Hence, the cultural assumptions underlying Beers's public diplomacy made her efforts counterproductive in that they were actually *more likely* to generate anti-Americanism. They were also dangerous because, by suggesting that the Middle Eastern values needed to be 'Americanized', they made people in the region feel that they were lacking valuable cultural resources of their own, thus fanning long-standing sentiments of humiliation and resentment.

Second, the State Department's attempt to 'rebrand' the USA treated values such as freedom and democracy as marketable commodities not unlike, say, a can of Pepsi or a Big Mac. Obviously, the intrinsic, non-instrumental value of liberty evaporates as soon as it is turned into a product to be bought and sold on the market. By commodifying people's deepest civic aspirations, Beers's campaign unwittingly lent some credence to Osama bin Laden's outlandish accusation that America was a soulless, materialist wasteland devoid of any genuine spirituality. In other words, the very means chosen by the Undersecretary to convey her message devalued 'Brand USA' in the eyes of many in the Muslim world.

Third, as Naomi Klein has pointed out, another serious obstacle facing the rebranding of America has to do with the nature of the marketing process itself. Successful branding requires a carefully crafted message delivered with discipline and consistency throughout the company's operations. Anything that threatens the homogeneity of the message dilutes the corporation's overall strength. But freedom, democracy and diversity are values that are inherently incompatible with 'discipline' and 'homogeneity'. Hence, Klein makes a convincing point when she argues that powerful marketing techniques driving businesses could be fatal when applied to politics: 'When companies try to implement global image consistency, they look like generic franchises. When governments do the same, they can look distinctly authoritarian.'[33] In short, celebrating difference by employing sameness turns out to be a counterproductive endeavour that undercuts the very values it tries to 'sell'.

Finally, and perhaps most importantly, no marketing technique in the world can compensate for a flawed product. This is not to say that freedom and democracy are not noble and worthwhile values; quite the opposite. However, by failing to incorporate these norms on a consistent basis, American foreign policy has generated much anger and frustration around the world. This is especially true in the Middle East, where the USA's employment of 'double standards' has been painfully visible for decades. For example, the vast majority of the 9/11 hijackers came from authoritarian Saudi Arabia. Moreover, Saudi money has financed scores of radical Islamist organizations around the globe. And yet Saudi Arabia has been treated by the Bush administration as a 'staunch ally' in the global War on Terror. Much of the same is true for Pakistan, a country ruled by a military junta that stockpiles weapons of mass destruction, including nuclear arms. The USA waged war on the tyrannical regime of Saddam Hussein in the name of 'liberating' an equally undemocratic regime in Kuwait. And the list goes on, culminating in the biased American approach to the Israel–Palestine conflict. Easily discernable by local people, the instrumental mode by which the USA picks friends and foes and pursues its interests in the region clearly contradicts its professed ethical commitment to 'American values'. Unfortunately, by insisting that she was not shaping foreign policy but merely carrying out policies made elsewhere, Undersecretary Beers was in no position to address the central problem of 'double standards'.

Towards an alternative public diplomacy

There is nothing wrong with the core objectives of US public diplomacy: namely, to improve America's global image and to enhance its international credibility as a world leader. In order to achieve these goals, however, public diplomacy should be afforded much higher priority in the State Department. It must not be relegated to the subordinate role of merely 'selling' flawed foreign policies and culturally insensitive metaphors to various 'target audiences'. Instead, public diplomats must become *active* and *critical* players in the collective effort of shaping America's relationship with the rest of the world. Public diplomacy's enhanced status should, therefore, correspond to an increased level of funding. In order to keep pace with the budgetary priorities currently in place in comparable countries, the US government would have to approve a tenfold increase from the current $1.2 billion to at least $12 billion. This figure may sound exorbitantly high, but it must be kept in mind that it amounts to only 3 per cent of the total US military budget.[34]

Having thus affirmed the *ends* of US public diplomacy, I will close this chapter with a brief consideration of its *means*. After all, this is where significant change must occur if its stated goals are to be realized in the foreseeable future. A new public diplomacy campaign employing alternative means must begin by abandoning Charlotte Beers's Madison Avenue approach. But which programmes should be given top priority and how should the responsible agencies implement them? Briefly, I suggest adopting the following three broad imperatives: (1) facilitate genuine multicultural dialogue in place of the current ideological monologue of American globalism; (2) pursue legitimate American security interests within a multilateral public diplomacy framework that seeks to counter global threats such as terrorism by addressing its local roots; (3) eliminate as far as possible existing 'double standards' in American foreign policy.

The implementation of the first imperative stands and falls with the government's genuine willingness to take into consideration views and opinions expressed outside its borders. Virtually all investigations into the failed Beers campaign found that the USA made a serious mistake by adopting a one-way advertising strategy rather than opting for a two-way 'engagement approach' that involves dialogue and relationship building as well as increasing the amount and effectiveness of public opinion research.[35] As Joseph Nye put it succinctly, 'To communicative effectively, Americans must first learn to listen.'[36] There are many tried and tested ways of facilitating multicultural encounters conducted globally in the inclusive spirit of mutual learning, including the creation of new dialogic institutions connecting the governmental and non-governmental sectors of the international community, the dramatic expansion of academic and cultural exchange programmes, the organization of high-profile conferences on intercultural understanding, and so on. However, the success of these programmes critically depends on the willingness of Americans to turn away from exceptionalism and recognize that freedom and democracy are not 'American values', but common norms to be polished through cross-cultural dialogue. Unfortunately, it is difficult to imagine such significant change in American culture in the current climate of nationalist fervour and imperial arrogance so clearly manifested in the neoconservative Bush administration.

The second imperative constitutes an extension of the first into the arena of national security. It is anchored in the recognition that public diplomacy programmes centred on global dialogue and cultural exchange have the potential to provide better security for the American people than Apache helicopters, laser-guided missiles or unmanned surveillance drones. For example, the creation of a sizeable US public diplomacy corps operating in *local* settings and committed to solving concrete problems such as poor sanitation, inadequate education and crumbling infrastructure might change the image of America in 'crisis regions' more dramatically than superficial television commercials that showcase American Muslim celebrities such as Muhammad Ali. In general, US public diplomacy has not paid sufficient attention to the opportunities emerging from what James Rosenau describes as the 'interactively reinforcing processes of globalization and localization' in the turbulent early twenty-first century world.[37]

Finally, the third imperative makes public diplomacy the voice of conscience that holds US foreign policy accountable to its espoused values. To be sure, in the harsh world of power politics, there always remains a gap between policy and ideals. However, to let this unavoidable discrepancy turn into a systematic practice of double standards fatally undermines American credibility in the world. The treatment of suspects at Abu Ghraib prison in Baghdad and at the US prison camp at Guantanamo Bay, as well as the Bush administration's disdainful rejection of the World Court's ruling that Israel's so-called 'security fence' violated the human rights of Palestinians, are but recent examples of such double-standard policies that generate intense anti-American sentiments in the Muslim world. If the US government made a concerted effort to build its public diplomacy around these imperatives, its claim to world leadership would find a more receptive global audience than it does today.

Notes

1 *Le Monde*, 12 September 2001.

2 G. W. Bush, 'Address to Joint Session of Congress and Americans', 20 September 20 2001, in J. W. Edwards and L. de Rose, *United We Stand* (Ann Arbor, MI: Mundus, 2002), pp. 7–11; and 'Remarks in the National Cathedral', Washington DC, 14 September 2001, online at http://www.whitehouse.gov/news/releases/2001/09.html.

3 See E. C. Nisbet, M. C. Nisbet, D. A. Scheufele and J. E. Shanahan, 'Public Diplomacy, Television News, and Muslim Opinion', *Harvard International Journal of Press/Politics*, 9 (2004), 14. This article also lists the results of other major opinion polls on the subject conducted in 2002–3. The latest in this series of polls is a comprehensive world opinion poll conducted between November 2003 and February 2004 in 19 countries. It found that 55 per cent of respondents believed that the United States exerts a negative influence in the world. See World Public Opinion Poll published by The Program on International Policy Attitudes (PIPA), 4 June 2004, online at http://www.pipa.org/OnlineReports/Global_Issues/globescan_press_06_04.pdf.

4 For an enlightening discussion of the neoconservative 'Project for a New American Century', see T. Barry and J. Lobe, 'The People', in J. Feffer (ed.), *Power Trip: U. S. Unilateralism and Global Strategy after September 11* (New York: Seven Story Press, 2003), pp. 39–49, and C. G. Ryn, 'The Ideology of American Empire', *Orbis* (Summer 2003), 383–97.

5 See, for example, P. G. Peterson, 'Public Diplomacy and the War on Terrorism', *Foreign Affairs*, 81 (2002), 77; C. Ross, 'Public Diplomacy Comes of Age', *The*

Washington Quarterly, 25 (2002), 75–83; and A. J. Blinken, 'Winning the War of Ideas', *The Washington Quarterly*, 25 (2002), 101–14.

6 Elsewhere, I define 'globalism' as a market ideology endowing the buzzword 'globalization' with norms and meanings that not only legitimate and advance neoliberal interests, but also seek to cultivate consumerist cultural identities in billions of people around the world. Since power elites concentrated in the USA constitute the main proponents of this ideology, globalism has a decidedly 'American' flavour. In my most recent study on the subject, I use the term 'imperial globalism' to refer to the post-9/11 militarized version of American globalism. See M. B. Steger, *Globalism: Market Ideology Meets Terrorism*, 2nd edn (Lanham, MD: Rowman & Littlefield, 2005), and *Globalization: A Very Short Introduction* (Oxford: Oxford University Press, 2003).

7 For various definitions of 'public diplomacy', see J. B. Manheim, *Strategic Public Diplomacy and American Foreign Policy: The Evolution of Influence* (Oxford: Oxford University Press, 1994).

8 P. van Ham, 'War, Lies, and Videotape: Public Diplomacy and the USA's War on Terrorism', *Security Dialogue*, 34 (2003), 429.

9 R. Holbrooke, 'Get the Message Out', *Washington Post*, 28 October 2001. For an excellent study of public diplomacy as rhetoric, see S. McEvoy-Levy, *American Exceptionalism and US Foreign Policy: Public Diplomacy at the End of the Cold War* (New York: Palgrave Macmillan, 2001).

10 J. Brown, 'The Anti-Propaganda Tradition in the United States', *Bulletin Board for Peace* (June 29, 2003), online at http://www.publicdiplomacy.org/19.htm.

11 A. A. Bardos, '"Public Diplomacy": An Old Art, a New Profession', *The Virginia Quarterly Review*, 77 (Summer 2001), 424.

12 Ibid., p. 433.

13 J. Fousek, *To Lead the Free World: American Nationalism and the Cultural Roots of the Cold War* (Chapel Hill, NC: The University of North Carolina Press, 2000), p. 7.

14 McEvoy-Levy, *American Exceptionalism and US Foreign Policy*, p. 24. For a comprehensive exploration of 'American exceptionalism', see S. M. Lipset, *American Exceptionalism: A Double Edged Sword* (New York: W. W. Norton, 1997).

15 Van Ham, 'War, Lies, and Videotape', p. 430.

16 Ibid.

17 Their preference for 'soft power' methods does not mean that American globalists disavowed the imposition of their 'Washington Consensus' through economic pressure exerted by US dominated, international lending institutions such as the IMF and World Bank. While the terms 'hard power' and 'soft power' have been coined by Joseph S. Nye, the power dynamics in question have been described and analysed in different words by generations of political thinkers influenced by the writings of Antonio Gramsci. For the latest elaboration of Nye's perspective on power, see his *Soft Power: The Means to Success in World Politics* (New York: Public Affairs, 2004).

18 For a detailed discussion of globalism's core claims, see Steger, *Globalism*, ch. 3.

19 J. S. Nye, Jr, 'The Decline of America's Soft Power: Why Washington Should Worry', *Foreign Affairs*, 83 (2004), 17.

20 For an informative overview of the organizational structure of US public diplomacy, see R. Smyth, 'Mapping US Public Diplomacy in the 21st Century', *Australian Journal of International Affairs*, 55 (2001), 421–44.

21 W. P. Kiehl, 'Can Humpty Dumpty be Saved?', 13 November 2003, online at http://www.publicdiplomacy.org.
22 Associated Press, 'New Office Aims to Bolster U. S. Image', *New York Times*, 21 January 2003.
23 Charlotte Beers interviewed by Alexandra Starr in 'Building Brand America', *BusinessWeek* online, 10 December 2001, online at http://www.businessweek.com/bwdaily/dnflash/dec2001/nf20011210_2325.htm.
24 Ibid.
25 Colin Powell cited in N. Klein, 'Failure of Brand USA', *InnerSelf Magazine*, September 2002, online at http://www.innerself.com/Essays/brand_usa.htm.
26 Van Ham, 'War, Lies, and Videotape', p. 434.
27 C. Beers, 'U.S. Public Diplomacy in the Arab and Muslim Worlds', Remarks at the Washington Institute for Near East Policy, Washington DC, 7 May 2002, online at http://www.state.gove/r/us/10424.htm. See also C. Beers cited in R. Satloff, 'Battling for the Hearts and Minds in the Middle East: A Critique of U.S. Public Diplomacy Post-September 11', *Policywatch*, 657 (17 September 2002), online at http://www.washingtoninstitute.org/watch/Policywatch/policywatch2002/657.htm; and C. Beers cited in B. Zorthian, 'Public Diplomacy Is Not the Answer', 12 June 2004, online at http://www.publicdiplomacy.org/29htm.
28 C. Beers, 'Funding for Public Diplomacy', Statement before the Subcommittee on Commerce, Justice, and State of the House Appropriations Committee, 24 April 2002, online at http://www.state.gov/r/us/9778.htm.
29 Pew Research Center for the People and the Press Poll (16 March 2004), online at http://www.preople-press.org/reports.
30 C. Beers cited in Associated Press, 'Senators Urge Bush to Work on U.S. Image', *New York Times*, 27 February 2003.
31 J. M. Blaut, *The Colonizer's Model of the World: Geographic Diffusionism and Eurocentric History* (New York: Guilford Press, 1993). See also E. Said, *Orientalism* (New York: Vintage, 1978).
32 M. Mandelbaum, *The Ideas that Conquered the World: Peace, Democracy and Free Markets in the Twenty-First Century* (Washington, DC: PublicAffairs, 2002), p. 79.
33 Klein, 'Failure of Brand USA'.
34 Nye, *Soft Power*, p. 123. As Nye points out, France and the UK each spent about 3 per cent of their total military budget on public diplomacy (p. 124).
35 See, for example, the reports submitted by Peter G. Petersen, Chair of the Independent Task Force on Public Diplomacy sponsored by the Council on Foreign Relations, 'Public Diplomacy and the War on Terrorism', 74–94; and Ambassador Edward Djerejian, Chair of the Congressional Advisory Group on Public Diplomacy, 'Statement to House Committee on Appropriations', 4 February 2004, online at http://www.appropriations.house.gov.
36 Nye, 'The Decline of America's Soft Power', p. 20.
37 J. Rosenau, *Distant Proximities: Dynamics Beyond Globalization* (Princeton, NJ: Princeton University Press, 2003).

15
Global Justice, the World Trade Organization and Free Trade

Darrel Moellendorf

Introduction

One important by-product of globalization, which is sometimes lost on critics, is that the increased association of persons around the global economy makes credible the claim that these persons have duties of justice to one another.[1] I shall not fully defend that view here, as I have discussed it in detail elsewhere.[2] The salient point for present purposes is that whatever the evils that globalization produces, and they are considerable to be sure, there also two important related moral facts, if I may use that term loosely, that globalization also produces: the evils can be criticized as injustices; and standards of justice may provide guidance in offering alternatives.

After discussing the relationship between duties of egalitarian distributive justice and global associations, and defending a global egalitarian orientation, I turn to a discussion of the World Trade Organization (WTO) and free trade. The road to a moral assessment of the WTO is littered with many hazards: the considerations are multiple and various; the jurisprudence and practice of the WTO in certain important areas are still developing; and fundamental empirical theories are subject to on-going debate. Nonetheless, WTO regulations already constrain the policy of nearly all states. This suggests that a moral assessment, even if incomplete and somewhat provisional, is desirable.

The global economic association and Egalitarian Justice

Let me begin by stating a few assumptions. First, I assume that all persons are owed equal respect. This is, of course, a substantive moral assumption. I do not believe that it follows from this assumption alone that we owe duties of social justice to all persons. I doubt that we have such duties to persons with whom we are not associated. I take duties of social justice, then, to be associative duties. They exist, when they do, because we owe persons equal respect and we are in a common association with some people.[3]

The global economy has profound effects on persons throughout the world. Consider the effects far beyond Asia of the Asian economic crisis in the late 1990s. The crisis did extensive damage to emerging markets. Eventually Russia defaulted on its debt and Brazil narrowly avoided complete financial collapse. States with economies heavily dependent upon exporting basic resources such as petroleum and precious metals expected dramatic declines in their GDP as a result of the Asian crisis, 14–18 per cent in Angola and Kuwait and 9 per cent in Zambia.[4]

The extent of globalization can be seen in terms of foreign direct investment (FDI), trade, and international lending and currency transfers. In 1997 FDI was 64 per cent of the world's gross fixed capital formation,[5] but this figure may fail miserably to indicate the full effect of foreign investment in domestic economies since foreign investment is often a condition of domestic financing as well as financing from third party countries. Total FDI related investment after adjusting for these other sources could be as much as four times that normally measured in official statistics.[6] Additionally, the United Nations Development Programme (UNDP) has observed that 'The pressures of global competition have led countries and employers to adopt more flexible labour policies, and work arrangements with no long-term commitment between employer and employee are on the rise.'[7]

Foreign trade as a percentage of the global domestic product has been increasing in recent years. The UNDP reports that world exports averaged 21 per cent of a state's gross domestic product (GDP) in the late 1990s as compared to an average of 17 per cent of a smaller GDP in the 1970s.[8] Moreover, the poorest countries are the most deeply integrated into world trade. For example, sub-Saharan Africa had an export to GDP ratio of 29 per cent as compared to 15 per cent for Latin America.[9] Multilateral rules now govern trade relations between the overwhelming majority of countries. As of April 2003, the WTO comprised 146 member countries,[10] accounting for over 97 per cent of world trade.[11]

There has also been an increase in international lending and currency transfers. International bank lending grew from $265 billion in 1975 to $4.2 trillion in 1994. Meanwhile, the daily turnover in foreign exchange markets increased from $10–20 billion in the 1970s to $1.5 trillion in 1998.[12] Between 1980 and 1998 the International Monetary Fund (IMF) and World Bank made at least 126 loans.[13] Between 1987 and 1991 loans to the low-income, debt-distressed countries in Africa – most of these having relatively little FDI – amounted to 15.4 per cent of the countries' real GDP and 75 per cent of real imports.[14] The conditionality associated with IMF and World Bank loans from the 1980s onwards gave these financial institutions considerable voice in the policies of poor countries that in other ways were not greatly integrated into the global economy.

Regardless of whether persons are directly engaged with the global economy, their local economy is profoundly affected by FDI, international trade, and international lending and currency exchange. The global economic association produced by these activities is massively unequal. The UNDP notes that the total income of the world's richest 1 per cent of people is equal to that of the poorest 57 per cent.[15] The assets of the richest three people in the world are more than the combined gross national product of all of the least developed countries.[16] Nearly half of the world's population lives in abject poverty on $2 PPP per day.[17] Worse still, 1.15 billion people live on less than $1 PPP per day.[18] Some 1.3 billion people lack access to clean water; and 840 million children are malnourished.[19]

These huge inequalities have dramatic effects on the life prospects of persons. One important example of this is longevity. According to the World Health Organization (WHO), 'Over 60% of deaths in developed countries occur beyond age 70, compared to about 30% in developing countries.'[20] The United Nations International Children's Emergency Fund (UNICEF) reports that 30,500 children under five die every day of mainly preventable causes.[21] Indeed, the condition of the world's poorest children provides evidence of growth in global inequality. In the 1990s children in sub-Saharan Africa were 19 times more likely to die than children in the world's richest countries. By 2003 this figure had grown to 26 times.[22] According to the WHO, 'In one hour over 500 African mothers lose a child; had they lived in a rich European country, nearly 490 of these mothers and their children would have been spared the ordeal.'[23]

The immense disparity of the life prospects of members of the global economy appears inconsistent with the requirements of equal respect. A commitment to equal respect places constraints on possible justifications for inequality. For example, respecting persons equally is inconsistent with telling some that they must endure lesser life prospects than others with whom they are associated merely so that the life prospects of these others may be enhanced.[24] The justificatory constraints of equal respect seem to have strongly egalitarian distributive implications. But libertarian critics of egalitarianism argue that an institutional arrangement that constrains the prospects of the most advantaged persons so that, for example, the prospects of the disadvantaged may be improved use advantaged persons merely as a means to benefit the disadvantaged.[25] The rhetorical power of this claim derives in large part from the assumption that deviations from the status quo of inequality require justification. I deny that a commitment to equal respect requires this. Rather, a commitment to equal respect takes equality as the benchmark and limits the kinds of justifications that may be offered to deviate from that benchmark.

Criticism and response

Global egalitarianism has been challenged on a number of grounds. An adequate survey and response to all of the strongest of these challenges is an important task, but one that I cannot complete here. Instead, I shall briefly discuss one challenge, which has some popularity, especially in analyses of public and international policy. This is the argument that the sources of inequality and poverty are largely domestic and therefore not the proper purview of global justice. In its 17 January 2004 survey of sub-Saharan Africa, *The Economist* argues that the reason for African poverty is 'bad government'.[26] In *The Law of Peoples*, John Rawls asserts that 'the causes of the wealth of a people and the forms it takes lie in their political culture and in the religious, philosophical, and moral traditions that support the basic structure of their political and social institutions, as well as in the industriousness and cooperative talents of its members, all supported by their political virtues'.[27] Consider the following argument against global egalitarianism along these lines:

1 The sources of inequality (relative to the developed world) and poverty in the developing world are primarily endogenous.
2 Duties of justice apply only to those who are casually responsible for some part of the harm that persons suffer.
3 Therefore, persons in the developed world have no duties of justice to relieve the inequality and poverty from which persons in the developing world suffer.

Thomas Pogge provides a response to this argument that involves accepting the normative claim in the second premise, but denying the empirical claim in the first. Pogge contends that under existing international law any group that controls the state's coercive apparatus, regardless of how the group came to power, enjoys 'the privileges freely to borrow in the country's name (international borrowing privilege) and freely to dispose of the country's natural resources (international resource privilege)'. In this way international law 'provides powerful incentives toward coup attempts and civil wars in resource rich countries'.[28] This undercuts the second challenge in many cases. But as insightful as Pogge's response is, its force is limited to regimes that came to power via coups and civil wars and to those that operate under the threat of military usurpation.

Criticism of the first premise could be broadened if, as I shall argue in the penultimate section, there are aspects of WTO practice, such as protectionism in the developed world and global intellectual property protection, that contribute to misery in the developing world. Additionally if the infant industry argument, which I discuss briefly in the final section, is correct, then premise one is further weakened by the liberalizing requirements of the WTO.

Another response involves challenging the normative premise, and is therefore potentially more far-reaching in scope. The claim that duties of justice apply only to persons who are causally responsible for some part of the harm that persons suffer seems to take duties of justice as wholly compensatory, but this is too limiting. For one, it does not explain why there are duties to prevent injustices from occurring. Moreover, it cannot explain why, say, the federal branch of a state has a duty to remedy a local rights violation. Finally, the normative principle does not cohere with several norms of international law that require international responses to domestic injustices, most famously perhaps the UN Convention on Genocide. Thus the normative premise is too limited to be plausible. A more plausible normative view, I believe, is the one that I discussed in the previous section, namely duties of justice arise among persons who are co-members of associations of the required type.

The World Trade Organization

The WTO was founded in 1995 as a result of the Uruguay Round of meetings of the signatories to the General Agreement on Tariffs and Trade (GATT).[29] The purpose of the WTO is to administer multilateral trade treaties, especially GATT 1994, which includes the amended GATT 1947, the General Agreement of Trade in Services (GATS) and the Agreement on Trade-Related Intellectual Property Rights (TRIPS).

The WTO's functions include implementing multilateral trade agreements, providing forums for negotiations on trade issues, facilitating dispute settlements and cooperating with the World Bank and the International Monetary Fund to achieve 'greater coherence in global economic policy-making'.[30] Decision-making in the WTO is formally egalitarian; all members have a voice. For matters other than amendments to existing agreements and general principles, decision-making is based upon negotiation and consensus. Consensus requires that no country represented in a meeting be 'decisively against' an issue.[31]

Members of the WTO must abide by negotiated trade rules that are guided by four basic principles: (1) non-discrimination, (2) reciprocity, (3) market access and (4) fair competition. Non-discrimination has two aspects. First, members must treat all other members as most favoured nations (MFNs), which requires that a country treat the products originating in or destined for any other county no better than like products originating in or destined for a member country.[32] Second, non-discrimination requires conformity to the national treatment rule, stipulating that after importation, foreign goods be treated no less favourably than domestic goods in terms of taxes and regulations.[33]

Reciprocity requires that trade liberalization between members be accomplished on a mutual basis.[34] Reciprocity also applies when countries join the WTO, which in practice means that countries that join the WTO are required to liberalize access to their markets. Market access requires that members agree to negotiate tariff reductions. This amounts to members being bound to schedules of tariff concessions agreed to at multilateral trade negotiations.[35] Fair competition is meant to ensure competition on a level playing field. For example, if a government subsidizes the export of an item, then those items may be subject to an anti-dumping duty by the importing country, thereby increasing the price of the item to compensate for the subsidy that lowered its price.

Free trade and egalitarianism

According to neoclassical economic theory trade liberalization should increase overall economic efficiency and lead to increases in aggregate production and consumption. The basic idea is that international competition provides incentives for efficient production. The law of comparative advantage holds that the most efficient strategy for a state to pursue involves producing only those goods and services for which it has a comparative advantage.[36] One characterization of the efficiency gains of free trade is the following: 'A high rate of economic interaction with the rest of the world speeds the absorption of frontier technologies and global management best practices, spurs innovation and cost-cutting, and competes away monopoly.'[37] Sometimes the efficiency argument in favour of liberalized trade is dismissed as merely an appeal to an economic good. But it cannot be so easily dismissed since more efficient production involves either more goods being produced with the same effort or the same goods with less effort.

It may come as a surprise to some that classical Left-wing theorists, such as Karl Marx and V. I. Lenin, were supporters of free trade.[38] Marx, as is well known, was impressed with the efficiency gains of capitalism achieved through the constant revolutionizing of the means of production. 'The bourgeoisie cannot exist without constantly revolutionizing the instruments of production, and thereby the relations of production, and with them the whole relations of society.'[39] He took the increases in efficiency that capitalism produces as a necessary precondition for socialism. '[T]his development of productive forces... is an absolutely necessary practical premise because without it want is merely made general, and with destitution the struggle for necessities and all the old filth business would necessarily be reproduced.'[40] In addition to eschewing the national chauvinism that accompanies protectionism, a belief in the efficiency of free trade probably was the basis for Marxian support for it.

Even if we suppose that free trade does produce efficiency gains, it could not be the whole of an egalitarian international trade regime. Two equally optimal distributions may be appraised very differently with respect to distributive justice. Market distributions alone cannot realize the aims of egalitarian justice. One reason for this is that parents who do well in the market can pass on the advantages that they have to their children through spending and inheritances. Without institutions that remedy this, market advantage will result in inequality of opportunity.

Equality of opportunity is probably insufficient to meet the egalitarian justificatory requirement that persons not be required to accept an institutional arrangement that assigns them lesser life prospects than others merely to enhance the life prospects of the others. A principle that reduces the degree of disadvantage that one can suffer is probably also required.[41] Market transactions alone will not realize such a reduction. Additionally, egalitarians criticize market inequality as productive of other severe social evils, such as exploitation and inequality of political influence.[42] So, even assuming that the goal of trade liberalization could be defended as efficiency promoting, such liberalization is far from sufficient on egalitarian grounds.

Four criticisms of WTO practice

Let's examine four criticisms of WTO practice on the basis of unfairness to the poor. First, there are serious concerns that poorer countries are marginalized in WTO decision-making procedures. This is in part due to inequalities in resources:

> Poor countries participate little in the formulation and implementation of the new rules that govern global markets. The 1994 Uruguay Round of GATT shows the difficulties facing small and poor countries. Of the 29 least developed countries in the WTO, only 12 had missions in Geneva, most staffed with a handful of people to cover the gamut of UN work...Many small and poor countries had difficulty even ensuring representation at meetings.[43]

A straightforward solution to this problem would be for the WTO to subsidize the participation of the least developed countries.[44] The demand for subsidization of the least developed countries is fully consistent with the Marrakech Agreement Establishing the WTO, which recognized 'that there is need for positive efforts designed to ensure that developing countries, and especially the least developed amongst them, secure a share in the growth in international trade commensurate with the needs of their economic development'.[45] The WTO procedural requirement of consensus has also been criticized as a means of ensuring that developing world interests cannot be pursued if this involves burdening the developed world.[46] Although the criticism has some force, it fails to appreciate that veto power also can be wielded to protect the interests of the developing world.

The second criticism concerns agricultural tariffs. One feature that distinguishes the WTO from the GATT is the former's commitment to liberalizing trade in agriculture, yet developed world protectionist agricultural policies (import tariffs and export subsidies) permitted by WTO rules have seriously restricted the possibilities for developing world agricultural producers to find markets for their goods. The United Nations Conference on Trade and Development (UNCTAD) estimates that low technology countries are losing out on $700 billion per year in export earnings due to developed world protectionism. This amounts to more than four times the annual capital inflow into the developing world due to FDI.[47] But due to lack of resources, developing countries have been unable adequately to subsidize their smallholding farmers while 70 per cent of the world's poor live in rural areas.[48] Moreover, 800 million people in the world currently suffer from hunger.[49] Despite the WTO's stated commitment to market access, its trade regime permits protectionism that results in mass hunger.

The third criticism of the WTO is that its practice prioritizes economic efficiency over all other values. Peter Singer has examined this criticism in light of the WTO's application of the principle of non-discrimination.[50] Since whether products are discriminated against affects employment opportunities, the principle of non-discrimination would seem to serve the purpose of reducing discrimination against persons on the basis of their national origin.

Singer charges, however, that the application of the principle of non-discrimination by the WTO erodes the ability of states to legislate in accordance with environmental and other values. He cites as evidence the 1991 GATT *Tuna-Dolphin* dispute between the USA and Mexico.[51] The context of this dispute involves the US Marine Mammal Protection Act, which sets standards for dolphin protection in the harvesting of tuna. A country exporting tuna to the United States must meet the dolphin protection standards set out in US law, otherwise the US government may embargo all imports of the fish from that country. Mexico's exports of tuna to the USA were banned under the act. Mexico then complained in 1991 in accordance with the GATT dispute settlement procedures. In its defence the USA cited GATT Article XX, which allows exceptions at (b) to protect animal or plant life or health and at (g) to conserve exhaustible natural resources.[52] In September of 1991 a GATT panel found that the USA could not embargo Mexico tuna on the basis of the process through which it came to the market. In effect, the decision was that similar products must get equal treatment regardless of a dissimilar production process.[53] Singer observes that non-discrimination with respect to processes erodes a state's ability to legislate to secure environmental and safe production processes. In 1994 a second GATT panel concurred with the earlier decision in a second dolphin dispute, *Son of Dolphin Tuna*, this time between the EU and the USA.[54]

However, Singer's criticism may not have as much basis in law as he suggests. Neither *Tuna-Dolphin* nor *Son of Dolphin Tuna* are precedent-setting for in neither case was the decision adopted; rather it was merely circulated. Moreover in a subsequent similar case, *Shrimp-Turtle*, although the WTO found against the USA, it upheld the right of states to legislate in accordance with environmental values.[55] This would appear to be an evolving area of WTO jurisprudence and it may be too early to tell how the law will eventually be decided. It would seem too early to determine whether Singer's criticisms are warranted.

The fourth criticism concerns TRIPS. Consisting of seven major parts, TRIPS governs a variety of intellectual property. Prior to ratification there was significant disagreement about TRIPS between developed countries – major exporters of intellectual property – and developing countries who were importers of intellectual property.[56] US pharmaceutical, entertainment, and information industries were largely responsible for getting TRIPS on the negotiating agenda, and developing countries – many of which had little or no legal protection for intellectual property – were concerned that an intellectual property rights regime would make important goods, such as medicine, prohibitively expensive to their citizens in need.[57]

Part I, Article 3 of TRIPs applies the national treatment principle to intellectual property.[58] Article 4 applies the MFN principle.[59] Part II, Section 5 protects patent rights.[60] According to Article 28, patent protection shall prohibit the 'making, using, offering for sale, selling, or importing' without consent of the patent-holder.[61] In effect, holding a patent gives the holder monopoly power in the market for the period of the patent. According to Article 33 this period shall last for 20 years.[62] Members have one year from the date of entry to implement the TRIPs requirements; developing countries have five years (but only one to implement the MFN principle); and least developed countries have ten years, and may request extensions.[63]

Consider the case of a country such as India, which previously provided patent protection for pharmaceutical processes for only seven years and provided no patent protection at all for pharmaceutical products.[64] The lack of product patent protection allowed firms to reverse engineer pharmaceutical products and produce them according to their own processes. Since typically this is done without investing as much in research and development as is required for invention, prices for pharmaceutical products are driven down, thereby allowing greater access to existing pharmaceutical products for the poor of India. With the advent of TRIPs, one can expect the price of pharmaceutical products to steadily rise in the developing world.

In 2000 The Sub-Commission on the Promotion and Protection of Human Rights under the auspices of The United Nations Commissioner for Human Rights declared:

> since the implementation of the TRIPS Agreement does not adequately reflect the fundamental nature and indivisibility of all human rights, including the right of everyone to enjoy the benefits of scientific progress and its applications, the right to health, the right to food

> and the right to self-determination, there are apparent conflicts between the intellectual property rights regime embodied in the TRIPS Agreement, on the one hand, and international human rights law, on the other.[65]

The Sub-Commission cites the *Human Development Reports* of 1999 and 2000, by the United Nations Human Development Programme, as studies evidencing the deleterious implementation of TRIPs on the stated rights.[66]

The knowledge of the chemical structure of pharmaceutical products would appear to be a public good; the supply does not diminish with consumption. It would seem to be most efficient to have this knowledge held as widely as possible. What reasons then favour patent protection? Most often, the need to provide an incentive for the initial outlay of research and development is cited.[67] By granting monopoly-pricing power, a patent regime provides incentives for original, inventive and innovative work. Without such an incentive, the most economical strategy would be to wait for others to make the initial outlay and then to reverse engineer their products.

TRIPS seeks to balance incentives to invention and innovation against the needs of consumers by providing a number of exceptions to patent protection. Article 27 seems to allow leeway for exceptions in matters of public health:

> 2. Members may exclude from patentability inventions, the prevention within their territory of the commercial exploitation of which is necessary to protect *ordre public* or morality, including to protect human, animal or plant life or health or to avoid serious prejudice to the environment, provided that such exclusion is not made merely because the exploitation is prohibited by their law.
> 3. Members may also exclude from patentability:
> (a) diagnostic, therapeutic and surgical methods for the treatment of humans or animals.[68]

Article 30 allows for exceptions provided that they 'do not unreasonably conflict with a normal exploitation of the patent and do not unreasonably prejudice the legitimate interests of the patent owner'.[69] Article 31 requires that exceptions be for a limited time and only after failure to gain permission on satisfactory terms from the patent holder.[70] It is impossible to know in advance of test cases and WTO dispute resolution whether Part II, Section 5, which protects patent rights, strikes a balance that will provide protection for the most important interests of consumers in the developing world.

It is doubtful, in any case, that the incentive argument for pharmaceutical patents has much purchase in the developing world. In order for the there to be a market-based incentive to produce a commodity, there must be effective demand for that commodity. Given the abject poverty of the developing world, it is extremely unlikely that under present conditions there can be effective demand for pharmaceutical inventions for many diseases. Indeed, according to one study, only 15 of the new medicines patented between 1975 and 1997 were for tropical diseases.[71] Moreover, access to existing pharmacological therapies is sometimes much more important in the developing world than incentives for innovation. For example, of the six million people in the developing world currently in need of antiretroviral treatment, only 400,000 have access.[72]

Two criticisms of free trade

Criticisms of WTO practice and structure could perhaps lead to appropriate reforms given sufficient political will or strategically mobilized pressure. I have been assuming, without the benefit of economic analysis, that there is an egalitarian defence of trade liberalization on the basis of efficiency. The argument of the previous two sections suggests that whatever the WTO's merits on efficiency grounds, egalitarians should nonetheless seek certain reforms; but perhaps there is a more fundamental critique. In closing, I examine two arguments against free trade itself.

The first invokes the interests of workers who enjoy relatively high wages and safe conditions globally and citizens who enjoy the enforcement of comparatively strong environmental standards. Persons in these situations may find themselves at a comparative disadvantage in the global market. This leads to the criticism that liberalized trade produces a race to the bottom for labour and environmental standards.[73] This would seem to be a particularly important criticism in light of the importance of strong labour and environmental standards.

Nevertheless the argument is hard to square with the global egalitarian principle that an institutional arrangement cannot be justified to those whom it assigns lesser life prospects merely on the grounds that it enhances the life prospects of others. Policies that protect the jobs and environment of the relatively privileged at the expense of job creation for the less privileged constitute a prima facie violation of that principle. Egalitarians should, however, be sympathetic towards the worry expressed in the criticism. One alternative to restricting trade would be to engage in cross-border organizing.[74] This requires a strategy that plausibly will benefit those whose employment and environmental situation is comparatively worse as well as safeguard the employment and environmental standards of the comparatively better-off workers.

The second criticism of trade liberalization concerns its impact on development. This criticism appeals to economic history. In the course of pursuing development, the countries of the developed world systematically protected their infant industries.[75] Indeed, protectionism may have been an essential policy for successful development. If this is the correct reading of history, multilateral arrangements that require developing countries to liberalize their trade policies may consign the poor in the developing world to lesser life prospects than would well-crafted protectionist policies.

At this point in the argument the political philosopher must defer to the economist since the fundamental issue is empirical: is trade liberalization or protectionism in the developing world more conducive to development, broadly construed, in the developing world? Suppose that the appeal to history is more credible than the claims of neoclassical economic theory. Egalitarians would then be required to argue against the claim that trade liberalization is necessary, even if not sufficient, for global justice. In this case, whatever the virtues of the WTO's commitment to non-discrimination, its commitment to market access would be objectionable. The following principle would then seem to be required by the egalitarian position: a country may be justified in protecting its economy *vis-à-vis* a more developed country, but not *vis-à-vis* a less developed one.[76] But a political philosopher is in a poor position to pronounce on the relevant empirical issues.

Notes

1 A version of this chapter was presented to the Political Theory Project and the Watson Institute at Brown University. I am grateful to the participants of that session for the comments that have helped me to improve the argument. I would also like to thank the James Hervey Johnson Charitable Educational Trust for support as I was finishing this chapter.
2 Cf. my *Cosmopolitan Justice* (Boulder, CO: Westview Press, 2002), ch. 3.
3 I have not said nearly enough here about the kind of associations that generate duties of justice. For more see my 'Persons' Interests, States' Duties, and Global Governance', in H. Brighouse and G. Brock (eds), *The Political Philosophy of Cosmopolitanism* (Cambridge: Cambridge University Press, 2005).
4 United Nations Development Programme, *Human Development Report 1999*, p. 41, online at http://hdr.undp.org/reports/global/1999/en/.

5 V. S. F. Sit, 'Globalization, Foreign Direct Investment, and Urbanization in Developing Countries', in S. Yusuf, S. Evenett and W. Wu (eds), *Facets of Globalization: International and Local Dimensions of Development* (Washington, DC: World Bank, 2001), p. 12.
6 Ibid., p. 13.
7 UNDP, *Human Development Report 1999*, p. 37.
8 Ibid., p. 25.
9 Ibid., p. 31.
10 See http://www.wto.org/english/thewto_e/whatis_e/whatis_e.htm.
11 See http://www.wto.org/english/thewto_e/whatis_e/inbrief_e/inbr02_e.htm.
12 UNDP, *Human Development Report 1999*, p. 25.
13 W. Easterly, 'The Effects of IMF and World Bank Programs on Poverty', World Bank, 31 October 2000, online at http://www.imf.org/external/pubs/ft/staffp/2000/00-00/e.pdf.
14 World Bank, 'Special Program of Assistance: Launching the Third Phase' (Washington, DC: World Bank, 1994) as cited in D. E. Sahn, P. A. Dorosh and S. D. Younger, *Structural Adjustment Reconsidered* (Cambridge: Cambridge University Press, 1997), p. 4.
15 UNDP, *Human Development Report 2002*, p. 19, online at http://hdr.undp.org/reports/global/1999/en/pdf/chapterone.pdf.
16 Ibid., p. 38.
17 World Bank, *Global Economic Prospects and the Developing Countries 2002*, p. 30, online at http://www.worldbank.org/prospects/gep2002/chap1.pdf. $2 PPP means the local currency equivalent of what one could purchase with $2 in the USA.
18 Ibid.
19 UNDP, *Human Development Report 1999*, p. 28.
20 WHO, *Global Burden of Disease in 2002: Data Sources, Methods and Results*, p. 44, online at http://www3.who.int/whosis/menu.cfm?path=whosis,burden,burden_estimates&language=english.
21 United Nation's International Children's Emergency Fund, *The State of the World's Children 2000*, online at http://www.unicef.org/sowc00/.
22 UNDP, *Human Development Report 2003*, p. 39, online at http://www.undp.org/hdr2003/pdf/hdr03_chapter_2.pdf.
23 WHO, *Global Burden of Disease in 2002*, pp. 44–5.
24 Cf. J. Rawls, *A Theory of Justice*, rev. edn (Cambridge, MA: Harvard University Press, 1999), Section 17.
25 Cf. R. Nozick's *Anarchy, State and Utopia* (New York: Basic Books, 1974), ch. 7.
26 'How to Make Africa Smile', *The Economist*, 17 January 2004, p. 4.
27 J. Rawls, *The Law of Peoples* (Cambridge, MA: Harvard University Press, 1999), p. 108.
28 T. Pogge, *World Poverty and Human Rights* (Cambridge: Polity, 2002), pp. 112–13.
29 Marrakech Agreement (1994), online at http://www.wto.org/english/docs_e/legal_e/04-wto_e.htm.
30 B. M. Hoekman and M. M. Kostecki, *The Political Economy of The World Trading System* (Oxford: Oxford University Press, 1995), p. 38.
31 Ibid., p. 40.
32 GATT 1994 Article I:1, online at http://www.wto.org/english/docs_e/legal_e/legal_e.htm#finalact.

33 Ibid., Article III:1, 2 and 4.
34 Hoekman and Kostecki, *The Political Economy of The World Trading System*, p. 27.
35 Ibid., p. 31.
36 The classic statement is D. Ricardo, *The Principles of Political Economy and Taxation* (London: J. M. Dent & Sons, 1973), ch. 7.
37 J. Frankel, 'Globalization of the Economy', in J. S. Nye Jr and J. D. Donahue (eds), *Governance in a Globalizing World* (Washington, DC: Brookings Institute Press, 2000), p. 60.
38 K. Marx, 'Speech on Free Trade', in D. McLellan (ed.), *Karl Marx: Selected Writings* (Oxford: Oxford University Press, 1977), pp. 269–70; V. I. Lenin, 'The Economic Content of Narodism', in *Collected Works*, vol. 1 (Moscow: Progress Publishers, 1960), p. 436 and 'Re. the Monopoly of Foreign Trade', in *Collected Works*, Vol. 33 (Moscow: Progress Publishers, 1966).
39 K. Marx, *The Communist Manifesto*, in D. McLellan (ed.), *Karl Marx: Selected Writings*, p. 224.
40 K. Marx, *The German Ideology*, in D. McLellan (ed.), *Karl Marx: Selected Writings*, pp. 170–1.
41 For a discussion of this see Gillian Brock's criticism of my views in her 'What Does Cosmopolitanism Demand of Us?' and my reply in '*Cosmopolitan Justice* Reconsidered' both in *Theoria*, 104 (2004).
42 Cf. M. Pendlebury, P. Hudson and D. Moellendorf, 'Capitalist Exploitation, Self-Ownership, and Equality', *Philosophical Forum*, 32 (2001), and, 'Equal Liberty and Unequal Worth of Liberty', in N. Daniels (ed.), *Reading Rawls* (Stanford, CA: Stanford University Press, 1989), pp. 253–81.
43 UNDP, *Human Development Report 1999*, pp. 34–5.
44 S. P. Shukla, 'From the GATT to the WTO and Beyond' in D. Nayyar (ed.), *Governing Globalization* (Oxford: Oxford University Press, 2002), p. 281.
45 Marrakech Agreement.
46 W. Below, *The Future in the Balance: Essays on Globalization and Resistance* (Oakland, CA: Food First Books, 2001), pp. 28–9.
47 UNCTAD, 'Industrial Countries Must Work Harder for Development if Globalization is to Deliver on its Promises' (1999), online at http://www.unctad.org/Templates/webflyer.asp?docid=3082&intItemID=2021&lang=1.
48 Ibid., p. 8.
49 J. Fraser, 'EU to Seek Reform of Agriculture Policy', *Business Day*, 15 February 2002.
50 P. Singer, *One World: The Ethics of Globalization* (New Haven, CT: Yale University Press, 2002), pp. 57–70.
51 For the WTO's account of the dispute see http://www.wto.org/english/tratop_e/envir_e/edis04_e.htm.
52 See http://www.wto.org/english/tratop_e/envir_e/issu3_e.htm#gattart20.
53 See http://www.wto.org/english/tratop_e/envir_e/cte03_e.htm#productvprocess.
54 See http://www.wto.org/english/tratop_e/envir_e/edis05_e.htm.
55 *United States – Import Prohibition of Certain Shrimp Products*, 1999 (38) *International Legal Materials* 118. See also http://www.wto.org/english/tratop_e/envir_e/edis08_e.htm.
56 Hoekman and Kostecki, *The Political Economy of The World Trading System*, p. 152.
57 Ibid., p. 156.

58 TRIPS Annex 1C of the Marrakech Agreement Establishing the World Trade Organization (1994), online at http://www.wto.org/english/docs_e/legal_e/27-trips_03_e.htm.
59 Ibid.
60 Ibid., http://www.wto.org/english/docs_e/legal_e/27-trips_04c_e.htm.
61 Ibid.
62 Ibid.
63 Hoekman and Kostecki, *The Political Economy of The World Trading System*, p. 155.
64 Ibid., p. 154.
65 See http://www.unhchr.ch/Huridocda/Huridoca.nsf/0/c462b62cf8a07b13c12569700046704e?Opendocument.
66 Ibid.
67 Hoekman and Kostecki, *The Political Economy of The World Trading System*, pp. 145–6. Nozick defends patents on natural rights grounds in *Anarchy, State, and Utopia*, p. 182. S. Sterckx powerfully criticizes various justifications of the TRIPS protection in 'Patents and Access to Drugs in Developing Countries: An Ethical Analysis', *Developing World Bioethics*, 4 (2004), 58–75.
68 See http://www.wto.org/english/tratop_e/envir_e/cte03_e.htm#productvprocess.
69 Ibid.
70 Ibid.
71 D. G. McNile, Jr, 'West's Drug Firms Play God in Africa', *Mail and Guardian*, 26 May–1 June 2000. Originally published in *The New York Times*.
72 UN AIDS, 'AIDS Treatment – A Focus on "3 by 5"', online at http://www.unaids.org/en/media/fact+sheets.asp.
73 J. Brecher *et al.*, *Globalization from Below* (Cambridge, MA: South End Press, 2000), pp. 4–10.
74 Ibid., pp. 47–59; K. Moody, *Workers in a Lean World* (London: Verso, 1997), pp. 269–92; and R. Munck, *Globalization and Labor* (London and New York: Zed Books, 2002), pp. 154–73.
75 F. List, *The National System of Political Economy* (New York: Augustus M. Kelley, 1966), Book 1. The argument has been revived by Ha-Joon Chang, *Kicking Away the Ladder: Development Strategy in Historical Perspective* (London: Anthem Press, 2002).
76 This principle was first suggested to me by E. A. Brett.

16
A Cosmopolitan Perspective on the Self-Determination of Peoples

Daniele Archibugi

Introduction

Over the last few years, the demand for the self-determination of peoples has once more acquired considerable force.[1] In consolidated states no less than in states that are falling apart, more or less dominant political groups have appealed to self-determination to support their own political projects. Statistics recorded on the issue tell us that at the beginning of 2003 there were 22 on-going armed conflicts for self-determination, 51 groups using conventional political means to pursue self-determination, and 29 groups using militant strategies short of armed violence.[2] Such demands have pursued a variety of goals, ranging from the attainment of multilinguism to greater tolerance for the religions, habits and customs of minorities, and even the review of borders and the setting-up of new states. Different and often contradictory aspirations have thus been grouped under the single banner of self-determination.

If we take a closer look at such demands, we find that 'the right to self-determination' spans three very different categories. The first is the self-determination of colonial peoples, which is how the term is used in the United Nations Charter and in many other sources of international law. The entire world political community supports this meaning, bar a few exceptions. The second meaning is associated with secession, and encompasses the demands of minorities which intend to break away from the state they belong to; this has been the meaning most in vogue since the end of the Cold War and also the one most directly associated with armed conflicts and civil wars of the last decade. It is the second meaning, in particular, that clashes with the concept of state sovereignty. The third meaning, finally, refers to certain ethnic or cultural groups which, while intending to continue to remain part of the state they belong to, wish to achieve given collective rights. This latter is the most innovative meaning and, in democratic states especially, has triggered a fierce debate.

While all theoretically and politically valid, the three meanings hide political and intellectual pitfalls. In all three, self-determination is a subjective right which fails as yet to be precisely matched by a body of law. The thesis I argue here is that to be put into full effect, the right to self-determination cannot be self-assessed by conflicting political communities. If this is the case, the outcome will probably reflect the power of the contending parties rather than the interest of peoples and it will lead to violent conflicts. In order to retain its validity, the concept of self-determination should be fitted into a legal system far broader than that of single states and even of interstate law. If it is to play a progressive role in the global community, self-determination requires a cosmopolitan legal order. Without such an order, the principle risks being out-of-date and reactionary, stirring up particularistic and chauvinistic demands contrary to fundamental human rights. Such a cosmopolitan legal order is unlikely to be achieved shortly but, even in the absence of such an order, I suggest that third and independent parties should assess the conflicting claims of political communities regarding self-determination.

Some milestones in the relationship between states and peoples

The concept of the self-determination of peoples is founded on the premise that peoples themselves are the holders of given rights. This means instituting rights different from those recognized to both states and individuals. The problem is by no means a new one: on various occasions in the evolution of meta-state law,[3] the need has been perceived for legal categories different from state public law and interstate public law. The Romans, the Spaniards at the time of the discovery of the New World and the European states before and after the French revolution felt the need to guarantee certain rights to 'peoples' even if they were devoid of a 'state'.

At the beginning of the twentieth century a major divide between 'states' and 'peoples' took place. At the end of the First World War, both the Bolsheviks and President Wilson preached the self-determination of peoples, albeit with slightly different meanings. The Bolsheviks referred, above all, to self-determination from the inside, believing that the principal factor of division among peoples was the dominion of autocratic governments and a minority oppressing the majority of the population. President Wilson, instead, promised he would achieve the self-determination of peoples from the outside, partly by redefining borders to create state communities that were, as far as possible, culturally, ethnically, geographically and linguistically homogeneous. Nevertheless, it thus emerged that the self-determination of peoples could not technically entail the creation of one state for every people. In a Europe built round nation-states, new states were created with very strong ethnic minorities: Czechoslovakia, Yugoslavia, Poland and the Baltic republics became new countries in which different peoples were forced to live together.[4]

The great powers were aware that this could have led to problems, and at the Paris Conference they persuaded the governments of the new states to pledge to recognize and guarantee certain rights to minorities. The new states also had to accept a limitation on the exercise of their sovereignty domestically, allowing the newborn international institution, the League of Nations, to act as a guarantor of the rights of minorities. As Arendt noted, to speak of minorities and their rights and, indeed, establish that an institution external to states was necessary to guarantee such rights, actually meant declaring a condition of 'political minority' for minorities.

It was arguably because the memory of the inconclusive evaluations of the Paris Conference were so fresh that, after the tragedy of the Second World War, the Charter of the United Nations was much more cautious in accepting the dichotomy between states and peoples. By 'peoples', it refers principally to those of the Third World which ought, in a more or less distant future, to become states (see, for example, Article 73). It failed, though, to address the problem of ethnic minorities inside already existing states. If it were the United Nations' intention to protect the given rights of peoples, they did so through the protection of the individual rights established in the Universal Declaration and subsequent acts.[5]

Peoples and their self-determination

The concept of self-determination is one which arouses a great deal of sympathy; no one in the contemporary world is in favour of the 'hetero-determination' of a people any more. But, for the concept of self-determination of peoples to acquire an accomplished meaning, it is also necessary to define exactly what is meant by 'people'. Ever vague and arbitrary, the definition of 'people' has become all the more so today, now that the entire planet is subdivided into compounded states.

When we refer to a state, there is no ambiguity involved: we know what its borders are, what the law in force is and, in many cases, which international laws it has pledged to respect. States can be defined, classified and counted. Any definition, classification and count of peoples will involve a much higher degree of subjectivity.

All the states on the planet represent peoples imperfectly in two different senses: on the one hand, they can represent more than one people (the United States comprises dozens of peoples, a fact which has become a motive for national pride). On the other, states do not necessarily represent a people *in toto*, in the sense that the members of that people may be citizens of more than one state. By Irish, for example, we may refer to citizens of Eire or of the UK or of the USA.

An objective criterion by which people could be defined has never existed, and never will. Attempts made by individual scholars could help,[6] but the acid test will not come from a shared academic definition, but when such definitions are taken for granted by conflicting political communities. Language, religion, race and shared faith fails to provide a solid method to identify the boundaries of a people. Basques, Northern Irish, Palestinians, Kurds, Armenians, Georgians, Quebecois, Serbs, Croats, Chechens, Aborigines, Luxemburgers, American Indians, Sardinians, Ladins, Val d'Aostans: which of these is a people? From the cultural and sociological point of view, nothing can stop any community which recognizes itself in a given identity from defining itself as a people. The ability to do so belongs in fact to the sphere of individual liberty.

If there were one state for every people in the world, and if each of these peoples lived solely and exclusively within the boundaries of its own state, it would not be necessary to resort to the notion of people's rights. The traditional notions of state and interstate law would suffice per se, and the concept of self-determination would be valid exclusively inside and not outside states. Yet history and geography force us to take account of the fact that state and people do not coincide. The United Nations boasts 192 independent members, but there are about 600 active linguistic communities and more than 5,000 ethnic groups in the world.

Let us try to imagine what it would take to form 600 linguistically homogeneous states, or, going even further, to create 5,000 politically and ethnically homogeneous communities. The international community would have no major problem in assimilating such a transformation: the diplomatic system, intergovernmental organizations, the United Nations included, would be able to work with 600 or even 5,000 member states instead of 192. In short, the interstate system would be able to work even with a much larger number of members.

Problems would arise, above all, inside states, which would have to redraw their frontiers and hence do violence to their history and geography. In other words, it would be necessary to resort on an unprecedented scale to means that are out of the question such as war, ethnic cleansing, forced deportation or even genocide. Hardly anyone today would be prepared to accept such methods. In short, the idea of redrawing the frontiers of states to make them correspond to a 'people' is simply unthinkable.

This does not mean that states as they stand are the ideal political solution to serve the needs and interests of individuals and peoples, but it will never be possible to cure a state's maladies merely by redefining its frontiers and modifying the way in which its population is constituted. The present limits of the state have to be solved much more radically, taking measures both internally and externally: on the one hand, making the state itself a truly multiethnic and multicultural political community; on the other, making it part of a world community founded on legality and cooperation.

The three meanings of 'self-determination of peoples'

The concept of the self-determination of peoples harbours too many perils. More precisely, it is fair to point out that the subjective right to self-determination can be interpreted in at least three different ways:

(a) the right of colonial peoples to become a state;
(b) the right of minorities of a state (or more than one state) to become an autonomous (or to join another) state;
(c) the right of ethnic minorities to benefit from certain collective rights.[7]

The three different categories are obviously interconnected, and a given people can assert its rights by using any one of the three meanings as circumstances demand. A people can, for example, demand certain collective rights from its own state (third meaning), and if such demands are ignored or even repressed, it can claim political independence as a means of achieving such rights (second meaning). This is the case of the Kurds, who have exerted pressure to establish themselves as a sovereign state directly proportional to the repression which states (whether Turkey, Iraq, Iran or Syria) bring to bear on their cultural, religious and linguistic identity. On the basis of the policy it implements towards minorities, a state may thus find itself having to deal with demands of the second or third type.

Demands of the first and third type may also be alternative one to another. Some of the peoples colonized by European powers have not asked to become autonomous states because they are satisfied with the degree of domestic self-determination allotted to them. Greenland, for example, continues to be an autonomous territory of the Danish crown precisely because, thanks to the autonomy it has achieved on the basis of the third point, it has no desire to become an independent state.

It is difficult to draw a clear line of demarcation between the first meaning and the second. Many nationalist political movements which aspire to independence (certain Basque factions or Catholics in Northern Ireland, for example) argue that they have been colonized. It is nonetheless possible to note a difference between an ethnic minority within a state and a colonized people. In the first case, the state accords the same rights and duties to the ethnic 'minority' as it does to the ethnic 'majority', whereas, in the second case, the state envisages certain rights and duties for the 'colonized' and others for the 'colonizers'. The following sections discuss these three different meanings.

The right of colonial peoples to form a state

It is no coincidence that the principle of self-determination has returned to the fore in the postwar years as a reaction to the colonial dominion of Western states. In the 1950s, 1960s and 1970s, the principle of self-determination was interpreted mainly as the right of peoples to become states, a reiteration of the conceptual and legal categories used to reorganize European society after the First World War.[8] In fact, the largest group of UN members comes from the achievement of self-determination in this meaning.[9] In cases such as those of India or Algeria, self-determination meant allowing such peoples to become sovereign states against the states that had conquered them. Britain and India or France and Algeria had no cultural, geographical, ethnic or religious affinities, and the rights granted to Indian or Algerian citizens were very different from those granted to British or French ones. In such cases, the notion of a people's right takes on a provisional configuration. As soon as the people in question wins its sovereignty, state and interstate law replace the right of peoples.

The process of decolonization has gone a long way over the last half century, and has been crowned by remarkable successes in terms of the achievement of formal sovereignty by Third World states. Yet today, precisely because all colonial peoples have become states, it is possible to review the story of their self-determination with a pinch of criticism. The liberation movements which aspired to become states sought to achieve self-determination externally. During national liberation struggles, there was much less talk about achieving self-determination internally.[10] Even world public opinion, which rallied in favour of Indian and Algerian independence and in respect of the sovereignty of states such as Vietnam and Cambodia, demanded self-determination achieved from the outside, confident in the fact that, once it had been achieved, the liberation movements in question would allow it from the inside too.

At best, overstressing ways of achieving *internal* self-determination when these peoples were under the colonial yoke would have appeared paternalistic; at worst, it would have seemed an instrumental means of conserving the imperialist domination. There can be no doubt that Indians and Algerians had something to learn from the democratic systems in force in the UK and in France, but the matter was secondary and subordinate to the indisputable demand of these countries to pursue their own self-determination from the outside. Moreover, 'noble' Western liberal democracies ceased to be taken seriously as models of democracy by peoples of the Third World at the very point at which they sullied themselves with colonialism.

Now that, at least formally, the decolonization process is over, hypocrisies abound with regard to self-determination processes. The first is that of the Western states which used to apply high degrees of self-determination internally (it is worth reflecting on the fact that countries of the great democratic revolutions – the UK and France – were also the main colonialists), but denied the same internal self-determination to the peoples they had initially dominated. Their approach, indeed, also cast a sinister light on the way in which countries exerted their power internally (how many times has it been repeated that a people which oppresses another cannot be free?). The second hypocrisy is that of national liberation movements which, after fighting to achieve their own self-determination from the outside, conquering power and setting themselves up as states, have often resorted to force to prevent self-determination from developing internally and established dictatorial regimes.

In short, decolonization has proved that external and internal self-determination do not necessarily coincide, a fact which has often created considerable political difficulties. For years, world public opinion supported certain liberation movements to assert the right of peoples to self-determination from the outside (suffice to mention the tragic case of Cambodia), but it was forced suddenly to back off when it saw that they were denying the right of peoples to self-determination from within. The full self-determination of peoples would have meant achieving both the external and the internal version. Today we have to admit that, unfortunately, the process of decolonization has achieved many successes of the first kind but far fewer of the second.

One further aspect needs to be stressed. Although often opposing Western colonial powers with arms, national liberation movements accepted the frontiers they had inherited from those powers even when they were established arbitrarily. What made India a homogeneous political community? Why did it become one single state and not, for argument's sake, three or 25 different states? In the event of divergences within local communities, who, in the final analysis, was called to solve them? Kaveli Holsti is not wrong when he points out that, 'The elites who led independence or national liberation movements under the doctrine of national self-determination often had no nation to liberate. Rather, they had a collection of communities that, aside from their dislike of colonialism, had little in common, and certainly no common identity.'[11] Even in the widely accepted case of the self-determination of colonial peoples, it thus emerges that the notion of the right of peoples is not enough to solve two essential problems: that of internal self-determination and that of the redefinition of existing frontiers. It would appear apt therefore to fit it into a broader legal framework, that of a fully-fledged cosmopolitan legal system.

The right of minorities to form a state

Since the 1980s another type of demand has gained weight; that of ethnic, linguistic, religious or simply cultural minorities that aspire to become states.[12] Croatians, Chechens, Basques, Quebecois, Scots and even Padanians have invoked the right of peoples to secede from their state of origin and become autonomous states. Even more complex is the story of peoples such as the Kurds whose territory is split up among a number of different states.

In a few fortunate cases, new states have been formed and recognized without conflict.[13] In many others, the aspirations of some peoples to become autonomous clashed with other aspirations. In the most controversial cases, which, sadly, have multiplied since the end of the Cold War, demands for secession have provoked civil wars and bloody conflicts. This is not surprising if we bear in mind that the configuration of modern states is such that any secession is bound to generate a new ethnic minority.[14] It is no coincidence that the few cases of separation without bloodletting (Slovakia from the Czech Republic or Slovenia from Yugoslavia, for example) have been the ones in which no significant ethnic minority was present inside the new state in the making. Until we reach the paradoxical point of one state for every individual, we shall have to come to terms with multiethnic political communities.

The former Yugoslavia was the tragic 'laboratory' for this process.[15] All the groups that took part in the conflict in the former Yugoslavia appealed to the right to self-determination of their own people. Those who wanted the separation of Croatia or Kosovo claimed the right of the Croat or Kosovar people to form a sovereign state, those who wanted to conserve the federal state appealed to the rights of the constituent Serbian minorities in Croatia and Kosovo, those who wanted to form an independent Bosnian state appealed to the right of the Bosnian people, those who wanted a union of Serbians appealed to the right of the Bosnian–Serbian people, and so on. Alas, the appeal to the principle of self-determination failed to offer practical solutions.

All the various counterpoised demands for self-determination were met in the most brutal and traditional way possible: by resorting to military force. Each ethnic community, real or presumed, fought with every ounce of energy to achieve sovereignty over a given territory. The international community proved incapable of proposing solutions that would on the one hand define the borders of states, and on the other hand guarantee the rights of ethnic minorities and individuals. The international community was even less capable of imposing peace and the respect for human rights within each political community.

The lesson we have learnt from the former Yugoslavia and the wave of ethnic nationalism that we have witnessed over the last decade is that a people's claim to form an autonomous state does not necessarily solve the problem of respect for individual rights. What was lacking was a *super partes* arbitral power capable of providing a peaceful solution and guaranteeing each community. The legitimacy and functionality of the claims of the various ethnic groups should have been based on three criteria, as explained below.

The first criterion is a people's effective intention to become an autonomous state. Its demand for secession must be deemed null and void if the majority of the citizens involved make no deliberate claims of this kind. The cases of the 1990s demonstrate how scarcely representative political groups can claim to speak on behalf of a people and adopt a deliberate strategy to create tension and force a majority relatively indifferent to a secession to take sides. If it is established that the majority of the population effectively intends to form an autonomous state, the demand has to be pursued on the basis of existing constitutional norms.[16] If they are not envisaged in, or even banned by, the constitutional systems, as in the Italian case, it is necessary to activate the channels envisaged by the international system.

The second criterion is the protection of individual rights and minorities. It is impossible to form a new state without preventively guaranteeing the rights of groups which, in the state-to-be, would constitute ethnic minorities. Turning it into an oppressive majority cannot solve the problem of a minority that feels oppressed. Even the fight for territory might become much less fierce if, before discussing the possible formation of new states or the modification of frontiers, the contending parties were to agree on guarantees designed to protect individual and collective rights. In the many republics that sprang up after dissolution of the Soviet Union, the resident Russian populations were oppressive majorities one day and oppressed minorities the next. To put it bluntly, sacrificing one people in place of another is no way of asserting a right.

The third criterion is monitoring and control by supranational institutions. A state's secession of a region cannot be considered as merely an internal problem. Where sharp conflict exists between the state and ethnic groups aspiring to autonomy, the main element for a peaceful settlement – reciprocal mutual trust – is lacking. In such cases, the jurisdictional and arbitral intervention of the international community is needed. It is unlikely that problems such as the delimitation of new boundaries and the attribution of rights to minorities can be solved peacefully without the intervention of a third *super partes* political authority. However, two questions remain unsolved: (1) what legal principles must such an authority be based on, and (2) which institutions of the international community should perform such interventions?

So far, the international community (i.e., the community of sovereign states and their intergovernmental organizations, including the United Nations) has been rather reluctant to take a more active role in issues concerning secession. The review by Crawford shows that the international community is reluctant to 'accept unilateral secession outside the colonial context. This practice has not changed since 1989, despite the emergence during that period of 22 new States. On the contrary, the practice has been powerfully reinforced.'[17]

It is no surprise that the international community, composed of states' representatives, is unwilling to recognize new states without the prior consent of the states they belonged to. For states, sovereignty should be respected and interference should be avoided. But such a passive role is not necessarily a good thing: it leaves, in fact, conflicting parties (that is, existing states on the one hand and movements for independence on the other hand) with no other choice than to use force. The world community could be much more helpful in intervening as an *ex-ante* arbitrator whenever frontiers are redrawn, and as a guarantor of individual rights and minorities, rather than with an *ex-post* recognition of the de facto condition.

Rights of peoples as rights of minorities

A third and final meaning of self-determination is the one used by groups which demand not to become states, but simply to achieve the recognition and protection of given collective rights. Such peoples do not question the fact that they belong to their state of origin yet, in so far as they are minorities, they believe valid reasons exist for obtaining special protections. In this meaning, the rights of peoples are claimed mainly from the territorial state of belonging. This is the case of some indigenous peoples: for example, Aboriginals in Canada, the USA, and Australia.[18] Similar situations also arise when ethnic communities settle in foreign countries, as in the cases of the Turkish community in Germany or the Arab community in France. The migrations of the contemporary era and the increasingly populous ethnic communities in foreign countries (Berlin is a city with one of the largest Turkish populations in the world) will make this type of claim increasingly frequent. The principle of self-determination is not associated with a request to form a state but is, instead, addressed at the state of belonging to achieve, for example, the right to decide which language one wishes to be educated in, autonomy for given cultural or religious norms and so on.

In our globalized age, states do not have much choice: either they opt for ethnic cleansing, isolationism and the forced standardization of minorities, or for multicultural and multiethnic integration policies.[19] This meaning of the right of peoples is thus an important legal instrument for helping states to manage communities with sharply different cultural traditions and values.

This third meaning of the right of peoples concerns not so much international law as internal public law.[20] When internal public law does not provide sufficient protection, minorities can seek protection also in international law and institutions.[21] A state is founded on the equality of citizens before the law although, as members of given peoples, some citizens could receive additional rights that others are not entitled to. Cases of this kind are highly topical: in Alto Adige, German-speaking Italians receive from the state certain benefits which are not received by Italian-speaking citizens. In Canada and Australia, Aborigines have rights that are not enjoyed by other citizens. No matter how far this meaning of the right of peoples presents itself as a subset of human rights, it risks entering into conflict with the notion in so far as it counterposes individual rights against collective ones.[22]

Furthermore, guaranteeing the rights of ethnic minorities may create conflicts with the communities in which such minorities live. In France and Germany, some French and German citizens of Arab origin and Muslim religion applied for the right to send their daughters to school wearing the chador. Albeit with some reluctance, often stronger among the liberal and progressive public opinion, the request was granted. But should European countries be just as tolerant if French Muslims claim the right to practise infibulation?[23] And what if their requests were to go even further and they were to demand the right to stone adulterous wives? And, more importantly, who is going to decide?

It is sufficient here to point out that the conflicts between the norms of a state and the claims of special ethnic and cultural communities inside them will tend to increase. A truly multiethnic and multicultural state ought to envisage methods of tackling and solving these conflicts internally. Yet, at the same time, it is hard to imagine minorities being prepared to recognize sufficient legitimacy of state institutions. A French court which has to pronounce on the chador will be seen by Muslim minorities as being overrespectful of the cultural traditions of its own people. There can be no doubt that judicial institutions representing the citizens of the world would be more authoritative. To be entirely valid, this meaning of self-determination requires some cosmopolitan law and institutions capable, as the need arises, of establishing which norms need to be allowed for minorities and which banned.

How to deal with self-determination?

Is there any way to allow the requests for self-determination to be addressed in a non-violent way? An ideal way would be to devolve competencies about self-determination to cosmopolitan legal institutions that should represent the views of citizens of the world as much as they represent that of states and single peoples. These institutions could be understood as a reformed World Court or a new World Parliament.[24] They would have the advantage of being impartial, and being seen as such by the different peoples. These institutions would be more inclined to deliberate according to the general interest rather than particular interests. It is, however, unlikely that such institutions could be established in the near future since states still dominate the world political stage.

Even in absence of such a cosmopolitan institutional setting, however, there are methods that can be used to minimize the recourse to violence. This implies that the contending communities should accept the independent assessment of third parties. Let's look at how this could work in each of the three meanings singled out.

The first meaning, that of the right of a people to become a state, is the one evoked by national liberation movements. Its value is provisional seeing that it conspires to override itself: more precisely, at the moment in which peoples achieve self-determination externally, they form states and thus replace the vindicated right of peoples with the law of a state. The problem of external self-determination ought, however, to have been combined with that of internal self-determination. Historical experience shows, in fact, that the liberation movements which achieved self-determination externally were often unprepared to grant internal self-determination. Peoples in decolonized countries ought to have drawn advantage from legal norms and institutions offering, at one and the same time, arguments in favour of independence from the outside and democracy from the inside. Independent institutions should have helped in this process. When the bulk of decolonization occurred, the UN was reluctant to interfere in internal affairs of the newborn states and the values of democracy were not yet universally shared as they are today.

On the basis of the second meaning, the right of peoples refers instead to cases in which ethnic or cultural groups ask to secede from the state they belong to or else to become a state themselves. It is extremely difficult to establish when such requests are legitimate, since redefining the boundaries of states necessarily means creating new minorities. This process demands that, in the first place, the rights of individuals and minorities are guaranteed, and that the arbitral and jurisdictional function of settling the opposing claims of ethnic groups is exercised by impartial institutions. It would certainly be an advantage if constitutions were to include 'a duly constrained right to secede'[25] since this would allow existing states to deal with the issue autonomously. But only a few constitutions allow for it. Third parties can help in avoiding a vicious circle where discrimination of minorities leads to radicalism and vice versa. Third parties should suggest practicable solutions on boundaries, individual and collective rights and the ways to guarantee them. It would signify enormous progress if the parties involved, that is, states on the one hand and separatist groups on the other hand, were willing to listen and follow the advice of independent parties. But this would require states to be willing to give up their sovereignty, and independent parties their claims to a self-assessment on their rights.

The third meaning touches on the collective rights that ethnic groups claim from the state they belong to (and from which they have no intention of seceding). This is a problem more of public law than of interstate law, and the supporters of multiculturalism have had a lot to say on the subject. Within this connotation, some collective rights may clash with individual rights. In this case too, third parties could play an important function, maintaining the right balance between people's collective rights and individual rights. This would allow the state to inform its norms and policies on the basis of an external opinion, and the minority groups to feel that their claims are not assessed by state-institutions only. Of course, third parties alone cannot non-violently solve a crisis without the willingness of conflicting communities; but often opposite communities can be induced to search for a positive solution if a third party mediates this.

Conclusions

I want to point out that, under conditions of globalization, the principle of self-determination of peoples is becoming the opening for a new form of tribalism[26] and it is encouraging some of the most reactionary tendencies present in contemporary society. If we wish to prevent this, we need to include its demands in a legal framework shared both by the community claiming self-determination and by the community that is rejecting it. The legal orders of single states as well as the interstate system are insufficient. It is thus necessary to change it in such a way as to give space to these demands. Liberal democracies are making significant steps to envisage in their legal systems both the collective rights of minorities and norms to regulate the devolution of some regions (see the significant case of Canada *vis-à-vis* Quebec). Progressive states can develop constitutional norms to deal both with claims of independence as well as to guarantee collective minority rights.

Elsewhere I have outlined the ambitious project for cosmopolitan democracy, ideally eligible to examine the demands of various peoples for self-determination. But even without a cosmopolitan legal order, the parties to the case which appeal to self-determination ought to accept the principle whereby their claims have to be examined by impartial institutions. This simply means accepting the principle that no one can be a judge of their own case. Without fully-fledged cosmopolitan institutions (representing, that is, citizens directly without the intermediation of their state), the parties to the case could turn to the intergovernmental organizations they trust. An organization potentially capable of performing this function is the Permanent Peoples' Tribunal.[27] If the states and collective groups which appeal to the principle of self-determination were prepared to hear an impartial opinion, we would already be on the road to the peaceful resolution of conflicts.

Notes

1 A previous version of this chapter has been published in *Constellations*, 10 (2003), 488–505.

2 I use the data collected by D. Quinn and T. R. Gurr, 'Self-Determination Movements: Origins, Strategic Choices, and Outcomes', in M. G. Marshall and T. R. Gurr (eds), *Peace and Conflict 2003: A Global Survey of Armed Conflicts, Self-Determination Movements, and Democracy* (College Park, MD: Center for International Development and Conflict Management, University of Maryland, 2003).

3 By meta-state law, I mean law different from the law in force inside states. This includes different categories which have emerged in the history of legal thinking, such as the law among states and suprastate law.

4 See the vivid account by H. Arendt, *The Origins of Totalitarianism* (London: The Trinity Press, 1950), especially ch. 9, section I: 'The Nation of Minorities and the Stateless People'.

5 I do not address here John Rawls's approach to the law of peoples since his analysis is explicitly designed to describe a 'particular political conception... that applies to the principles and norms of international law and practice'; see *The Law of Peoples* (Cambridge, MA: Harvard University Press, 1999), p. 3. In other words, Rawls does not address in his research how political communities have been established and how they could or should be modified, but only how political communities should interact among themselves. I think that his approach would have been better described by the terms 'the political philosophy of inter-state law'. The debate generated by Rawls's theses is critically reviewed in S. Caney, 'Cosmopolitanism and the Law of Peoples', *Journal of Political Philosophy*, 10 (2002), 95–123.

6 See, for example, D. Miller's attempt in *On Nationality* (Oxford: Clarendon Press, 1995).

7 This taxonomy is different from those suggested by D. Ronen in *The Quest for Self-Determination* (New Haven, CT: Yale University Press, 1979), pp. 9–12, and A. Cassese, *Self-Determination of Peoples: A Legal Reappraisal* (Cambridge: Cambridge University Press, 1996), pp. 316–17. It unifies similar categories and takes into consideration the internal/external relationship in each.

8 See the excellent overview in Cassese, *Self-Determination of Peoples*. The crowning moment of this phase was the Charter of Algiers. Cf. F. Rigaux, *La Carta d'Algeri* (San Domenico di Fiesole: Edizioni cultura della pace, 1988).

9 J. Crawford, 'State Practice and International Law in Relation to Secession', *The British Yearbook of International Law*, 69 (1999), 90.

10 By 'internal self-determination', I mean the possibility for citizens to participate in the choice of government and the formulation of their own policies; in other words, the democratic system. Cf. D. Held, *Democracy and the Global Order* (Cambridge: Polity, 1995), p. 147.

11 Cf. K. J. Holsti, 'The Coming Chaos? Armed Conflict in the World's Periphery', in T. V. Paul and J. A. Hall (eds), *International Order and the Future of World Politics* (Cambridge: Cambridge University Press, 1999), pp. 283–310.

12 Cf. the carefully pondered review by A. Buchanan, 'Theories of Secession', *Philosophy and Public Affairs*, 26 (1997), 31–61. On the capacity of some groups to become 'imaginary' ethnic communities, see the fundamental observations of B. Anderson, *Imagined Communities: Reflections on the Origins and Spread of Nationalism* (London: Verso, 1983). I thus find that the criterion proposed by D. Miller in *Citizenship and National Identity* (Cambridge: Polity, 2000), to judge the requests of secessionist groups on the basis of their national identity, is not feasible in theory and in practice.

13 Crawford, 'State Practice and International Law', p. 86, draws a useful legal distinction between secession, which is unilateral, and devolution or grant of independence, which follows an agreement among the parties.

14 As Habermas has noted, establishing new borders serves only to produce new minorities. See J. Habermas, *Kampf um Anerkennung im Demokratischen Rechtsstaat* (Frankfurt: Suhrkamp Verlag, 1996).

15 See M. Kaldor, *New and Old Wars* (Cambridge: Polity, 1999).

16 On the need to contemplate the right to secession (or, to adopt the terminology suggested by Crawford, the grant of independence), see D. Weinstock, 'Constitutionalising the Right to Secede', in *Journal of Political Philosophy*, 9 (2001), 182–203.

17 Crawford, 'State Practice and International Law', p. 114.

18 A number of essays are dedicated to these cases in J. Crawford, *The Rights of Peoples* (Oxford: Clarendon Press, 1988).

19 This is the learnt lesson received from Canadian scholars such as W. Kymlicka, *Multicultural Citizenship: A Liberal Theory of Minority Rights* (Oxford: Clarendon Press, 1995); J. Tully, *Strange Multiplicity: Constitutionalism in an Age of Diversity* (Cambridge: Cambridge University Press, 1996); C. Taylor, *The Politics of Recognition* (Princeton, NJ: Princeton University Press, 1992); A.-G. Gagnon and J. Tully (eds), *Multinational Democracies* (Cambridge: Cambridge University Press, 2001).

20 Although, as rightly stressed by I. M. Young, 'Self-determination and Global Democracy', in I. Shapiro and S. Macedo (eds), *Designing Democratic Institutions* (New York: New York University Press, 2000), some ethnic minorities within states could also claim to have an autonomous voice in international organizations (as in the case of the Roma people in Europe).

21 For an analysis of these cases, see B. Kingsbury, 'Reconciling Five Competing Conceptual Structures of Indigenous Peoples' Claims in International and Comparative Law', in P. Alston (ed.), *Peoples' Rights* (Oxford: Oxford University Press, 2001).

22 In this context of self-determination see I. M. Young, 'Two Concepts of Self-Determination', in A. Sarat and T. R. Kearns (ed.), *Human Rights: Concepts, Contests, Contingencies* (Ann Arbor, MI: University of Michigan Press, 2001),

pp. 25–44; Young differentiates between non-dominating and non-interference.

23 As a matter of fact, infibulation is a criminal offence in the majority of Western countries. See http://www.unfpa.org/index.htm.

24 The prospects for such global institutional buildings are discussed in an increasingly vast literature. See, for example, D. Archibugi and D. Held (eds), *Cosmopolitan Democracy: An Agenda for a New World Order* (Cambridge: Polity, 1995); Held, *Democracy and the Global Order*; D. Archibugi, D. Held and M. Köhler (eds), *Re-imagining Political Community: Studies in Cosmopolitan Democracy* (Cambridge: Polity, 1998); B. Holden (ed.), *Global Democracy* (London: Routledge, 2000).

25 Weinstock, 'Constitutionalising the Right to Secede', p. 202.

26 As pointed out by T. Franck, 'Postmodern Tribalism and the Right to Secession', in C. M. Brolman, R. Lefeber and M. Y. A. Zieck (eds), *Peoples and Minorities in International Law* (Dordrecht: Martinus Nijhoff, 1993).

27 G. Tognoni (ed.), *Tribunale permanente dei popoli. Le sentenze: 1979–1998* (Verona: Bertani editore, 1998). The Tribunal's web site can be consulted online at http://www.grisnet.it/filb/tribu%20eng.html.

Index

Made in the USA
Monee, IL
13 September 2026

62976824R00164